Becoming an Archaeologist

Becoming an Archaeologist: A Guide to Professional Pathways is an engaging handbook on career paths in the area of archaeology. It outlines in straightforward fashion the entire process of getting a job in archaeology, including the various career options; the training required; and how to get positions in the academic, commercial, and government worlds. It also includes a discussion of careers in related heritage professions, such as museums and conservation societies. The book includes a series of interviews with real archaeologists, all young professionals who began their careers within the past ten years. These insider guides offer essential tips on how they got their first jobs and progressed in their careers. Written in an accessible style, the book is essential reading for anyone interested in the realities of archaeology in the twenty-first century.

Joe Flatman is the County Archaeologist of Surrey in southeast England and a senior lecturer at the Institute of Archaeology, University College London. He has published widely on issues of archaeological practice, ethics, and law in archaeology. His most recent books include *Ships and Shipping in Medieval Manuscripts* and *Archaeology in Society: Its Relevance in the Modern World* (coedited with Marcy Rockman).

To my parents, Frances and Martin Flatman
With my love and thanks for providing a unique grounding in the pleasures
and perils of professional life
"Not all Greeks were Spartans"

Becoming an Archaeologist

A Guide to Professional Pathways

Joe Flatman
Institute of Archaeology, University College London

CAMBRIDGE
UNIVERSITY PRESS

CAMBRIDGE UNIVERSITY PRESS
Cambridge, New York, Melbourne, Madrid, Cape Town,
Singapore, São Paulo, Delhi, Tokyo, Mexico City

Cambridge University Press
32 Avenue of the Americas, New York, NY 10013-2473, USA

www.cambridge.org
Information on this title: www.cambridge.org/9780521734691

First published 2011

Printed in the United States of America

A catalog record for this publication is available from the British Library.

Library of Congress Cataloging in Publication data
Flatman, Joe.
Becoming an archaeologist : a guide to professional pathways / Joe Flatman.
p.   cm.
Includes bibliographical references and index.
ISBN 978-0-521-76772-9 (hardback) – ISBN 978-0-521-73469-1 (paperback)
1. Archaeology – Vocational guidance.   I. Title.
CC107.F53   2911
930.10023–dc22   2011002261

ISBN 978-0-521-76772-9 Hardback
ISBN 978-0-521-73469-1 Paperback

Contents

Contents

Contents

Tables and Figures

Tables

Figures

Tables and Figures

Preface and Acknowledgments

I wrote this book primarily to help prospective archaeologists (in particular, archaeology students) better plan their futures. However, this book is also borne of my frustration at the widespread misunderstanding of the practice of archaeology and lifestyle of archaeologists in the modern world. As a consequence, although I have tried to paint a balanced portrait of archaeology throughout the book, this is, inevitably and unashamedly, partly a personal perspective – one to which some readers may take exception. I make no apologies for that. One thing that I would emphasize in particular, however, is that although this book is about "professional" archaeology, it is absolutely not a call for a solely paid archaeological sector in which all voluntary/amateur/avocational/community/independent involvement has been driven out of existence. As a long-standing member of the UK's Council for British Archaeology (dating back to my teenage membership in the Young Archaeologists Club), and lately and very proudly serving on that organization's board of trustees, I would emphasize my belief in the key place of the independent individual or group in archaeology, and that archaeology – and wider society – are big enough places to see both paid and unpaid archaeologists working to the highest professional standards. I do not believe that these two ways of doing archaeology are mutually exclusive, as some commentators suggest. Nor do I believe that the improved living and working standards so many archaeologists urgently deserve can only and inevitably come through the loss of the volunteer. As I highlight repeatedly throughout this book, I sincerely believe that the single best thing that anyone can do to get involved in archaeology is to join his or her local archaeological or historical society.

In terms of acknowledgments, first and foremost I am extremely grateful to Beatrice Rehl at Cambridge University Press for seeing the potential of a book on this subject, commissioning it, and then editing it, as well as to her assistant Amanda Smith for much other hard work in bringing the book to fruition. Thanks also to James Dunn, Production Controller at Cambridge University Press, for keeping us all on track. Barbara Walthall, the Project Manager at Aptara responsible for this book, must then particularly be thanked for her exceptional work in preparing this book for publication; Deborah Wenger, who so diligently copyedited this work; as well as other – alas unnamed – production and proofreading staff are thanked. Similarly, I wish to give special thanks to my managers, Patricia Reynolds at Surrey

County Council and Stephen Shennan at University College London, for providing the professional support and time to allow this book to be written. The anonymous peer reviewers of this book's proposal and draft also made a number of exceptionally useful comments, for which they should be thanked.

Dozens of friends and colleagues around the world have – often unknowingly – contributed to this book through conversations, conference papers, e-mails, Web-sites, and blogs. Many students whom I have taught in the UK and Australia also made passing comments that became the germs of issues explored here. Consequently, a full list of contributors is impossible to provide – too many issues that eventually made it into this book began life as random comments and fleeting moments. To anyone who reads this book and thinks that he or she may have been the first to mention an issue or idea to me – my apologies for not formally acknowledging you here: next time we meet, remind me of my failure and I shall attempt to make amends! In particular, however, I wish to thank my colleagues at Surrey County Council and University College London, especially Emily Brants, Giles Carey, Phil Cooper, Martin Higgins, Tony Howe, Gary Jackson, Sophie Unger, and David Williams at the former; and Cyprian Broodbank, Ian Carroll, Lisa Daniel, Charlotte Frearson, Andy Gardner, Sjoerd van der Linde, Kris Lockyear, Roger Matthews, Judy Medrington, Gustav Milne, Norah Moloney, Gabriel Moshenska, Kirsty Norman, Darryl Palmer, Dominic Perring, Matthew Pope, Andrew Reynolds, Bill Sillar, Kathryn Tubb, Tim Williams, and Sarah Wolferstan at the latter. I am in the uniquely privileged position of working across two employers in, and sectors of, archaeology, and there is simply no way that I could have written this book without the advice of such dedicated colleagues at these organizations.

Special thanks and acknowledgments should also be made in relation to the photos reproduced, including Jeremy Ashbee (Figure 26), Kath Buxton (Figure 27), Ian Carroll (Figures 2, 11, and 21), Leanne Chorekdjian (Figure 7), Nathalie Cohen (Figure 31), English Heritage (Figure 27), Brendan Foley (Figure 4), Charlotte Frearson (Figure 10), Andrew Gardner (Figures 20 and 32), Elizabeth Graham (Figures 6, 7, and 8), Tony Howe (Figures 23 and 24), David Jeffreys (Figure 21), Dominic Perring (Figures 5, 9, 13, 14, 15, and 16), Brett Seymour (Figures 28 and 29), Dean Sully (Figure 33), Chris Waite (Figure 32), and Lynley Wallis (Figures 17 and 18). In addition, thanks specifically to Archaeology South East, Nick Blows, Andres Diaz, Alice Gomer, Vanessa Saiz Gomez, Louise Holt, Amy Lindsay, the Marco Gonzalez Project, Danny Markey, the US National Park Service, the Petrie Museum, the Portable Antiquities Scheme, Stephen Quirk, Kyle Rice, Matt Russell, Elizabeth Saunders, Jane Siddell, Rachel Sparkes, the Thames Discovery Programme, UCL Institute of Archaeology, Jenny Walsh, Rachael Warren, and Andrew Wright.

An array of other individuals who have made a marked or formal contribution to this book must also then be thanked, including Jon Adams, Kenny Aitchison, Mark Beattie-Edwards, Paul Belford, Marc-André Bernier, Heather Burke, Dan Carsten, Martin Carver, Nathalie Cohen, Dave Conlin, Kara Cooney, Steve Cross, Ian Cundy, Dominique de Moulins, Sarah Dhanjal, Amanda Evans, Robert Epstein, Paul Everill, Hannah Fluck, Brendan Foley, David Gaimster, Alice Gorman,

Erica Gittins, David Graham, Paul Graves-Brown, Lisa Gray, Lalage Grundy, Abby Guinness, Mary Harvey, Jon Henderson, Don Henson, Nigel Hetherington, Mike Heyworth, David Hinton, Peter Hinton, Fred Hocker, Tim Howard, Tom Irvin, Hilary Jackson, Peta Knott, Rebecca Lambert, Chris Loveluck, Colin Martin, Paula Martin, Miriam Miller, Chris "Bazooka" Morris, Tom Munnery, Courtney Nimura, Aidan O'Sullivan, Mike Page, Richard Perry, Cass Philippou, Julian Pooley, Rob Poulton, Nathan Richards, Isabel Rivera, Marcy Rockman, Blake Sawicky, Barney Sloane, Claire Smith, Mark Staniforth, Lynley Wallis, Gareth Watkins, Rebecca Weiss, Howard Williams, Michael Williams, and Elliot Wragg. Special thanks also to the members of the Kentish Town Yacht Club for moral support and worldly advice, in particular to its founder members Geoffrey Craig, Bethan Crockett, Joanne Gillis, Mark Gillis, Kyra Larkin, Ali Naftalin, and Matt O'Neill.

Last but not least, thanks to my wife, Jennifer Young, for all her support, encouragement, and constructive criticism. It was once said: I thank you for bringing me here.

Introduction

One of the things that most archaeologists hate about archaeology is how misunderstood it is; we meet people all the time who have never met an archaeologist, or who did not realize that one can have a career as an archaeologist, or who think that archaeologists spend their time digging up dinosaurs. Almost as bad, we meet people who have heard of archaeology and perhaps even have met real archaeologists, but who have a misconceived notion of the discipline and its practitioners.

The myth of archaeology runs from the adventure of tomb raiding at the one extreme to the tedium of unending work in dusty archives at the other. The reality is, of course, far more complex. Thus, this book is an introduction not to what archaeology *is*, but to what archaeologists *do*, and, therefore, to what the archaeological community is like. To that end, this book is about the profession of archaeology, because modern archaeology is a vocation akin to law or medicine; the various chapters of the book discuss the different jobs open to budding archaeologists.

Although the main users of this book are likely to be prospective archaeologists – archaeology students, in particular – the intention is that this book will be of interest and use to anyone who has ever wondered what archaeologists actually do on a daily basis. Friends and family of current archaeologists might thus find this book of use; so too should anyone in industry, business, government, or the nonprofit sector who has contact with archaeologists, as well as colleagues in related disciplines and professions such as geography, geology, and history (who may identify some similarities in outlook and lifestyle). This is a potentially very large audience, which says something about how much archaeology has an impact on people's daily lives, whether they realize it or not.

Why Archaeology Matters – Archaeology in the Real World

In a book about the profession of archaeology, it is as well to address early on the significance of archaeology: why archaeology matters in the real world. At the time of this writing, the world is embroiled in crises, both human and natural – wars, social and economic disaster and disorder (especially the ongoing impacts of the global economic crash of 2007 onward), unexpected environmental disasters, and human-created incidents. It is thus a fair question to ask: Why does archaeology matter? Why should people spend their time studying archaeology, and why should society at large fund and support archaeology through various means? Should not this time and these resources be spent on something else, something potentially more "useful" to society? As the wonderfully named archaeologists Fritz and Plog (1970: 412) once wrote:

> We suspect that unless archaeologists find ways to make their research increasingly relevant to the modern world, the modern world will find itself increasingly capable of getting along without archaeologists.

True in 1970 and equally true now, the following sections highlight the major reasons that archaeology is relevant to society and why archaeology is a justifiable thing on which to spend scarce time and resources (see Sabloff 2008 for a more detailed explanation of this).

Studying, Exploring, Protecting, and Managing the Past for Present and Future Generations Is a Moral Obligation of Any Civilized Society

Taking its lead from the issue of "birthright," there is demonstrable evidence that humans have shown an interest in their past since the very origins of humanity itself – that such an interest is one of the self-defining features of humanity, a characteristic that makes us what we are. As a starting point, it is reasonable to suggest that a society with no respect for its past is no society at all. Imagine, not a world, but just a single country, without any heritage – no books or TV shows; no historic sites to visit; no imagination, thoughts, or cares about the past. This imaginary world is dystopian – close to that depicted by George Orwell in his novel *1984*. An appreciation of the past, of history – of *archaeology* – is integral to civilized society. Archaeology is part of the fabric of society – not a desirable extra, but a quintessential part. It is in the interests of archaeologists in particular, and the public in general, to better acknowledge this.

Archaeology Tells Us about the Past, and the Past Tells Us about Both Our Present and Possible Future Worlds

If archaeology tells us about our ancestors and ourselves, it follows that it can also be used to help us shape the future in ways that we want, including trying to avoid the worst aspects of the past. As Sabloff (2008: 17) writes:

> Archaeology can play helpful roles in broad, critical issues facing the world today. Archaeological research not only can inform us in general about lessons to be learned from the successes and failures of past cultures and provide policy makers with useful contexts for future decision-making, but it really can make an immediate difference in the world today and directly affect the lives of people at this very moment.

There is, for example, a growing body of work on archaeological lessons of climate change – how human adaptation to past climate change can be used to inform modern decisions about responses to climate change in our and future worlds. This is the type of "critical issue" identified by Sabloff. Archaeology demonstrates, time and again, that humans are resourceful, inventive, and above all adaptive: as a species, we are good at dealing with change. Archaeology helps give both "broad brush" and "little picture" examples of how humans can adapt to climate change, from entire civilizations down to individuals – for example, how we can live in a more sustainable manner in more energy-efficient buildings. The problem is that archaeology is rather bad at highlighting this supremely practical use of its knowledge. The global community of archaeologists needs to work much harder at demonstrating this use to decision makers in government and industry alike.

Archaeology, of all the sociohistorical disciplines, is uniquely good at connecting with people, because it deals with things – with real, tangible objects. Telling a story with images and objects; learning through handling and especially doing things; having a physical connection with a place, culture, and past by exploring an ancient site are demonstrably some of the best ways to engage with both the past and the present. Such types of active learning are also among the best types of learning in terms of engagement and data retention, those types of learning most recommended by educational psychologists. Thus, if archaeology can contribute to planning for critical issues such as climate change, it can do so in ways that really connect with people. Climate change, in particular, is an issue that can seem insurmountable – a problem too big and complex for any community, let alone individual people, to deal with. However, one of the key lessons of archaeology – and one of its unique advantages – is the human scale: archaeology can be used to humanize responses to climate change; to take responses down to a personal, individual level; to show how we as individuals and small groups such as families can make changes in our own lives that matter collectively – things such as energy efficiency, recycling, and so on that were done in the past and need to be done more now and in the future.

Archaeology Contributes More to Any Economy Than It Takes from Any Economy: Archaeology Is a Net Contributor to Many National Economies

This is the ultimate, market-led reality of archaeology, and in the brutal economic circumstances of the early twenty-first century it sometimes appears to be the only argument that holds much sway. Here is an indicative example of the purely economic value of broader heritage in contemporary society comes from the UK for the financial year 2009–10 (see Davies 2010 citing HLF 2010; Heritage Alliance 2010) (similar data exist for other countries as well – see Chapter 1):

- Tourism is the UK's fifth largest industry and its third largest export earner; specifically, heritage tourist spending (including that on attractions, food, and accommodations) directly generates £4.3 billion of GDP and employment for 113,000 people – making heritage tourism comparable to the film, motor vehicle manufacturing, and advertising industries.
- The wider impacts of heritage tourism on the UK economy (i.e., supply-chain impacts on goods and services) increase this heritage tourism contribution to £11.9 billion of GDP and 270,000 jobs (some estimates put this figure even higher, as much as £20.6 billion of GDP and 466,000 jobs [Heritage Alliance 2010]).
- More than 31 million paying visits a year are made to heritage attractions in England alone; 69 percent of the population of England (29 million people) visited an historic site in 2009-10 (figures for Scotland and Wales are not available).
- Historic sites are a key driver of international tourism in the UK: more inbound tourists plan to visit historic sites than to visit the theater, museums and galleries, or sporting events. Ten million holiday trips are made by overseas visitors to the UK each year – and four in ten of these visitors cite heritage as their primary motivation for visiting the UK.

Archaeology Is Fun – and Fun Is Too Important a Thing Not to Be Taken Seriously

Countless studies have demonstrated that a society that has adequate leisure time is healthier in both mind and body. Moreover, people want to be involved in the study and protection of the past. As an example, more than ten times as many people belong to heritage organizations than belong to political parties in the UK: in the summer of 2009, membership of the National Trust (a key voluntary sector heritage body in the UK) reached an all-time high of 3.8 million people. In total, some 66 percent of the historic environment of the UK is supported, managed, or owned privately or by civic heritage bodies, and there are more than 2,000 community archaeology groups with more than 200,000 members.

Archaeology matters for all these reasons. It is worth doing, and is worth studying. It is worth paying for, and worth protecting. It is worth fighting for when placed under threat.

What Is This Book About?

This book provides a short guide to the profession of – careers in – archaeology in, primarily, the UK, US, and Australia. The following chapters outline, in as straightforward a fashion as possible, the entire archaeological career process in these nations – the various job options, the training that is required, and how one gets positions in the academic, commercial, and government worlds. Focused on archaeological employment (i.e., work connected directly to the understanding of past societies through the recovery and study of material culture), the book also includes discussion of careers in related heritage professions such as museums and conservation sciences – although it does not go into great detail about these, which are too specialized not to be the subject of an entirely different book. To this end, the book includes interviews with real archaeologists currently at work across the UK, US, and Australia, all young professionals who began their careers within approximately the past ten years.

Although the case studies in this book are focused on the UK, US, and Australia, these are not the only places where archaeologists live and work – these are merely the locations where the author has contacts and experience. As discussed in Chapter 1, there are archaeologists at work in almost every nation of the world – and more now probably at work in nations such as India and China than in most of the rest of the world combined. A second version of this book published in ten years' time will tell a very different story of the experiences of this growing global community of archaeologists, for the situation changes almost daily; so too would a version of this book written, for example, by a Chinese or Indian archaeologist at work today, or a book written by an Indigenous archaeologist living and working in the US or Australia.[1] The amazing work of archaeologists at work across the many different nations of Africa, to name but one continent, for example, is almost entirely unknown outside a small circle of professional archaeologists – and although the results of their fieldwork are well published, the experiences of undertaking this fieldwork are not (although see, for example, the many contributions in Philips' (2005) *Writing African History*, and the work of Walz (2009) for a frank example of fieldwork in Tanzania).

Closer to home, only two hours away by train from the office in London in which this book was written, a French archaeologist writing in a Paris-based office would tell a very different story, for the archaeological community and career structure of France is profoundly different from that of the UK. And even just within Europe, the communities and career structures vary considerably – the aforementioned hypothetical French archaeologist works in a very different cultural environment from that of potential research collaborators elsewhere in Europe, far more so than

---

[1] See Ucko, Ling, and Hubert (2007) for evidence of the former in various nations around the world, including in China, Nigeria, Korea, Mexico, Southern Africa and Thailand; Smith and Burke (2007, chapter 6) for a discussion of working with Indigenous Australians; Watkins (2000) for an example of the Indigenous archaeology of the US; and Nicholas (2010) and Smith and Wobst (2005) for examples of people being and becoming Indigenous archaeologists around the world.

the differences in experience and career structure among archaeologists working in different parts of the US, UK, and Australia.

One of the sad facts of present life is that the professional community and general public alike grossly underappreciate the stories and experiences of these archaeologists' different lifestyles. There is shockingly little written about the lives of modern archaeologists anywhere in the world. This book focuses on the UK, US, and Australia partly because that is where the author has experience, but mainly because these are some of the only places where enough published literature exists for a consistent, verifiable story to be told. The author looked long and hard for published examples from other countries, and found virtually nothing – although a new series of books being produced in conjunction with the World Archaeological Congress, the Global Cultural Heritage Manual Series, is beginning to redress this balance (see Smith and Burke's (2007) first volume on Australia, with more to follow on other countries, and Nicholas' (2010) *Being and Becoming Indigenous Archaeologists*). As discussed elsewhere in this book, we do not even know how many archaeologists are currently at work around the world. Therefore, one of the wider aims of this book is to encourage more archaeologists out there to tell their stories – to write their own versions of this book.

A Note on Terminology

To make this book as readable as possible, it is structured into some broad over-arching chapters on the main sectors of archaeological employment (see Figure 1). These chapters' titles use the same terms for the different sectors discussed in the text. But archaeology is a complex international business, and not everyone uses the same terms, which can easily lead to confusion.

To try to keep things clear and simple, a glossary of archaeological terms is provided in Appendix 2, outlining official and unofficial terminology, concepts and meanings, legal terms, organizations, and acronyms. In addition, here is what is meant by the terms used throughout the rest of the book for the different sectors of archaeological employment:

- *Cultural resource management (CRM) archaeology*: archaeological employment undertaken as a consequence of various "polluter pays" laws and policies of different countries, legal requirements for archaeological work to be undertaken in advance of developments such as housing, industry, or transport development.
- *Academic archaeology*: archaeological employment undertaken within the setting of a university, college, or other place of higher education, and generally connected with teaching and research.
- *Local government archaeology*: archaeological employment undertaken within the setting of a state (in federal systems such as the US and Australia), county, borough, district, unitary, or other local authority settings, usually in relation to the provision of information to people and the enforcement of local heritage laws within a defined area.

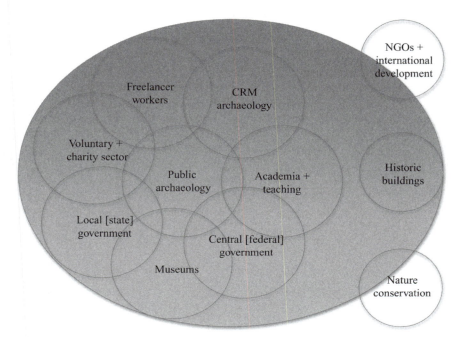

Figure 1. The structure and interrelationships of the archaeological job market and related disciplines.

- *Central government archaeology*: archaeological employment undertaken within the setting of regional or national government (the federal government level in those countries that have such systems), usually in relation to provision of information to people and the enforcement of national heritage laws.
- *Public and community archaeology*: archaeological employment undertaken within the setting of interaction with the general public. In truth, it is not a distinctive sector comparable with the preceding sectors, which all involve (or should involve) public and community archaeology. There are specialist skills relating to these practices, however, which is why these are considered separately in their own chapter of this book.

Chapter 1

What Is – and Isn't – Archaeology?

What Is Archaeology?

Archaeology is usually defined along the lines of "the study of past cultures through the analysis of surviving material remains"; if a historian is someone who studies surviving *documents* to understand the past, so an archaeologist is someone who studies instead surviving *things* (the formal term is "material culture"). Digging deeper, this means that an archaeologist might study, at the large scale, an entire landscape to look at traces of, say, ancient agriculture, and, at the small scale, the microscopic remains of plant pollen from a particular site in that same landscape to understand the species of plants propagated by the people who once lived there. Along the way, the archaeologist of this imaginary landscape is likely to look at a mass of other evidence, too, down to the broken pots dumped in a disused well by way of the outline of the houses in an abandoned village. It is likely, too, that the imaginary archaeologist will find evidence of trade and exchange – perhaps some worked beads made of a stone that is foreign to the study area and in fact come from only a few specific locations hundreds of miles away, perhaps even from across the sea.

In this brief picture-portrait, a host of different aspects of archaeology as a discipline, and archaeologists as a community, are touched on. Archaeology studies tangible, material things that one can pick up, touch, and feel; it also studies, through these surviving things, far more ephemeral concepts about people and places, cultures and communities: the aforementioned beads were worked by someone who had some artistic scheme for them in mind; the designs the beads carried appeal enough for someone else to trade them, perhaps multiple times, over a long distance until they ended up in their final location. The archaeologists who found the beads then did so after a series of other processes that took them to that one site, in that one landscape. They may have planned to visit that specific site after a long period of research and planning – or they may have been led to the site as a consequence of development or industry in the area or even as a result of a chance discovery by a passerby. The archaeologists had to have the training to be able to identify the beads and to excavate them in a controlled fashion so the beads' exact location was recorded in relation to hundreds, perhaps thousands, of other materials found on site; they also had to have equipment and resources to get to the site in the landscape, along with permission from various government and even private authorities to be there in the first place. Having completed their fieldwork, the archaeologists then had to take the beads away and analyze their structure in a laboratory to realize that the beads came from far away; they also had to compare their data with those of other archaeologists to understand the significance of the find. Having realized the significance of the discovery – or equally, having realized that the find is mundane and insignificant, because identical beads have been found on many similar sites both near and far away – the archaeologists will have written up the results of their exploration and discovery and published these results in a book or journal, and probably online as well. They may also have presented their findings in a lecture or at a conference, or even on a TV show. The beads, meanwhile, will have remained in a laboratory to be conserved before being put on display, or stored in a museum or archive.

This picture-portrait gives a sense of the different components of an archaeologist's life: project planning and management in advance of any work; fieldwork, exploring and excavating an archaeological site; lab work, analyzing remains; and desk work, thinking about the meaning of a discovery before writing, lecturing, and other forms of public engagement. A formalized understanding of all these skills can then be gained from the UK's *National Occupational Standards for Archaeology* (TORC 2010), which gives some idea of the diverse array of skills put into play by a modern archaeologist. There can be no doubt that it is this mix of practical and theoretical, physical and intellectual activities that represents one of the strongest appeals of archaeology to its practitioners.

So much for the basic truth of archaeology and archaeologists; what of the myth? Depending on whom you ask, archaeology is either incredibly lucky or utterly damned by being an eternally stereotyped profession – adventurous, perhaps even glamorous, and above all popular, considering the viewing figures for archaeology-themed TV shows and book sales: millions of people around the world are interested in archaeology. The profession has endlessly debated the rights and wrongs of this public perception of archaeology. This subject has even been tackled in a formal way by the über-archaeologist of archaeologists, Cornelius Holtorf (2005, 2007a). Back in 1999, the US-based Society for American Archaeology was so concerned about this issue that it even commissioned a report exploring public perceptions and attitudes about archaeology (see Ramos and Duganne 2000). It is not the purpose of this book to debate the rights and wrongs of the mass representation of archaeology, except in passing, by contributing this particular description of the profession in the early twenty-first century. A few "pop" characteristics can usefully be noted, however, that are of significance to the understanding of what archaeology is and, thus, what archaeologists do.

Key within this is simply the fact that people *do* care about archaeology and, by default, about archaeologists – many people are interested in both the process and people. Secondary to this is the fact that this interest is overwhelmingly positive. Archaeology is a field that enjoys a special place of enduring, affectionate popular myth: we are the "good guys," at least in European-influenced society; the populations of many other countries around the world do not always feel the same way, however, when the history of European colonial oppression means that archaeologists are often viewed with suspicion at best, and open hostility at worst. Despite this, not too many other professions have such an unequivocally positive place in popular culture; for every good TV cop or lawyer there is a bad one, for instance. Even in comparable academic settings, archaeology has an enviable position – there are plenty of historians who would kill for the kind of media attention that archaeology seems to be able to command at its whim.

Archaeology, truth be told, is incredibly lucky to be seen as a distinct and even glamorous field – it is rare to meet people who are cynical about archaeology and archaeologists. To use a political analogy, this makes archaeology a tiny country that "punches above its weight" on the global stage and enjoys a special relationship with many other nations. This is not bad for a discipline that is barely more than a century old.

Furthermore, this is an incredibly small community. Globally, there are no total recorded figures for professional archaeologists because the sector is too small for government statisticians to track the industry (although specific albeit partial figures for some nations do exist, as discussed later), but a fair guess would be no more than 40,000 people globally employed in archaeology, with perhaps another 40,000 students of various types (to this should then be added, however, hundreds of thousands, if not millions, of active volunteer archaeologists at work around the world, and many millions more passive consumers of archaeology through books, TV shows, and site visits). For example, the World Archaeological Congress (WAC; a nongovernmental, not-for-profit organization and the only representative worldwide body of practicing archaeologists) has a membership in the thousands, representing nearly every nation on earth. WAC's most recent meeting – the Sixth World Archaeological Congress, held in Ireland in 2008 – was attended by more than 1,800 archaeologists (professionals, volunteers, and students) from some seventy-five countries, with WAC supporting the attendance of around 230 participants from Indigenous groups and economically disadvantaged countries. Furthermore, the financial barriers to joining organizations such as WAC mean that there are many more professional archaeologists than there are members of such organizations, to a ratio of at least 2:1 or even 3 or 4:1 – so if WAC has, say, 500 members in any one country, it is a fair guess that there are at least twice as many practicing archaeologists in the same country, possibly three or even four times as many.

The History and Development of Archaeology as a Career

Until the early 1960s it was relatively simple to define both what archaeology was and who archaeologists were. Archaeology, from its antiquarian origins in the eighteenth century onward, involved a tiny group of people, all of them white, all middle or upper class, and virtually all of them men, working on the surviving evidence of past cultures, both excavated physical remains and surviving documents. The majority of these people were based in universities and museums in affluent early industrialized nations, particularly Britain and the United States but also other European colonial powers such as France and Germany, with a few schools scattered adjacent to the archaeology that these people were most interested in excavating, especially in major urban centers such as Rome, Athens, Jerusalem, and Baghdad (in the United States there was also dedicated research into the prehistoric civilizations of the Southwest – locations equally remote, both physically and conceptually in that period at least, from the urban centers of academia and government, where the majority of researchers were based). A few of these people were paid to be archaeologists, but most had private incomes of one sort or another.

Around these individuals then circulated a far larger band of semiprofessional archaeologists of very mixed background and ability, ranging from genuinely dedicated and able scholars to liars, charlatans, and thieves who saw in the burgeoning scientific discipline of archaeology a chance to get rich, get famous, or simply have a good time (see Hudson 1981 for a sample discussion of this in the United Kingdom; Patterson 1994 or Neumann and Sanford 2001: 3–23 for a discussion of this in the United States). This period was, by all accounts, a golden age enjoyed by a chosen few (Figure 2), and is the archaeological world depicted by people such as the novelist Agatha Christie, whose second husband, Max Mallowan, was one of the archaeologists in question (see Trümpler 2001). This is also the world that has inspired many modern depictions of archaeology, from the *Indiana Jones* and *Mummy* movies to the *Tomb Raider* video games and countless others.

Hesitantly at first in the 1950s ands 1960s, then speeding up in the 1970s and 1980s, a series of occurrences changed the world of archaeology forever. Some of these changes came about from within the discipline of archaeology; others came from outside and were the result of much larger changes to society as a whole. Undoubtedly, the biggest impact came from the rise of the "ownership debate," linked to the domestic reform of civil liberties on the one hand and the formalization of the legal protection of heritage sites on the other. A major external driver of this process was also the wider decolonization process following the breakup of European colonial rule around the world following World War II, where many newly self-governing nations saw the protection and promotion of their distinctive cultural heritage to be a key part of nation building.

11

Until the mid-1960s there was, effectively, no legal protection for antiquities in almost any country of the world – with precious few exceptions, the owners of land could pretty much do what they liked with historic materials on their property and, as long as they had permission from the landowner to be there and thus did not break broader laws of trespass and theft, so could anyone visiting a property. Although, technically, many nations had some basic laws to prevent the movement of historic materials outside of their home country (in the UK, for example, the Ancient Monuments Protection Act of 1882; in the United States, the Antiquities Act of 1906), in reality these laws were regularly flouted; in many cases a "scientific" justification of "research" was used for the removal of materials. As a result of a series of important sites being destroyed, however, there was an increasing lobby to better protect historic sites, both above and below ground. This lobby coincided with a far louder, larger, and fundamentally more important lobby for civil liberties, particularly for comprehensive legal (including property and voting) rights. A part of that battle included a fight, still shamefully not yet won in many corners of the world, for the control of cultural sites and remains by descendant, Indigenous Communities – particularly the Indigenous Communities of the Americas, Australasia, and elsewhere. This process includes battling for control of everything from entire landscapes covering thousands of square miles to the repatriation of stolen material items and even human remains. The latter, held in their thousands in major Western museums and archives since their "collection" by various colonial powers in the nineteenth and early twentieth centuries on the basis of, at best, pseudoscientific study, is one of the great historic crimes of archaeology, and remains an extremely emotive issue for descendant communities (see Colwell-Chanthaphonh and Ferguson 2008).

In terms of the practice of archaeology as discussed in this book, the reform of the legal system had a greater impact in a different way. Until the 1960s, people practicing archaeology usually worked outside their home countries. Although funding and facilities might be based in, say, the United States or UK (and although materials might be shipped back to those locations), the majority of actual fieldwork was being done in other nations, particularly in the Middle East but also in Central and South America, the Indian subcontinent, Africa, and Australia. In this work, these individuals were simply following the established principles of their respective colonial empires. Following (and in some cases as a result of) the destruction, rebuilding, and colonial collapse of World War II and its aftermath, however, more and more archaeological sites began to be discovered in "home" nations such as Britain and the United States. Some of these sites were discovered as a result of research, but an increasing number of discoveries came about as a result of accident, during new road or building construction, or in the course of major landscape works such as dam construction and even new farming techniques, such as the introduction of fully mechanized deep plowing in Britain, which led to countless sites being discovered in the postwar period. The rebuilding of many historic cities of Europe following the aerial bombardment and ground conflict of the war also led to such discoveries, as ruins were pulled down and new buildings, requiring deeper foundations, constructed in their place; our understanding of the ancient

Figure 2. The development of archaeology as a career: British archaeologist Mortimer Wheeler visiting an excavation while working as Director-General of the Archaeological Survey of India in the late 1940s. Wheeler was one of the first professional archaeologists and also one of the first ever "television archaeologists," appearing regularly on TV shows from the 1950s onward (© UCL Institute of Archaeology 2010, courtesy of Ian Carroll).

origins and layout of cities such as London was transformed as a result of such discoveries.

Meanwhile, postwar urban planners were also taking their toll on such heritage, as new road schemes, grids, and even entire new urban landscapes were laid out. The 1960's focus on domestic archaeology also saw new approaches to the new types of sites being discovered – indeed, an expansion of what society as a whole understood to be "archaeology." The dominance of classical archaeology began to wane under these circumstances, and new approaches and schools of thought emerged. On one hand, the detailed study of prehistoric civilizations became a key issue; on the other hand, "historical archaeology" began to drive a very different approach to both classical and prehistoric archaeology. The differences in philosophy and approach of these three strands of archaeology created a theoretical divide that remains, to some extent, in the present day, and is discussed in more detail later.

By the late 1960s, the often senseless destruction of historic sites led to the rise of what became known as "rescue archaeology" in the UK (and "salvage" archaeology in the United States and elsewhere). At the forefront of this movement in the UK at least were two organizations, RESCUE: the British Archaeological Trust (founded in 1971) and Save Britain's Heritage (founded in 1975). Philip Rahtz's famous book

Rescue Archaeology (1974) brought the plight of archaeological sites under threat to a wider audience, and poet John Betjeman's involvement in the campaigns to save Euston Arch and St. Pancras Railway Station in central London similarly brought to light threats to historic buildings, especially those of more recent construction, such as those from the Victorian period (see Jones 1984; Delafons 1997). Central to this process was lobbying to enhance the legal protection of historic sites, particularly to create legal instruments specifically associated with the protection and preservation of historic materials. In the United States, a cornerstone of this process was – and remains to this day – the National Historic Preservation Act (1966), which established several key institutions: the Advisory Council on Historic Preservation, the State Historic Preservation Office, the National Register of Historic Places, and the Section 106 review process, a series of organizations and policies further strengthened by the enactment, three years later, of the National Environmental Policy Act (1969) (see King 2002, 2004, 2005, 2009; Neumann and Sanford 2001). Similarly, in the UK, a series of Historic Buildings Councils (one each for England, Scotland, and Wales) was created via the Historic Buildings and Ancient Monuments Act (1953), the forerunners of the modern national heritage bodies in the UK of English Heritage, Historic Scotland, and Cadw that were established under the terms of the National Heritage Act (1983) and responsible, in particular, for key nationally important historic sites protected under the Ancient Monuments and Archaeological Areas Act (1979) (for archaeological sites and monuments) and the Planning (Listed Buildings and Conservation Areas) Act (1990) (for listed buildings) (see Hunter and Ralston 2006).

Even given such new legal protection, however, archaeology in this context remained woefully underprotected and underfunded for the next twenty years, until the formal rise of the "polluter pays" principle in the late 1980s and early 1990s – the principle that the activities and organizations adversely affecting a historic site should pay for its monitoring, study, protection, and preservation whether in situ (being left in place) or by record (destroying the site but creating an extensive documentary archive of what was previously there) (see King 2005: 60–62). Such a principle had its origins in much earlier, similar statutory protection for significant natural rather than historic environment sites and features such as parks and gardens, "green belt" sections of countryside on the fringes of cities and important woodlands, and coastal and other major landscape features. In the United States the drivers for such practices are laws such as the National Historic Preservation Act (1966, amended 1980 and 1992), the National Environmental Policy Act (1969), the Archaeological Resources and Historic Preservation Act (1974), and the Archaeological Resources Protection Act (1979) – at least, primarily when projects have an impact on federally managed lands and seas (also on projects in which there is some kind of federal involvement, in the form of federal funding or licensing arrangements). On private land in the United States, however, state laws and regulations (as well as Tribal and other local laws) that protect heritage vary very widely from state to state, and a similar situation is in place in many other federal systems, such as in Australia and Canada.

In Britain, the arrival of similarly dedicated protection for historic sites came about only in the 1990s thanks to a series of related pieces of government policy, Planning Policy Guidance (PPG) Notes No. 15 (*Planning and the Historic Environment*) (1994) and No. 16 (*Archaeology and Planning*) (1990) in England and Wales, Planning Advice Note No. 42 (*Archaeology*) (1994) and National Planning Policy Guideline No. 5 (*Archaeology and Planning*) (1998) in Scotland, and Planning Policy Statement No. 6 (*Planning, Archaeology and the Built Heritage*) (1999) in Northern Ireland. These finally enshrined the principle of statutory payment for work on historic sites in advance of development – in the UK's case, on all land, irrespective of government, private, or other ownership – and led to the formalization of the cultural resource management (CRM) archaeology environment of the present, alongside its corollary, the curatorial archaeological community charged with monitoring such work. In 2010, PPGs 15 and 16 in England and Wales were replaced with one overarching but essentially similar piece of guidance covering the entire "historic environment" (i.e., archaeological sites, historic buildings, and historic parks, gardens, and landscapes): PPS (Planning Policy Statement) 5: *Planning for the Historic Environment*.

Similarly, in 2010 in Scotland, PAN 42 and NPPG5 were replaced with Scottish Planning Policy, an overarching planning framework in which heritage is one component (as advised by the Scottish Historic Environment Policy [SHEP] of 2009). Similar laws, policies, and processes to those described previously for the United States and UK, such as the Commonwealth Environment Protection and Biodiversity Conservation Act (1999), exist in many other nations around the world, covering both terrestrial and maritime archaeology. There are also particularly strong laws protecting Indigenous archaeology in many nations, most famously the Commonwealth Aboriginal and Torres Strait Islander Heritage Protection Act (1984) and the Commonwealth Native Title Act (1993) in Australia and the Native American Graves Protection and Repatriation Act (1990) in the US.

Archaeology also began to undergo change from the 1960s onward as a result of broader social factors. Central to this was the rise of the "new" universities – linked to new social mobility, itself the result of the baby boomer population explosion of post-World War II – and within these a vast increase in the number of university departments in, and courses on, archaeology. Until the 1960s there were both very few courses on, as well as jobs in, archaeology; after the 1960s there were more of both. Although this process was most visible in countries such as the UK, US, and Australia, it was taking place in many other countries around the world.

Particularly in the UK, US, and Australia – and, to a more varied extent, in other countries – the changes discussed previously also created a greater need for professional CRM archaeologists to advise on work in relation to development; the new demand for university courses similarly created a greater need for professional academic archaeologists based in universities to teach and undertake research. Although this was at first a mutually agreeable situation, the realities of the different pay, working conditions, and social status of these different types of archaeologists soon began to lead to a literal split, reflecting the existing split in conditions and locations, of the practice, methods, and theories of archaeology. The uneasy relationship between CRM archaeologists on one hand and academic archaeologists on the other is something that is returned to later in this chapter, and has its origins in this period. Although all within the discipline agree that archaeology is, broadly, a social science tasked with studying the surviving physical remains of past societies, there can be no doubt that for certain sectors of the archaeological community, the primary focus is on research into these materials and the understanding these provide of their parent societies, whereas for other sectors of the archaeological community the primary focus is on managing and maintaining these historic materials (sometimes referred to as historic resources, and by default who "owns" these, either the items or data relating to them) in situ or by record. In truth, all archaeologists are involved, or at least should be involved, in all these different processes.

Archaeology, as a broader whole, has enjoyed an unprecedented intellectual, as well as technical, growth from the 1960s onward, a process that has further sped up in the past decade thanks to the incredible recent advances in computer technology. The archaeologist of today benefits from a wealth of different theories, methods, practices, tools, and techniques developed over the past fifty years. Some of these advances have come from within the community and are of immense practical benefit. For example, the resistivity meter, which uses variations in an electric current passed through these features and the soil surrounding them to reveal evidence for buried features and structures, is only really of use to archaeologists and has been developed and refined largely within the discipline. In comparison, other advances have been developed by archaeologists in conjunction with other disciplines that have use for a particular technology – such as different forms of scientific dating technique, from the commonplace, such as dendrochronology and carbon-14 dating, to the rare and specialized, such as thermoluminescence, electron spin, and potassium–argon dating. Archaeology has also been unafraid to benefit from techniques and technologies developed entirely independent of it, one of the most useful recent examples being LiDAR (**li**ght **d**etection **a**nd **r**anging), a form of ground-based and aerial laser-scanning survey.

Alongside such refinements to the ways in which archaeologists can find, identify, and interpret sites, there has been a great theoretical development in archaeology – how archaeologists think about the ways people lived their lives in the past. Archaeological theory often has a bad name, accused of being a self-serving, overly complex, and willfully confusing process designed to obscure, rather than interpret, the past. A detailed discussion of theory is outside the scope of this book, but at heart archaeological theory is a tool – just like the other, more immediately practical, tools discussed earlier – designed to help us better understand the past. Just as a practical technique such as a resistivity survey helps identify *where* walls or ditches once ran, so good archaeological theory can help give an insight into *why* people felt it necessary to construct those same walls or ditches. People's lives – and, particularly, motivations – are complex things at the best of times in present circumstances, where we share similar values, beliefs, and lifestyles; people's lives in the past, even the relatively recent past of only a few generations ago, are far harder to understand, and their motivations are incredibly difficult to identify. Archaeologists use theory to help try to explain at least some small part of the thoughts that lie behind the physical evidence of particular materials, places, or activities. An excellent – and genuinely fun – introduction to theoretical archaeology comes in the form of two mystery novels written by the archaeologist Adrian Praetzellis, *Death By Theory* (2000) and *Dug to Death* (2003) (a more conventional but easy-to-read introduction is Johnson's [2009] *Archaeological Theory: An Introduction*).

World Archaeology

Archaeology in the twenty-first century is a truly global profession. Virtually every nation on earth has some professional archaeologists at work, although as discussed earlier, no one knows how many there are in total. The focus of this book, as discussed in the introduction, is primarily the UK, US, and Australia, but this focus should not discourage any budding archaeologists reading this book anywhere in the world: if you really want to become an archaeologist, then although some of the circumstances described in this book may not fit your particular country, the basic principles of why and how we do archaeology remain the same. Moreover, archaeology is an international, inclusive discipline. Within this, it acknowledges its past mistakes – and the behavior of many European colonial archaeologists working in other countries in the nineteenth and twentieth centuries was disgraceful – and strives for a better future for all. No one, of any age, origin, or background, should ever feel discouraged from becoming involved in archaeology. No one should ever be told – at least not by an archaeologist – "you cannot be involved." The future of archaeology clearly lies in more and more archaeologists learning and working in their home nations around the world, rather than the current European–US–Australian dominance of practice and theory. The global growth areas for archaeology are the same as wider socioeconomic growth and leadership areas: Asia (especially China), the Indian subcontinent, Africa, and South and Central America. All these regions already have well-established archaeological communities, but there is no doubt that it is these communities that will experience distinctively greater growth, come to relatively greater prominence, and become leaders in both archaeological practice and theory in the future, more so than the longer established European–US–Australian archaeological communities. Although the practice of archaeology will undoubtedly continue in such locations, the future of archaeological leadership lies beyond these traditional centers of power of the discipline.

Thematic Routes in Archaeology

The thousands of archaeologists at work today around the world comprise myriad different approaches to – and training in – archaeology. The particular issues of this training are discussed in Chapter 2. However, it is worth briefly outlining the major different approaches – sometimes called schools or disciplines – of archaeology, how these approaches interrelate, and what the differences between these approaches mean for the employability of archaeologists (Figure 3). Although it is possible to work within more than one of these approaches, the reality is that most professional archaeologists end up fairly firmly fixed within one from an early stage – usually when they decide for which university courses to apply or, at the latest, when they choose to go on to specialize as postgraduate students. Archaeology is such a broad field that to thrive, people inevitably must specialize. These different approaches are also, however, theoretical – concerned with variations in the differing conceptual approaches involved in interpreting the physical remains of the past – and so at times are also ideological/political: some members of these different groups have fundamental disagreements with the philosophies and physical approaches to the past of other groups, in the same manner as other people have fundamental disagreements over political or religious outlooks and beliefs. This can be a deadly serious issue – very occasionally, people have come to physical blows over such disagreements, but much more often there is formalized confrontation at academic symposia and through specialized books and media. However, it should also be noted that partly this is an issue of geography – these approaches or schools of archaeological approach are at least partly drawn along national lines, and are also partly a question of regional environmental specialty – such as African, American, Asian, Australian, Chinese, European, or Indian archaeology.

Anthropological Archaeology

Anthropological archaeology is the study of the physical evidence of the human past before records began – an incredibly long span from millions (in terms of the general evolution of humans) and hundreds of thousands (in terms of the specific development of biologically modern humans) of years ago to, depending on where you look in the world, only thousands of years ago. In this sense, it is sometimes seen as the root of all other archaeological approaches – and it is certainly as influential (and contentious) as this implies. There are also marked differences in theoretical and practical approaches within anthropological archaeology and also among the anthropological approaches of different countries. In the US, where the term originates, this always has been the dominant force in academic archaeology and, indeed, the theoretical worldview of many other professional archaeologists – the focus of the majority of university departments and museums, a driving force of much theory and debate, and so the dominant influence on the majority of students. This is so much so that "anthropological archaeology" is virtually synonymous with simply "archaeology" in much of the US, as well as in other countries with strong ties to the US. In comparison, in the UK (and, to a lesser extent, in Australia and elsewhere), the term "anthropological archaeology" is not commonly used; in these locations, the related disciplines of archaeology and anthropology are more clearly delineated, and the term "anthropology" is usually used specifically for what, in the US, is often termed "cultural/social anthropology" (the study of living cultures through anthropological techniques). However, many of the theoretical and practical approaches of anthropological archaeology are shared with what is

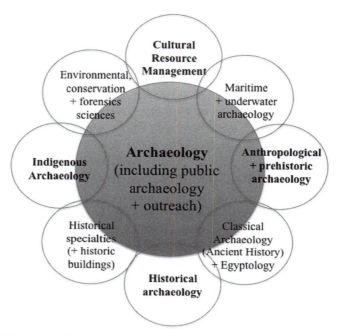

Figure 3. The major thematic groupings in archaeology and related disciplines.

commonly known as prehistoric archaeology in the UK and Australia. Akin to that in the US, prehistoric archaeology in these countries is also a major focus of the majority of university departments and museums, a driving force of much theory and debate, and so a dominant influence on many students. This is also true of many other locations in the world – many nations of Europe and Asia, as well as parts of the Americas and Africa, for example, have an extremely strong focus on the study of prehistory.

The incredibly long time span of anthropological archaeology means that it is a focus of much development both of theory and practice – hence, its driving influence of much of the rest of wider archaeology. In terms of theory, the absence of written evidence on one hand, and the complex, fragmentary, and ambiguous nature of the limited physical evidence on the other, drives debate about how people lived and thought thousands or even hundreds of thousands of years ago. This same relative scarcity of evidence also drives much conflict about different theoretical approaches to the past.

In terms of practice, anthropological archaeology works very closely with related subjects, including geology, biology, physics, and chemistry, in the study of ancient remains (including, in particular, with biology in the study of biological or physical anthropology – the study of human evolution and genetic/physical variations – and with physics in the study of the accurate dating of the past through different "absolute" techniques of radiometric dating (based on the constant rate of decay of radioactive isotopes). Anthropological archaeologists also work with social science and humanities subjects, such as linguistics, in the study of ancient languages, and with art history in the study of ancient arts.

The diverse range of skills associated with anthropological archaeology, combined with its dominance of the university sector, means that anthropological archaeologists are employed in all the different career sectors of archaeology described in the following chapters. The dominance of this approach in the university sector also means that many different pre-university backgrounds are considered suitable for study in this field: newly arrived undergraduate students will come from a diverse array of backgrounds – some from the liberal arts and humanities, others from the sciences. Students of the latter, in particular, find anthropological archaeology, with its focus on applied science, especially appealing.

Historical Archaeology

If anthropological archaeology is the study of the physical evidence of the human past before records began, then historical archaeology is its natural partner – the study of cultures with some form of self-created documentary record. This makes historical archaeology hard to define (the date of first appearance of such documents varies enormously around the world) and also politically problematic: for example, what is the exact definition of "writing" – the most commonly accepted form of documentary record – and how does this relate to other types of documentary evidence, such as art or even oral history? By seeking to define itself, historical archaeology runs the risk of making pejorative assumptions about different cultures and civilizations, of being biased toward documentary cultures and assuming that any culture without a written record is somehow lesser than others that possess such records. Historical archaeology also runs the risk of being biased toward Eurocentric approaches to the past in terms of documentary chronology – not a perception of the past in relation to the present shared by all civilizations and cultures. These are certainly the accusations that many Indigenous Communities in the US and Australia make against historical archaeology, and with good reason: the study of their civilizations by non-Indigenous, colonial archaeologists making such biased assumptions was a major contributor to the destruction of these same cultures in the past, as the "findings" of archaeologists about these communities' lack of what, at the time, was accepted as documentary evidence – and so these communities' implicit primitiveness – was used to justify their destruction. Only more recently have the astounding evidence of oral, art historical, and other records of these cultures and their ways of perceiving the relationship of the past and the present begun to be appreciated. Modern historical archaeology works hard not to be biased in these ways, but the scars of past harm and the distrust this produces remain strong in many places around the world. Historical archaeology remains a complicated theoretical approach, combining theories and approaches of both anthropological and classical archaeology (and arguably a part of broader historical archaeology) alongside some of its own special skills.

"Modern" historical archaeology emerged in the US in the late nineteenth and early twentieth centuries in the particular study of the physical evidence of European colonization of the Americas, meaning within this post-1492 European impacts across South, Central, and North America. At first, historical archaeology focused more on the earlier periods of historical archaeology – of the evidence of fifteenth-, sixteenth-, and seventeenth-century colonization and settlement. More recently, historical archaeology has expanded to encompass the study of the remains from the eighteenth, nineteenth, and even twentieth and twenty-first centuries, including sites of "living memory" such as remains and documents of World War II and Cold War structures (even space debris), as well as twenty-first-century sites such as Ground Zero in New York. Historical archaeology is also strong in other former locations of European colonization, in particular Australia, with the study of pre- and, in particular, post-1788 European arrival on the continent, as well as in some nations of Africa – in particular, South Africa, with its long history of Portuguese, Dutch, and later British colonization. Historical archaeology is also now a major focus of British archaeology (and, to a much lesser extent, elsewhere in Europe), with the study of the physical remains of the industrialization of that country and even its postindustrial world of the twentieth and twenty-first centuries.

Central to historical archaeology is an inclusive approach to evidence. Although led by archaeology – by the study of physical remains – historical archaeology also uses documents of all kinds (e.g., texts and photos), oral and art histories, and anthropological sources – everything produced in some format by past societies. The physically rich remains of these more recent pasts make for incredible, in-depth understanding of wider civilizations as well as smaller communities and even groups or individuals of a type rare in prehistoric archaeology. Historical archaeology also uses many of the techniques – in particular, types of radiometric dating techniques – first developed by anthropological archaeology. And historical archaeology includes a number of subdisciplines and relationships with other disciplines: of the former, some historical archaeologists are specialists in particular types of surviving physical evidence such as historic buildings or ships; of the latter, there is a particularly close working relationship between historical archaeologists and many historians and art historians.

Once seen as very much the "poor cousin" of anthropological archaeology, historical archaeology is now a significant focus of university departments and museums, a driving force of much theory and debate, and thus a significant influence on many students. The sheer mass of historical archaeology that surrounds us in many countries – from historic buildings to parks, gardens, and landscapes, to shipwrecks and even historic aircraft – also means that this approach to archaeology has growing political influence, as well as a growing part of the archaeological job market, with historical archaeologists employed in all the different career sectors of archaeology described in the following chapters. In some cases, anthropological archaeologists and historical archaeologists work together in the same university departments and other organizations (particularly true in the UK); in other cases, these groups work separately – for instance, in the US, many historical archaeologists work not in anthropology departments but in combined historical archaeology and history departments.

Prospective students of historical archaeology, just as prospective anthropological archaeologists, tend to come from a diverse array of backgrounds. However, there can be no doubt that this approach attracts particularly those with an existing interest in history and art history – more students from a liberal arts background than the more science-oriented approaches of anthropological archaeology.

Classical Archaeology (Ancient History) and Egyptology

As discussed previously, classical archaeology and Egyptology – the study of the physical remains of the civilizations of ancient Egypt, Greece, and Rome – are the origin of "professional" archaeology: this is where people were first paid a living to work as archaeologists. Since that heyday, and in particular in the last generation or so, the disciplines of classical archaeology and Egyptology have seen something of a decline of influence – falling student numbers, closing university departments, and a drop of interest in key related skills, such as ancient languages. Alongside this, however, has been a somewhat confusing trend toward greater popular interest in these subjects in terms of TV shows – turn on the Discovery Channel almost anywhere in the world and at any time of day and the likelihood is that you will find a show titled something such as "Secrets of the Mummy."

Classical archaeology remains a major force in global archaeology, in particular in terms of museum archaeology, where collections of classical era materials remain a key component of many major international museums, such as the British Museum in London and the Louvre in Paris. The same is also true of Egyptology, discussed here with its sister discipline, classical archaeology, for reasons of clarity and brevity, but in truth a distinct subject of its own. There are, however, relatively few jobs in these fields in comparison with anthropological and historical archaeology. Although it may seem unfair, the truth is that even though graduating university students with a degree in classical archaeology or Egyptology are just as well trained as their classmates in these other specialties, they face a genuine problem of employability within the archaeological community, at least – CRM archaeology firms and local and national government offices of the types discussed in the following chapters generally prefer what they see as the more directly transferable skills of anthropological and historical archaeology. The irony is that, as noted earlier, many of the approaches and skills of historical archaeology are also those of classical archaeology and Egyptology, with an inclusive approach to all kinds of physical evidence. In addition to this, students of classical archaeology and Egyptology also have additional language skills in one or more ancient and modern languages. Altogether, the package of skills presented by a classical archaeologist or Egyptologist should be extremely attractive to any prospective employer, archaeological or otherwise. But the fact remains that this is a – albeit gently – declining subject, for reasons no one quite understands. Either a cause or a consequence of this is that it also tends to be much more self-selecting than either anthropological or historical archaeology: those who choose to enter this field tend to have an existing interest in it, fed by specialist skills such as the language competency highlighted earlier.

Indigenous Archaeology

Nicholas (2008: 1660) defines Indigenous archaeology as "an expression of archaeological theory and practice in which the discipline intersects with Indigenous values, knowledge, practices, ethics, and sensibilities." In this sense, it arguably encompasses both non-Indigenous archaeologists who work with Indigenous Communities, and also Indigenous archaeologists themselves – although this is an extremely emotive issue, and some archaeologists and Indigenous Peoples alike might disagree with this definition. Indigenous archaeology emerged out of the broader civil rights movement among the Indigenous Peoples of the world that is still actively being fought to this day. The longest history of Indigenous archaeology is in the US on one hand and Australia on the other, although in various forms its fight continues in many nations of the world, and not just in commonly expected places such as former European colonies or in environmentally threatened locations such as the Arctic. For instance, some members of European groups such as Gypsy–Roma–Traveler communities certainly define themselves as Indigenous (and their distinctive cultures are under threat); to a different extent, there is also a move toward "Indigenous archaeologies" of more modern communities such as the modern "traveler" groups of the 1960s onward (distinct from the Gypsy–Roma–Travelers).

In terms of professional pathways in archaeology, it is the Indigenous archaeology, and Indigenous archaeologists, of the US and Australia that are the focus of this book. This is not meant to be pejorative – it is simply recognition of the distinctive history of Indigenous archaeology among these communities, including a long history of political activism as well as academic study and self-definition (see, for example, Watkins 2000; Nicholas 2010). That being said, even though advances have been made, Indigenous archaeology is likely to – and needs to – advance still further. There are relatively few Indigenous archaeologists at work around the world, and few dedicated university departments, museums, or government offices. The laws to protect such communities and their cultural heritage around the world also remain relatively weak (especially in comparison with other types of cultural and natural heritage protection). Thus, there is still something of a self-denying process at work here: few Indigenous People become archaeologists, not because they are not interested in archaeology, but because the opportunities for study and employment are too few. Meanwhile, in general, Indigenous People also remain underrepresented among university students because of glaring disparities in wealth and pre-university education, and thus access to university. The solution to this imbalance is, simply, additional investment by the public and private sectors alike – in schools, in university courses, and in jobs in and open to Indigenous archaeologists, an investment that, with luck, will make the twenty-first century the century of Indigenous archaeologies. In the meantime, the few Indigenous archaeologists who do work in this field more often than not have a background in broader anthropological or historical archaeology. To this they bring unique additional skills of use to all archaeologists at work everywhere in the world regarding Nicholas's aforementioned "values, knowledge, practices, ethics, and sensibilities." All archaeologists at all levels should thus be aware of at least the basics of Indigenous archaeology – take courses in, read books about, and ideally work alongside Indigenous archaeologists.

Cultural Resource Management

Given the preceding discussion of anthropological, historical, classical, and Indigenous archaeologies, this subsection on CRM might seem superfluous. As outlined earlier, all the aforementioned approaches to archaeology provide a broad-based university training that is sufficient for the majority of professional archaeologists – including those employed in the field of CRM itself. Nonetheless, this is a major – arguably, now *the* major – field of employment in archaeology, and as such there are a growing number of archaeology departments that offer specialized training in CRM skills, both theory and practice, as well as a growing number of dedicated CRM departments and other organizations in their own right. There is also, most crucially, a clear theoretical, philosophical basis for this approach to archaeology – allied to, but distinctive within, the broader archaeological mind-set and certainly as self-aware (the academic term is *reflexive*) as these anthropological, historical, classical, and Indigenous archaeologies. This is so much so that there is now even conflict in this field. As Shennan writes (Shennan 2002: 9):

> For a discipline supposedly concerned with the past, archaeology today is more than ever subject to the tyranny of the present . . . with the rise of the cultural heritage movement, key debates about interpretations have increasingly become centred on who owns them, rather than on their validity as representations of some aspect of past reality.

The origins of CRM were discussed earlier; what is increasingly in question, in the light of Shennan's and others' writings, is the place of CRM within archaeology – not whether CRM should or should not occur, but rather, whether CRM is a part of archaeology, something with its own intellectual focus, traditions, and concerns (see, for example, Smith 2001, 2006). This book is not the place to discuss this complex issue. It is an issue worth bearing in mind, however, not least in terms of professional pathways in archaeology, because the issue has an impact on the training of archaeologists.

Most archaeologists around the world gain a mixed array of training that covers, to a greater or lesser extent, anthropological, historical, classical, and Indigenous archaeologies. Included within these is usually some training in, or at least awareness of, CRM, without CRM being the primary focus of study. The question is whether, as some in the industry attest, the balance should be switched: that professional archaeologists, at least those intending to work in certain sectors of archaeology, should rather take training primarily focused on practical and theoretical applications of CRM as understood through anthropological, historical, classical, and Indigenous archaeologies. This is a subtle but key distinction, and the argument is made on the basis of employability – that too many university students graduate with a degree in archaeology but limited practical application suitable for a career in the world of CRM. The argument is that such students would be better off studying these other specialized approaches to archaeology within the more defined practical sphere of their application in real-world CRM circumstances, and included within this a theoretical/philosophical understanding of the uses of heritage in the past, present, and future worlds – a philosophical stance for CRM as clear-cut as that of the longer-established specialties of archaeology. Within this are major questions of the relationship of archaeology to related disciplines, not just within culture–historical studies such as history and anthropology, but, more broadly, the relationship of archaeology to the study and management of the natural environment, and thus how, in an increasingly uncertain and unstable world, we manage the environment in a sustainable and, above all, holistic (all-encompassing) manner. This is one of the major battlegrounds of the twenty-first-century archaeological community.

Maritime and Underwater Archaeology

Of all the different specialties of archaeology, maritime and underwater archaeology is one that is as well established in the public imagination as it is misunderstood by amateurs and professionals alike. For this reason, to clear up these misunderstandings, it is worth discussing here as a separate section, although in reality it is a part of the anthropological, historical, classical, and Indigenous approaches to archaeology explored earlier, with archaeologists from across these specialties using the tools and techniques described later.

Defining what this specialty is, first of all, the best description is also one of the earliest (Bass 1966: 15):

> Archaeology under water, of course, should be called simply *archaeology* [original emphasis]. We do not speak of those working on the top of Nimrud Dagh in Turkey as mountain archaeologists, nor those at Tikal in Guatemala as jungle archaeologists. They are all people who are trying to answer questions regarding [hu]man's past, and they are adaptable in being able to excavate and interpret ancient buildings, tombs, and even entire cities with the artefacts they contain. . . . The basic aim of all these cases is the same. It is all archaeology.

This quote comes from George Bass, the father of underwater archaeology, and author of what is arguably the first, and still one of the best, books on the subject, *Archaeology Under Water* (1966). Bass goes on to explain that "the problems presented . . . should be considered only as an extension of those already met and solved for dry land archaeology" (Bass 1966: 20).

Archaeology under water, therefore, is the subspecialty related to the technical practicalities of working in the marine zone – making sure one has the right planning, training, equipment, logistics, and backup to work safely and effectively in the marine environment (from the waterfront to the depths of the ocean), doing good archaeology with the right people, and bringing those people safely home at the end of the day (Figure 4). Related to this, however, is the specialty of maritime archaeology. This is not a practical or technical concern, but rather a theoretical concern: the rationale for excavating different types of sites relating to the marine zone, including sites on dry land that ostensibly have nothing to do with the sea. Another of the key names in this specialty, Keith Muckelroy (1978: 4), defined it thus: "Maritime archaeology . . . can be defined as the scientific study of the material remains of [hu]mans and [their] activities on the sea."

Maritime archaeologists and underwater archaeologists often work together, and often have the same skills, but need not – these two specialties are not indivisible. It is possible to do maritime archaeology on dry land (an example is Scandinavian Viking Age boat graves); it is equally possibly to do non-maritime archaeology under water (an example is the now-submerged remains of prehistoric settlements that were formerly on dry land but that became submerged owing to long-term sea level rise after the end of the last Ice Age). These definitions also help make clear what is *not* underwater or maritime archaeology: treasure hunting or looting. If any project – in any environment – involves as a primary objective the recovery of objects for sale or irretrievable dispersal, then, as discussed below in the section on ethics, this is not archaeology. Archaeology is a scientific discipline that undertakes systematic research into the human past for the common good of humanity. Randomly diving into the ocean to find things to sell does not meet these broad disciplinary aims.

In terms of professional pathways toward becoming a maritime or under-water archaeologist, therefore, it should be clear that prospective specialists in these fields need exactly the same skills as every other archaeologist – good schooling in a broad array of subjects allowing them to move on to at least a first, if not multiple, university degree in archaeology, anthropology, and related disciplines. Most undergraduate archaeology/anthropology degrees now include classes, in some cases optional courses, in underwater and/or maritime archaeology: there are also specialist MA/MSc programs around the world, and many active underwa-ter/maritime archaeologists also have PhDs in related topics.

The only things that can, in truth, be seen to distinguish underwater and maritime archaeologists from all other archaeologists are the following:

- *Conservation training*: Archaeological materials recovered from marine zone sites are often very fragile; certain types of "wet" sites (on land as much as underwater) also contain materials such as the remains of organic materials not commonly found on archaeological sites. The excavation, recovery, stabilization, and con-servation of such materials are complex, can be expensive, and require highly specialized training (see Robinson 1998).
- *Diving training*: Those wishing to become underwater archaeologists need to learn how to dive. Initially, and for many practitioners (such as most academics),

Figure 4. The realities of twenty-first-century maritime archaeology: taken in July 2006 aboard the Greek national research vessel *Aegaeo* (operated by the Hellenic Centre for Marine Research), the high-tech realities of modern-day maritime archaeology are visible here. Shown here are the human-occupied vehicle *Thetis* and the autonomous underwater vehicle *Seabed*. At the time, the *Aegaeo* was working off the coast of Milos in the Aegean, undertaking archaeological field-work (© Brendan Foley 2010).

this can be exactly the same training as for sports divers. There are numerous well-known international schemes that provide the qualifications to dive in most corners of the world – perhaps the best known of these is the Professional Association of Diving Instructors (PADI). However, for those wishing to work as CRM archaeologists in the marine zone, much more complex commercial dive training is necessary, required under various national laws, and the same as that for any other marine zone professional, from an offshore oil industry diver to a marine conservation officer. Such training can take weeks or months, is expensive (costing thousands of pounds/dollars/euros), and includes learning how to use surface supply rather than SCUBA diving equipment. In the UK, such training must be certified by the Heath and Safety Executive, in the United States by the Occupational Safety and Health Administration, and in Australia by the National Offshore Petroleum Safety Authority.

- *Excavation training*: Archaeology under water involves the use of specialized equipment that necessitates training. This is distinct from diver training. Such archaeologists use tools such as water or air dredges to help remove silt and sand from around archaeological sites; they also have to learn how to handle tools such as tape measures, drawing boards, and pencils in the weightless marine environment. Many of the skills that we take for granted on a land excavation, such as simply drawing a sketch of a site or taking some notes and measurements, have to be relearned for the underwater environment (see Bowens 2009).

- *Legal training*: Various distinctive laws govern the marine zone around the world. Some of these are generic and international – the most notable example is the United Nations Convention on the Law of the Sea (1982) that agrees to what the national marine boundary limits are and the rights of free passage through these areas. Other laws are national but generic – different laws on marine zone safety, environmental protection, and industrial regulation. Finally, many countries also have laws specific to marine zone heritage. In the UK, for example, there is the Protection of Wrecks Act (1973); in the US, the Abandoned Shipwrecks Act (1988); in Australia, the (Commonwealth) Historic Shipwrecks Act (1976). In addition, many separate federal states/territories of the US and Australia have their own similar laws. There are also distinctive government organizations involved in the management and monitoring of the marine zone, including its heritage – for example, in the UK, the Maritime and Coastguard Agency and the Marine Management Organization; in the US, the Bureau of Ocean Energy Management, Regulation and Enforcement and National Oceanographic and Atmospheric Administration; and in Australia, the Australian Maritime Safety Authority. There are also voluntary international agreements on maritime heritage – most notably, the UN Convention on the Protection of the Underwater Cultural Heritage (2001) (see Dromgoole 1999).

- *Marine zone safety training*: Working in the marine zone – anything from the edge of a river or lake, by way of the foreshore, right out to the middle of the ocean – requires an awareness of particular risks, and thus particular safety precautions, that need to be taken into consideration. At the most basic level, this might mean making sure that mobile phones work at the destination and that they are kept in a waterproof pouch alongside the phone number of the coast guard; at the upper end, this involves all the logistics of taking a suitably sized and equipped vessel into the deep ocean.

- *Survey training*: Marine geophysics – the science and technology of marine zone remote sensing and survey – is a distinctive, multibillion-dollar high-tech industry. Underwater and maritime archaeologists do not necessarily need to be specialists in this field, but they do need to have a sound working knowledge of the basic technologies and techniques that can be used to identify and survey archaeological sites in the marine zone.

- *Technical training*: One of the major focuses of maritime archaeology is the study of ancient watercraft. Humans have been building different types of rafts, boats, and ships for thousands of years: the oldest remains of such vessels date back only a few thousand years to around 6000 BCE, but there is circumstantial evidence for prehistoric sea crossings in locations such as Australasia as long ago as 60,000 to 100,000 years ago. Archaeologists who choose to study the remains of ancient vessels need extensive training in the technical minutiae of such craft – the tools and techniques needed to construct such vessels, the names of different components, and so on (see McGrail 2001).

- *Vessel-handling training*: Some underwater and maritime archaeologists also have vessel-handling training. As with diving training, this is the same type of training as for other marine zone users, and falls into amateur and commercial sectors. The amateur sector includes various yacht and powerboat handling/ratings and training, as managed by organizations such as the Royal Yachting Association in the UK, the US Sailing Association, or the Australian Sail Training Association. The professional sector includes a comprehensive array of larger vessel handling skills overseen by organizations such as the UK's Merchant Navy Training Board, the US Merchant Marine Academy, and the Australian Maritime College.

In terms of who works as an underwater or maritime archaeologist, all the chapter-based job sectors that follow in this book employ individuals with these specialist skills. Because these specialties are all part of broader archaeology (and because a great deal of the globe is covered by or adjacent to water in some manner), it would be odd for such jobs not to. CRM archaeologists specializing in the marine zone work all over the world in relation to marine zone industries such as the oil, gas, and minerals industries, as well as for shipping and dredging companies, and increasingly for energy companies, working in relation to offshore wind farms and tidal energy barrages (this is a distinctive growth area of marine zone CRM archaeology); academic underwater/maritime archaeologists research and teach these subjects; government underwater/maritime archaeologists advise developers and related sectors on maritime archaeology public policy and law and monitor the activities of other archaeologists; and public underwater/maritime archaeologists explain this subject to the wider community as well as involve people in fieldwork. As a consequence of the latter group, there are active avocational underwater/maritime archaeology groups around the world that anyone interested in these specialties can join. To name but three examples, in the UK there is the Nautical Archaeology Society, in Australia the Australasian Institute of Maritime Archaeology, and in the US, a host of regional societies, including the Advisory Council on Underwater Archaeology. Most other nations of the world have their own groups as well.

Archaeology as a Career: The Contemporary Archaeology Job Market

Ask the average people in the street who they think employs most of the archaeologists at work today and the answer is likely to be universities and museums. Follow up that question with the query "And do you think that industry is a major employer of archaeologists?" and the answer is likely to be, "I don't imagine that many archaeologists are employed by industry." In reality, almost the exact opposite is true, with, very broadly from most to least number of archaeologists employed, the running order being industry (by which I mean CRM archaeology – undertaking work in advance of new developments such as roads, houses, or pipelines), academia, local government, central government, professional and charitable (including educational and lobbying) organizations, and finally museums. The most recent survey of archaeological employment in Britain, for example, which was conducted from September 2007 to January 2008, produced the data shown in Table 1.

Broadly similar data are recorded from the Republic of Ireland (where CRM archaeology accounted for 89 percent of jobs in 2007) (McDermott and La Piscopia 2008) and Australia (where CRM archaeology accounted for 49 percent of jobs in 2004–05) (Ulm et al. 2005)). Only the US appears to buck this trend (with only 27.7 percent of jobs recorded in CRM archaeology, the largest percentage of jobs instead being recorded at 33.6 percent in academia) (ARI 2005), but its last such survey in 2004 had a bias toward the non-CRM archaeology sector in the way the data were collected (via the membership of the two largest archaeological organizations in the United States, the Society for American Archaeology and the Society for Historical Archaeology), and appears to have missed a significant proportion of the US CRM archaeological community.

Of these different sectors, industry not only employs the vast majority of the archaeologists, but it also controls the largest amount of money spent on archaeology, either directly in terms of payment for archaeological services or indirectly in terms of government grants and awards. Accurate data on the funding for archaeology in any country are extremely hard to find. However, for example, as outlined by Aitchison (2000), the major funding streams prior to the introduction of the Aggregates Levy Sustainability Fund in the UK include payment for developer-funded reactive fieldwork as well as central and local government support via English Heritage and other grant-giving bodies, including research councils and the Heritage Lottery Fund. Darvill and Russell (2002: chapter 7, especially illustration 37 and table W14) also provide various partial figures, including an

TABLE 1. Primary Archaeological Employment Sectors in the UK, January 2008

	CRM or Freelance	Local Government	Academia	Public Archaeology or Other	Central Government
Core employment	46%	31%	10%	8%	5%

Source: Aitchison and Richards, 2008.

estimate of around £35 million spent on "commercial archaeological projects" in 1996 (ibid., 52), and an estimate of some £22.25 million being the approximate financial turnover for twenty major CRM firms in England in 1999 (ibid., 62). Overall, although estimates vary, it is thought that some 90 percent of all the money spent on archaeology annually comes from industry in one form or another, and yet that 90 percent represents only approximately 1 percent of the total costs of the entire industry sector. Thus, that 1 percent goes a long way and makes an incredibly cost-effective contribution to our understanding of the past. Sadly, however, all that funding buys only so much, and of these archaeologists employed as a whole, fewer and fewer are on permanent contracts and many inhabit the perilous world of the freelance archaeologist, effectively self-employed.

Exact figures on any aspect of archaeological employment are few and far between; both the best and virtually the only reliable data come from the surveys periodically sponsored by different professional organizations, such as the Institute for Archaeologists in the UK; the American Cultural Resources Association, Register of Professional Archaeologists, Society for American Archaeology, and Society for Historical Archaeology in the US,; and the Australian Archaeological Association and Australian Association of Consulting Archaeologists in Australia. These published surveys are for very specific locations – no such comparable surveys have ever been undertaken for many nations of the world where thousands, if not tens of thousands, of archaeologists are at work. A survey of archaeologists at work in individual nations such as India or China, or at work in specific continents such as Africa or South America, would undoubtedly reveal very different patterns. Budding archaeologists in such locations should not be put off or misled by these very partial figures for specific places. The most recent, easily available of these sources are:

- Australia: Ulm, Nichols and Dalley (2005), "Mapping the Shape of Contemporary Australian Archaeology" (see also Smith and du Cros 1991) (a new survey for Australia was also under way in 2010).
- Great Britain: Aitchison and Richards (2008), *Archaeology Labor Market Intelligence: Profiling the Profession 2007–08* (see also Aitchison and Edwards (2003) and Aitchison (1999), also Everill (2009) for anecdotal evidence).

- Republic of Ireland: McDermott and La Piscopia (2008), *Discovering the Archaeologists of Ireland* (see also CHL Consulting Co. Ltd. (2002)).
- United States: the Society for American Archaeology and Society for Historical Archaeology Salary Survey (ARI 2005) and the Register of Professional Archaeologists Needs Assessment (ARI 2006) (see also Zeder 1997).

Such analyses are supported by additional broader disciplinary surveys in the UK, such as the All-Party Parliamentary Archaeology Group's (1993) *Current State of Archaeology in the United Kingdom* and the Association of Local Government Archaeological Officers' (2008) *Local Authority Archaeological Services* report. There has also recently been a Europe-wide survey of archaeologists, titled "Discovering the Archaeologists of Europe," which ran between 2006 and 2008, funded by the European Commission (see Aitchison 2009). The global recession of 2008 onward has, meanwhile, sadly led to detailed surveys of job losses by professional organizations such as the Institute for Archaeologists (IfA), monitoring the impact of the recession on the archaeology community. The IfA reported the disturbing statistics for the UK that:

> Following the loss of 345 archaeological jobs in the three months from 1st October 2008 to 1st January 2009, a further 195 jobs are estimated to have been lost from the profession in the period from 1st January 2009 to 1st April 2009. Since the summer of 2007, approximately 670 jobs have been lost. This figure represents 1 in 6 (16.5%) of all commercial archaeological posts, which equates to nearly 10% of all the jobs in professional archaeology that existed in 2007 (IfA, *Job Losses in Archaeology – April 2009 Report*, Aitchison 2009: 1).

The American Cultural Resources Association (ACRA) (2010) reported broadly similar data for the US in March 2010, with 44 percent of those surveyed reporting a drop in business over the previous six months (see also Schlanger and Aitchison 2010 for a review of the international situation in mid-2010).

Trying to draw any conclusions on career paths, pay, benefits, and working conditions in archaeology from this sporadic mass of data is extremely hard. The UK, for instance, may have the most recent and consistently comparable data, having undertaken periodic surveys via the IfA for the past decade, but in the most recent of these surveys only 23 percent of those surveyed replied (Aitchison and Richards 2008). In comparison, the best response rates have come from the 2004 and 2005 surveys undertaken in the United States, where, respectively, 53 percent and 70 percent of those surveyed replied (ARI 2005 and 2006), but those surveys are arguably much less representative than the IfA data: the latter are more recent, and most importantly, managed to reach the hard-to-contact younger, entry-level archaeologists, whereas the former was drawn from the membership of the US Society for American Archaeology, Society for Historical Archaeology, and Register of Professional Archaeologists (RPA), membership in all of which costs significant sums of money and, in the case of the RPA, sufficient professional experience, thereby likely excluding younger, poorer, and less experienced archaeologists and skewing the results in favor of more established practitioners (it is notable that to try to avoid this data imbalance, the 2005 RPA survey also surveyed 4,000 non-RPA members, but received only a 25% response rate to its survey – largely comparable to that of the IfA in 2008) (see ARI 2006 and Table 2).

Drawing the data from these surveys together, it becomes clear that the following conclusions may be drawn from these survey locations alone – *not* about the world as a whole:

Age: about 50 percent of archaeologists are aged between 20 and 40, with the majority of that group aged between 25 and 35.

Ethnicity: more than 99 percent of archaeologists define themselves as ethnically "white" (i.e., of European origin) (bearing in mind the previous qualifier that these data are gleaned from surveys in a few very specific counties, and do not represent the global situation, where many different people practice as professional archaeologists) (see Benjamin 2003).

Gender: the split is roughly 60 percent male/40 percent female overall, but with biases within sectors – CRM archaeology tends to have slightly more men, public archaeology slightly more women, and academia slightly more women (although anecdotal reports suggest that this is imbalanced internally, with more women in younger, junior positions and more men in older, more senior positions).

Pay, conditions, and benefits: the bottom 10 percent of archaeologists are paid under UK £15,000 a year (gross); a significant and worrisome minority of this 10 percent only earn around £11,000 (gross), or slightly more than £200/week (gross) (compared with the £12,862 national average wage in 2008). Although this is not at what the UK considers to be the poverty line (which, in 2007–08, was considered to be £115/week (gross) for a single adult with no dependent children), it remains an extremely, and unacceptably, low figure for individuals with such high education and other qualifications, and represents a poverty trap exacerbated by the disturbing fact that 23 percent of CRM archaeologists were on contracts of twelve months or less in the UK in 2007–08. The average annual wage for archaeologists lies somewhere between £22,000 and £34,000 (gross), heavily biased toward the lower end of this scale at about £22,000 to £28,000 (gross) (compared with the £29,999 national average wage in 2008). Meanwhile, the top 5 percent to 10 percent of all archaeologists are paid more than £50,000 a year (gross) (compared with the £47,747 national average in 2008), and a tiny top group of this 5 percent to 10 percent are paid more than £70,000. Data from the UK's Higher Education Statistics Agency for 2002–03, for example, noted that archaeology graduates were the least well paid of the sixty-one different subject areas compared in that study (see Aitchison 2006: 5; Jackson and Sinclair 2010).

Sector employment: CRM archaeology is consistently the largest sector, amounting for more than 50 percent of all careers, with academia and government following up as the second and third largest sectors.

TABLE 2. Comparison of the 2007 Irish, 2004–05 Australian, 2007–08 British, 2004 and 2005 US, and 2007–08 European Surveys of Archaeologists

Nation	Republic of Ireland and Northern Ireland	Australia	Great Britain	US 2004	US 2005	Selected European states (Austria, Belgium, Cyprus, Czech Republic, Germany, Greece, Hungary, Ireland, Netherlands, Slovak Republic, Slovenia, UK)
Survey period	June–August 2007	July 2004–July 2005	September 2007–January 2008	October–December 2004	September–November 2005	September 2007–January 2008
No. of surveys distributed	165 (organizations)	1,251	1,997	4,490	1,754 RPAs plus 4,000 nonregistered professionals (5,754 total)	No data, but total numbers of archaeologists in each country reported is: Austria 965; Belgium 1,232; Cyprus 491; Czech Republic 777; Germany 10,549; Greece 1,856; Hungary 620; Ireland 1,811; Netherlands 1,036; Slovak Republic 307; Slovenia 175; UK 7,731[1]
% of responses	26%	25%	23%	52.80%	70.4% RPAs; 24.7% non-RPAs	No data
Top two age groups	20–29, 56%; 30–39, 33.5% (89.5% younger than 40)	26–35, 29.5%; 46–55, 26.5% (57.2% younger than 45)	25–29, 40%; 30–34, 35% (75% younger than 35)	under 40, 25%; 40–49, 26% (51% younger than 50)	under 45, 39.2% (60.8% over 45 and average age 47.4 years)	20–29, 25%; 30–39, 30% (55% younger than 40)

Top two employment sectors	89% CRM; 5% (each) academia/central government	49% CRM; no additional data	45% CRM; 31% local government	33.6% academia; 27.7% CRM	49.8% CRM	No cumulative data
Gender split	60% M/40% F	52% M/48% F	59% M/41% F	59.7% M/40.3% F	54.4% M/45.6% F	No cumulative data
Annual gross salary minimums	€11,250 (£10,242)	2.5% M/2% F less than A$20,000 (£11,224)	£14,921 (lowest 10%) (compared to £12,862 national average)	Lowest reported US$29,893 (£16,774)	No data	No cumulative data
Annual gross salary mean	€37,680 gross (2.75% lower than national average) (£34,302)	18.5% M A$60–80,000 (£33,660–44,880)/ 16.5% F A$40–60,000 (£22,427–33,660)	£23,310 (compared with £29,999 national average)	No data	No data	€31,134 (£28,352)
Annual gross salary maximum	24% paid more than €35,000/year (£31,862) (unidentified % on over €80,000 [£72,829])	7% M/2.5% F over A$100,000 (£56,069)	Top 10% paid over £35,000 (compared with £47,747 national average)	Highest reported US$84,483 and 90,645 (£51,696 and 55,466)	No data	No cumulative data
Length of contract	No data	No data	23% of contract archaeologists on contracts of 12 months or less	No data	No data	No data
Highest qualification	1% PhD	15% PhD	10% PhD	53.1% PhD (39.7% MA/MSc)	47.4% PhD	37% MA/MSc (16% PhD)
Core qualification	80% BA/BSc; 41% MA/MSc	17% BA/BSc	44% BA/BSc (24% MA/MSc)	58.9% MA/MSc	32% BA/BSc

Sources: McDermott and La Piscopia 2008; Ulm, Nichols, and Dalley 2005; Aitchison and Richards 2008; ARI 2005, 2006; Aitchison 2009.

Training and education: the majority, between 40 percent and 60 percent, have a BA/BSc in archaeology or anthropology, and approximately 30 percent to 40 percent also have an MA/MSc in a related specialty; a notable minority – between 1 percent and 50 percent of those surveyed – have a PhD, and are usually among the highest wage earners.

Overall, a picture can be built of a young, dedicated, well trained, and talented archaeological community that works very hard but for limited reward, with pay, benefits, and working conditions all lower than usual for university graduates (for virtually all are) of this caliber. However, job satisfaction, quality of life, and all other indicators of general happiness seem high for archaeologists (see Everill 2009). This is the crux of the issue – ask most archaeologists why they first became involved in archaeology and later got jobs within the discipline and almost all will respond along the lines that they "love" or are "fascinated by" archaeology, have been since childhood, and rarely imagined doing anything else – a long-held dream made real. If asked about the pay or conditions, most will admit that these are at best a constant and niggling worry, at worse a genuine problem (particularly for those with non-archaeological family with whom they share financial responsibilities), but will quickly qualify this by noting that they "couldn't imagine doing anything else" or wouldn't want a "boring" or "normal" job "like everyone else." The conclusion seems to be that most archaeologists are poor but happy, love but are frustrated by their jobs, and are surrounded by friends and family who are pleased that their loved ones are so committed to their chosen career but sad that this career does not reward them better.

In terms of the prospective archaeologist considering a career in the discipline, the conclusion is then clearer-cut – archaeology is a vocation and, like all vocations, will involve sacrifice. But being a vocation, if you genuinely feel that this is your calling, then there is probably very little that will stop you from pursuing it, so the thing to do is to get the right mix of qualifications and experience possible to maximize your employability. The only people who should hesitate about pursuing a career in archaeology are thus those people already hesitating for a variety of reasons – if the vocational pull is not strong enough, or is not present at all, then no matter how exciting the subject, then ultimately those long hours, that poor pay, and that job insecurity are going to wear you down and you should know when to cut your losses and quit.

Within this, however, should come the qualifier of the unsurveyed minority, those former professional archaeologists who left the discipline to pursue careers elsewhere. There has never, to the author's knowledge, been a formal survey of such former archaeologists (especially as many continue on with archaeology in some informal capacity even after they leave paid archaeological employment), but anecdotal evidence suggests that the poor pay and job security are usually the driving forces in people leaving the profession but that no one had a particularly difficult struggle to find work in a different area after this, moving either directly, or after retraining, into employment that perhaps offers lower job satisfaction but provides at least much greater security and stability, and often much greater pay as well.

The Archaeological Mind-set: The Pleasures of Archaeology

The archaeologists Trent de Boer (2004) and Paul Everill (2009) have provided an excellent and detailed overview of, respectively, UK and US CRM archaeologists (whom de Boer calls "shovelbums" and Everill "diggers"). Similarly, Smith and Burke (2007) sum up many of the characteristics of the Australian archaeological community (see also Baxter 2002; Holtorf 2005, 2007a, 2007b; Membury 2002; Russell 2002a, 2002b; Talalay, 2004; Zarmati 1995). De Boer and Everill in particular, however, are focused on the specifics of the CRM archaeology community – the least known but undoubtedly most distinctive sector of the community rather than the wider whole.

Two things that archaeologists often get asked are, first, "Why do you do archaeology?" and second, in relation to this, "What is it like to do archaeology?" Although this entire book is broadly dedicated to answering the latter question, these questions are considered here briefly by making a few observations about the archaeological mind-set and so the pleasures of archaeology – those things that keep people coming into the profession and going to work each day (Figure 5).

Dealing with the pleasures of archaeology, for these are the more tangible of the two motivations behind being an archaeologist, one of the most commonly cited pleasures is undoubtedly the combination of mental and physical exercise that archaeology offers. The ability to, sometimes simultaneously, be involved in a deeply cerebral activity that also puts one out in the fresh air undertaking physical exertion is hugely addictive and is one of the great attractions of archaeological fieldwork. Within this is also the flexibility of working that archaeology often offers: get the right position, and one not only gets that balance of metal and physical exercise, but one also gets to choose where, and most importantly when, to exercise brain, brawn, or both together, which usually translates into picking the places one would most like to visit in the most pleasant seasonal weather those places offer.

Moving on, another commonly cited appeal of archaeology is one that everyone has experienced firsthand at some point: the thrill of discovery. For some people, that thrill comes from collecting clothes, books, or music – stumbling across that rare record or volume in a store somewhere. For others, the thrill comes perhaps from visiting new places, being the first to explore undiscovered or little-known locations, or spotting a rare animal – this is certainly what drives many cavers and divers to probe ever deeper into the depths of the earth and the oceans, or birdwatchers to spend days waiting in a blind. All these and many more examples can be drawn in comparison with archaeology.

Going back to the first point about the appealing mixture of the mental and physical in archaeology in relation to the thrill of discovery moves this discussion into the other, somewhat intangible, question of the archaeological mind-set.

Here, it is clear that two sometimes-contradictory motivations are at play. First, as Mortimer Wheeler (1954: 13) famously noted, "the archaeologist is digging up, not things, but people." Archaeologists have an inherent interest in people – all people, people now, but particularly people in the past, what they were up to, what they were thinking, and how those materials or physical marks in the landscape that survive reflect behavior and cognition. Politely, interest such as this can be called curiosity; impolitely, nosiness. This means that the archaeologist is always "at work" – every person met and every place visited has the potential to offer archaeological inspiration. This, in turn, is related to the generally outgoing character of most archaeologists, who like nothing more than to chat over a drink, to ponder at length on human nature. What makes the archaeological mind-set so contradictory, however, is the other side of archaeological practice that seems so at odds with this person-driven, outgoing perspective: successful archaeologists combine with the above an equal love of complexity – of puzzle and problem solving, of sifting and sorting data from many different sources in a gigantic, multispatial matrix. A love of detail for detail's sake plays a part in this, especially in fieldwork, in which accuracy of recording and repetition of a prearranged, systematized, routine approach is necessary if an archaeological site is to be recorded accurately and systematically. This focus on detail and repetition at times makes for what borders on obsessive-compulsive behavior among archaeologists, when rituals of repetition, collection and characterization can begin to look like a low-level disorder – a sort of occupational anal-retentiveness – that under other circumstances might be treated by medical practitioners. Such disorders, however, are commonly associated with *asocial* behavior. Thus, the archaeological mind-set is a contradiction – at once outgoing and human-oriented, in-looking and object-fixated. There is space within the community for all sorts – from the quiet and introspective to the loud and extroverted.

All of the above, then, give some sense of what it is like to do archaeology. The good days balance the mental and the physical, the social and asocial, the micro and macro perspectives at an interesting site in good weather, where the archaeologist works alongside responsive, enthusiastic colleagues to uncover new information. Under such circumstances, an archaeological project enjoys a unique and seductive rhythm of passing days, weeks, or even months or years, as the three-dimensional jigsaw of the site (or sites) being studied becomes daily more complex and the archaeologists have to daily respond to this – a real-time game infinitely more complex that any ever dreamed up by a computer-game designer, but with the same sense of quest, in some cases narrative, but above all an addictive lure. Into such a world are drawn the archaeologists at work around the world today.

What Isn't Archaeology? Archaeology and Ethics, Professional Standards, and Codes of Conduct

To conclude this chapter, it is worth defining what archaeology is *not*. The sad truth remains that archaeology is one of those fields of study, as well as forms of

Figure 5. The archaeological mind-set: the pleasures of archaeology are clearly visible here, where a CRM archaeologist uses an upended wheelbarrow as an improvised seat while updating site records on a sunny day in southeast England. Note, however, the amount of dried mud on the archaeologist's clothing – it had not been sunny all the time (© Archaeology South East UCL 2010, courtesy of Dominic Perring).

employment, that is surrounded by a fog of simply wrong- or at least muddle-headed thinking, pseudoscientific half-truths and outright lies, snake-oil merchants and con artists. Much of this is harmless and amusing; archaeologists should be no more worried about the latest TV show or film that misrepresents them than lawyers, doctors, or police officers should be concerned about comparable representations of their respective vocations. But there is a fringe, often a vociferous one, that is more harmful and is, frankly, a real worry.

On the one hand, such fringe activity involves the misrepresentation of archaeological (as well as broader scientific) data in support of a variety of myths and fables, some of these very ancient, such as various creation myths to do with a rich spread of gods, monsters, and aliens alike being responsible for the origins and antiquity of earth and/or humankind. Material such as this sells amazingly well in the popular press and is irritating to archaeologists, although rarely directly harmful to actual archaeological sites (see Fagan 2006; Lovata 2007). Most people who write such junk thankfully seem to like to do so from the comfort of their homes rather than from the rigor of the field, office, or lab, and rarely if ever are willing to go out and check data to verify their misguided hypotheses.

On the other hand, there is a small but influential fringe involved in actual physical activity on archaeological sites that is by varying degrees damaging, destructive, and, frankly, disastrous. Some of this is state sanctioned (such as the Taliban destruction of the two statues of the Buddha carved into the cliffside at Bamiyan in Afghanistan in 2001) or even government licensed (Florida is burdened by a relic law of the 1960s that licenses treasure hunting off its coastline), but much is the result of private enterprise driven by the pursuit of short-term financial profit – looting and treasure hunting. At one end of a sliding scale, this can comprise lone individuals or small groups looting on single sites or across small areas (see King 2005: 120–22). At the opposite end of the scale is well financed and formalized looting of archaeological sites by commercial organizations. Often working under the guise of what they would term legally legitimate salvage – increasingly and erroneously phrased as "commercial archaeology" – these organizations feed the international trade in illicit antiquities, and some items eventually pass hands a sufficient number of times for them to become "clean," entering the legitimate antiques trade in a similar way to money laundered by international crime and terror organizations. Such salvage occurs all over the world, above, across, and below water, and has of late spread into the deepest abysses of the oceans; there is no location or time period that is free from this scourge.

What is interesting is that in their own activities, and especially in their publicity, many such salvage organizations demonstrate that they do, in fact, know right from wrong and recognize that what they are doing is harmful and damaging. Numerous treasure hunting organizations go to great ends to justify their activities by insisting that their work is necessary to protect heritage because such sites are already under threat from either human or natural processes, such as low-level looting, storm damage, and erosion – in other words, they argue, "it is better that we pull this stuff out of the earth and sell it than if we do not, as it is going to get destroyed no matter what." Such organizations also frequently attempt to give at least a veneer of archaeological respectability to their work, either employing archaeologists (or at least, people with a range of real, as well as spurious, archaeological qualifications) or working with what, in passing, appear to be archaeological techniques, such as using site grids or recording finds in situ prior to recovery. When attacked by real archaeologists in the media or in other outlets such as government inquiries, such groups are also prone to vociferously claim persecution from an elite intellectual cabal bent on controlling sites in the protection of their own self-interests, a claim that collapses in the face of the overwhelming evidence discussed elsewhere in this book that most archaeologists are woefully underpaid and insecure in their jobs (if there was an international archaeological "mafia" that decides who is in and who is out, would we not have sorted the labor laws in our favor ages ago?).

Thankfully, it is relatively easy to judge whether an individual or an organization is undertaking genuine archaeological work. There exist a wide variety of domestic, as well as international, codes of ethics and conduct, professional standards, treaties, conventions, and statutes for archaeologists (see Vitelli and Colwell-Chanthaphonh 2006). Choosing to undertake work that meets the terms of such standards costs an individual nothing – one does not have to pay a fee or join any organization to personally abide by such standards of ethics or codes of practice, although one can choose to formally join such groups – and adherence to such good practice can usually be demonstrated easily. For individuals and organizations, these standards are most commonly defined by the codes of conduct of various professional organizations that regulate archaeologists and their work. Examples of these include the Australian Archaeological Association's Code of Ethics, the UK's IfA's Code of Conduct, the American Anthropological Association's Statements on Ethics: Principles of Professional Responsibility, the US RPA's Code of Conduct, the Society for American Archaeology's Principles of Archaeological Ethics, and the US Society for Historical Archaeology's Ethical Principles.

For entire nations, the situation is far less clear-cut, mainly because international law runs more on precedent than enforced statute – that is, nations tend to pick and choose what laws and treaties they sign on the basis of a variety of interests, and even if they do sign a treaty, ensuring – especially enforcing – and even simply monitoring good practice can be extremely difficult. However, some of the better-known and wider-ranging examples include, in chronological order:

- ICOMOS (1964) International Charter for the Conservation and Restoration of Monuments and Sites.
- UNESCO (1970) Convention on the Means of Prohibiting and Preventing the Illicit Import, Export and Transfer of Cultural Property.
- UNESCO (1972) Convention Concerning the Protection of the World Cultural and Natural Heritage.

- Council of Europe (1985) Convention for the Protection of the Architectural Heritage of Europe (the Grenada Convention).
- Council of Europe (1992) Convention on the Protection of the Archaeological Heritage (the Valetta Convention).
- UNECE (1998) Convention on Access to Information, Public Participation in Decision-making and Access to Justice in Environmental Matters (the Aarhus Convention).
- UNESCO (1999) Convention for the Protection of Cultural Property in the Event of Armed Conflict.
- Council of Europe (2000) European Landscape Convention.
- UNESCO (2001) Convention on the Protection of the Underwater Cultural Heritage.
- UNESCO (2003) Convention for the Safeguarding of the Intangible Cultural Heritage.
- Council of Europe (2005) Framework Convention on the Value of Cultural Heritage for Society (the Faro Convention).

Real archaeology, in fact, comes down to a relatively simple range of basic good practice, of personal ethics. Although much argued about, none of these are particularly radical suggestions – not unlike all other forms of good behavior in any community, it comes down to people choosing to act in a thoughtful and responsible manner, respecting one another and the environment, and trying to make as small an impact as possible. This is no different from the basic "campfire rule" (i.e., leave a site as good as, or ideally better than, you found it). What this means for professional archaeologists is the following, paraphrasing from the IfA Code of Conduct (IfA, October 2009):

Maintain, develop, and promote the highest standards of professional practice: archaeologists try to be well informed, preparing for projects in advance by reading relevant literature. Throughout their career, this means that they will keep up to date on advances in archaeological ideas and techniques (a process known as continuing professional development [CPD]), and they will not agree to undertake archaeological work for which they are not adequately qualified. Once on a project, they will try their utmost to present archaeology to one another, as well as to the public, in a responsible and timely manner – they will tell people about their work quickly and in a clear and straightforward manner, keep a detailed and thorough record of their work, store materials and records appropriately, and reference as well as give appropriate credit for work done by others in final publications, which again they will seek to publish quickly and make easily available in different formats – for instance, in books, in journals, and on the Internet.

This means that it should be easy for anyone to find out more about any archaeological project's location, aims, objectives, team members, funding sources, fieldwork, outcomes, conclusion, and the final site of deposit of the project archives. Any project for which this is not possible is, frankly, suspect.

Actively discourage and combat the trade in illicit antiquities: archaeologists know and comply with all laws applicable to their professional activities. As a consequence, they do not engage in illicit or unethical dealings in antiquities, which means that if they have even the slightest doubt about the origins of an object brought or offered to them they will not buy or sell the artifact. More broadly, this means that they will be cautious about any financial benefits resulting from their work, especially if this seems to relate, in any way, to the recovery or sale of objects of materials recovered during archaeological fieldwork. But this does not mean, for instance, that they cannot be paid to work on an archaeological site in advance of a new housing development – as long as the primary intention of the project is to analyze a site in advance of its development, rather than recover materials for their own sake or to sell them to make a profit, then such work is allowed.

This means that anyone involved in selling or buying materials recovered from an archaeological site, whether named or unnamed, is not an archaeologist. This also means that if an individual or project sets out with a primary motive to recover materials for sale, then that project is not an archaeological project and that person is not an archaeologist.

Work to preserve the scientific integrity of a total site: archaeologists strive to conserve archaeological sites and material as a resource for study and enjoyment now and in the future and encourage others to do the same.

This means that when it is not possible to leave a site untouched or materials in place, they will seek to ensure the creation and maintenance of an adequate record through appropriate forms of research, recording, and dissemination of results. It also means that when destructive investigation is undertaken, they will endeavor to ensure that this destruction has the smallest possible impact on the archaeological site or remains.

Recognize the rights of communities to control access to and information on their cultural heritage: archaeologists will take account of the legitimate concerns of groups whose material past may be the subject of archaeological investigation.

This means that archaeologists will work with communities that are involved in an area – be these communities near or far away – to plan any project, and will work with such communities to ensure that materials recovered from a site or other archives that result from a project will be placed in the best possible location for community access in the future. This means involving descendant communities from the outset and acquiescing to their cultural mores – even if this runs against common archaeological practice. Communities, not archaeologists, own their cultural heritage, and real archaeologists recognize the overarching right of descendant communities to control remains as they see fit.

Interviewee: Joe

How did you first become involved in archaeology?

I realized that I was interested in the subject when studying for my A levels; my school didn't offer archaeology as an A level, so I joined the local branch of the

Young Archaeologists Club as the best way to get involved in archaeology. I went on to study archaeology at university, and decided to try to make a career in the discipline at the end of my undergraduate studies, when I chose to undertake postgraduate studies in archaeology.

What is your present job?

I am the County Archaeologist for the British county of Surrey, where I lead the team that advises residents of the county on their archaeology and built heritage and enforces the planning laws that apply to such sites. I am also a Senior Lecturer in Archaeology at University College London (UCL) Institute of Archaeology in London.

What qualifications do you hold? Where and what did you study?

I have a BA in archaeology and history, an MA in maritime archaeology, and a PhD in archaeology, all from the University of Southampton in the UK. I am also a member of the Institute for Archaeologists (IfA), the UK professional organization for the discipline, as well as an elected Fellow of the Society of Antiquaries of London, a learned society for the study of the past.

What are your terms of employment, working conditions, and other job benefits?

For my UCL job, I am on a 0.5 (2.5 days a week) permanent contract, but my hours are not specified; I am on a similar contract for my Surrey job, although there I am restricted to working 18 hours a week. Both jobs also pay into private pension funds, and thanks to the UK's excellent National Health Service, I do not need private medical insurance.

How did you get your current job? What do you feel was most helpful to you in gaining this position?

I got both my jobs as a result of seeing them advertised in the professional press and applying via a CV and covering letter. In each case I then had to give a presentation on my plans for the job and also have an interview – in both cases the most stressful interviews of my life, some really tough questions! I undoubtedly got these jobs because I have a broad range of archaeological skills, having worked on both terrestrial and marine sites across the world, for universities, government, and as a freelance archaeological professional. As a result, I already had most of the skills and specialisms required by each post and could hit the ground running, not needing much training on arrival.

What is the best thing about being an archaeologist?

The best thing is the fact that in both of my jobs I have a direct impact on how people come to understand and appreciate the place they live in and how people lived in the same place in the past. Archaeology shows us that people haven't changed all that much in many ways – and that for all the bad things humans have done to their landscape and to one another, they have done some amazing things too.

What is the worst thing about being an archaeologist?

I work very long hours – 60 to 70 hours a week spread between my two jobs is not uncommon, and I've done even longer weeks than that on occasion. It is rare for me to have both days of any weekend off, and I've never taken more than a fortnight's holiday a year.

What do you consider to be your greatest achievement in or contribution to archaeology so far?

Personally, my greatest achievement so far is getting a PhD – my dad was so proud that he cried at my graduation; no one in my family had ever done so well academically before. Professionally, my greatest achievement was working at a site called Myos Hormus (near modern-day Qusier) on the Egyptian coast of the Red Sea. The project I was involved with there changed how we understand ancient trade routes from India to the Middle East, and the site was an amazing and beautiful place to live and work.

What is the one thing that you would change about archaeology if you could?

I'm one of the really lucky archaeologists who is properly paid and in a secure post, but some of my friends are still on frankly awful wages and fixed-term contracts. So I'd find a way to enforce improved pay and conditions. Archaeology is one of the poorest paid professions in existence, despite the fact that most archaeologists have multiple higher degree qualifications; I do not see why archaeologists should not get paid the same as similarly skilled professions such as law or engineering.

What is your top tip for pursuing a career in archaeology?

Develop a wide range of skills and be willing to use these – all the people I know who are doing well in the profession have a detailed knowledge of more than one archaeological specialty, be these time periods, geographic locations, or practical or theoretical skills. As a result, they get jobs.

What do you see yourself doing in ten years' time?

I'd like to be doing one job in archaeology – juggling my two current jobs is fun but really tiring! I think, on balance, I'd like to be full-time in a university but working closely with government to help advance the cause of archaeology in that sector.

Chapter 2

Skills and Training

Introduction

The archaeological job market, as can be inferred from the discussion in Chapter 1, is akin to a small island on a geologic fault line: community-based with a nice lifestyle and amazing opportunities, but also volatile, owing largely to factors outside the population's control. One consistent outcome of all the different professional surveys of archaeologists, though, is that of training and education. The modern archaeologist is exceptionally well trained, with at least one (and often several) degree and qualifications in archaeology or a related subject, backed up by a raft of different experience.

Until even fairly recently it was still possible to get a job in archaeology with a lot of experience but only a little learning. The opposite is now true, however – statistically, a lot of learning and a little experience are the defining characteristics of the young professional archaeologist. Many would argue that this is a bad thing – that archaeologists with real, well-honed field experience are in shorter and shorter supply and that this is harming the practice of archaeology at a fundamental level. This is certainly a recurrent theme of meetings and conferences of CRM archaeologists, who feel that the university sector is letting them down, churning out ever more graduates from the academic "sausage factory" who simply do not have the skills required for the posts that need to be filled. Such a debate is not within the scope of this book. Here, all that can be stated are the facts as presented by various professional surveys; these surveys demonstrate that more and more professional archaeologists hold multiple degrees in the subject or its related specialties.

It appears that if one wants to get ahead in archaeology, with a degree but not much field experience there is at least a chance of getting a job, but with a lot of field experience but no degree the chance of finding a job is minimal.

Why Study Archaeology?

Many students come to formal archaeological study with a burning passion for the subject. To them, the answer to the question "Why study archaeology?" is simple: *because they want to*, and in many cases they have done so from an early age. Such individuals may well go on to take multiple university degrees in archaeology and become professional archaeologists themselves. But for others, the situation may be less clear-cut, be this at school, college, or university. Many people may be uncertain about studying a subject with what seems, at first glance, limited wider applicability. This section is for these people in doubt.

Archaeology is worth studying, from the school level right up to and even beyond a bachelor's degree, because it offers an unrivaled array of transferable skills that can be used in virtually any corner of the world and in all job sectors. The UK's Universities and Colleges Admissions Service (UCAS), for example, provides profiles, including employability skills profiles, of all the different subjects available in UK universities. The profile for archaeology (UCAS 2010a) includes the following transferable – that is, non-archaeological – skills:

- Apply scholarly, theoretical, and scientific principles and concepts to specific problems.
- Use diverse sources of evidence to formulate an argument.
- Appreciate the importance of recovering primary data through practical experience.
- Critically apply methodologies for quantifying, analyzing, and interpreting primary data.
- Understand the concepts and application of scientific methods used in collecting, analyzing, and interpreting data.
- Interpret spatial data.
- Select and apply appropriate statistical and numerical techniques.
- Marshal and critically appraise other people's arguments.
- Produce logical and structured arguments supported by evidence.
- Communicate effectively orally, visually, and in writing to diverse audiences.
- Use IT, information retrieval, and presentation skills effectively in a variety of graphical media.
- Execute research, working independently.
- Collaborate effectively in a team.
- Be sensitive to different cultures and deal with unfamiliar situations.
- Be able to critically evaluate one's own and others' opinions.

UCAS also provide details (more than eleven pages' worth) of specific employability skills (UCAS 2010b). These include a wide array of cognitive (i.e., thinking) skills matched with practical (i.e., doing) skills. This is also an observation backed up by successive government reviews of the subject within higher education, most recently in 2007, when the UK's Quality Assurance Agency for Higher Education (QAA) last surveyed the subject and published its report (QAA 2007). At that time, the QAA commented:

> The broad-based nature of the subject and of the skills it gives graduates provide a strong grounding for a wide range of career paths: the archaeology graduate is extremely well equipped with transferable skills from the mix of humanities and science training, engagement with theory and practice, and individual and team-based learning, together with the intellectual curiosity to continue learning, and the skills to benefit from challenging work environments. Archaeology also offers much non-professional involvement, via continuing education courses, local societies, museums, heritage groups and so on, so graduates not employed within archaeology have many opportunities for lifelong learning and to share their expertise within the community.

It is also notable that archaeology scores highly across the different types of learning styles that have been modeled. To take one example, the VARK neurolinguistic model breaks learning styles down into: (1) visual (learning through seeing), (2) auditory (learning through listening), (3) reading/writing, and (4) kinesthetic/tactile (learning through doing) styles of learning. Archaeologists, and thus archaeology students, get to use all these different learning styles in their training and professional development, which makes archaeology an extremely engaging subject to study. As Indiana Jones put it: "It's not the years . . . it's the mileage": archaeologists get a very diverse array of attractive transferable skills under their belts, and get to practice these skills on a regular basis.

Put another way, studying archaeology gets a big bang for the buck in terms of skills (see Jackson and Sinclair 2010). Archaeology is obviously worth studying because of one's love for the subject, but even if one is only a little bit in love with it, studying it is not going to harm one's future career prospects – indeed, the opposite may be true. Archaeology courses provide skills that can set someone up for life, and be interesting too. And archaeology, lest we forget, is also simply cool. How many people at a party do not want to meet an archaeologist?

Archaeology and Disabilities

The Americans with Disabilities Act (1990), Australian Disability Discrimination Act (1992), UK Disability Discrimination Act (1995), and similar laws in place around the world make it unlawful to discriminate against people with respect to their disabilities in relation to employment, the provision of goods and services, education, and transport. Impairments in this sense may include physical, sensory, and cognitive or developmental disabilities.

There has never been any survey of archaeologists with disabilities anywhere in the world. There has, however, been at least one guidance document produced on this subject, supported by an extensive website (see Philips et al. 2007). That being said, even without laws in place to protect people with disabilities, archaeology

49

has, overall, a good track record of inclusivity. Numerous archaeologists (famous, as well as not so famous) have had successful careers in which disability has not been a barrier to their involvement. Indeed, archaeology can at times provide an unusually adaptable and supportive environment.

The key is clearly that no one, including anyone with any type of disability, should ever feel excluded from archaeology. The physical demands of archaeological fieldwork might be perceived as a barrier to full involvement, for many different reasons – disability is merely one reason that people may be cautious or nervous about pursuing an interest in archaeology. In truth, however, very few disabilities, of any type, are so influential that they cannot be worked around or mitigated in some manner when involved in archaeology. Doing some specific jobs, or access to some specific sites, may be a problem but there are, as outlined in this book, many different jobs and many different sites in archaeology. Health and safety laws and regulations may also have an impact on the possibilities of work. The key is full and frank discussion with individual people who are, or may feel themselves, to be disabled about their needs in advance of planning or undertaking fieldwork. Flexibility during a project, by both planners and participants, is also necessary, as is "a recognition that ability is an attribute that will change and develop with experience and time" (Philips et al. 2007: 19) and also that "simple, common sense solutions are usually the most successful" (ibid.).

To take one particular and very common example of a disability, many prospective archaeologists with dyslexia might be worried that this prevents a career in a subject for which a university degree is a virtual necessity. Reading, and especially writing, long essays and reports can seem like an insurmountable barrier to someone with dyslexia. There are plenty of archaeologists with dyslexia, however, and it is almost always something that can be overcome with various types of mitigation, from special types of computers and computer software to simply taking more time to plan and write work (and being given more time in exams).

As a different case study, people with mobility issues may similarly feel potentially excluded from undertaking archaeological fieldwork. Again, in reality, this is rarely a problem. For example, plenty of people who use wheelchairs have worked on a variety of archaeological sites, on land as well as under water. The secret, as for everyone in archaeology, is dedication – those who want to succeed will do so, potential barriers can be overcome, and no one in the community will ever use a disability as an excuse to bar involvement.

Going on Your First Archaeological Project

Irrespective of the circumstances – school or college, local society, university or other – the following general advice is useful for all those individuals embarking on their first archaeological project. *It is worth reading this section if you are unsure about going on archaeological fieldwork – if the following does not sound like it appeals, then are you really sure that archaeology is the way forward for you?*

Prior to any project there will usually be a meeting of all the participants that gives a detailed briefing on the project, its aims and objectives, methodologies, and also the logistics and practicalities – plus, most important, what equipment each participant is expected to bring (see Figure 6) and how they are expected to get to the project site (see Figure 7). Assuming that a student's first field experience is to be on a traditional university-led survey/excavation project, a few commonalities of all projects can be highlighted here (in alphabetical order) that may be of use:

- *Accommodations*: These can vary from the luxurious to the basic. At the top end it might mean (usually shared) hotel rooms with en suite facilities; the sliding scale then runs down through rather less amazing motels, dorms, and bunkhouses to tents – although a well-tended tent in the middle of a green field beats a sketchy motel in a rundown neighborhood any day of the week.
- *Activities*: A good project director will move participants around so they learn both general principles of excavation and specific skills such as surveying, section drawing, photography, and the like (see Figure 8). Such a director will also challenge students to apply their classroom thinking to the site's interpretation, understanding, and presentation: Why is the site structured the way it is? What might the differential scatters of find types around the site say about social structures? How can we best present this site and its data to the public? Once in the field, if you do not feel that you are getting this kind of support, then do not be afraid to (politely) say so. On a training project you need to experience a variety of different roles and skills; you will learn very little if you end up digging the same section of a trench for three straight weeks.
- *Catering*: This is usually organized communally (often on a rotation basis) and arranged by the project team itself; quality depends on the project's finances on one hand, and the ability of the cooks on the other. If the food you are being given is awful and you think you can do better, offer to take a turn shopping and cooking – it beats doing the washing up, another regular chore! Given that fieldwork is usually physically demanding, expect hearty food; do not be afraid to eat it even if you are officially on a diet – if you are not used to sustained physical labor (most people these days are not), your body is going to need this fuel to prevent collapse. Vegetarians and vegans are usually well provided for – some digs may be totally vegetarian if the project director is. Picky eaters have a harder time of it, although if you have a genuine food allergy, this can be dealt with. Food will usually be purchased for you, but additional snacks such candy will be up to you to provide. Remember to drink lots – and lots – of water when doing fieldwork, even in cool/wet weather; there should be extensive supplies of potable water provided on site.
- *Drugs*: Social mores vary from country to country. Plenty of excavations (as, indeed, people and nations) around the world have a zero-tolerance approach to all and any drugs, including alcohol, and you will get into major trouble if you sneak drugs onto such sites – illegal substances and fieldwork do not mix and can lead to your being thrown out of the project at best or arrested, tried, and ending up with a criminal record and resultant sentence at worst. Such a crime could jeopardize the entire project. Project directors will make clear the rules for alcoholic consumption in particular, and if you cannot abide by those rules, you

Figure 6. Fieldwork training in action. Field training takes place in many different environments around the world. Here, students record stone platform terraces at the Marco Gonzalez site, Ambergris Caye, Belize, in July 2010. The students in the background are excavating stone risers of another structure, and are also digging down in front of the risers in the hope of discovering a preserved plaza floor – which they ultimately did (© Elizabeth Graham 2010, courtesy of the Marco Gonzalez Project).

Figure 7. The realities of fieldwork, part 1. Field training often means novel travel arrangements. Here, students travel to the Marco Gonzalez site, Ambergris Caye, Belize, in July 2010 via their normal mode of transport: the back of a truck. They have just been picked up from their hotel and are passing the dig house and lab (behind the white fence on the right). It is about five and a half miles from the site of the photo to the excavation – the concrete road soon ends, replaced by a sand road (© Elizabeth Graham 2010, courtesy of Leanne Chorekdjian and the Marco Gonzalez Project).

should not come on the project. That being said, many archaeologists enjoy an alcoholic drink *after* a hard day's work (never on site). If you do not like alcohol, or if your beliefs prohibit its consumption, then do not worry – no one will hassle you to partake, but you should at least be comfortable sitting alongside others who do, matching a soft drink to their hard drink to be sociable – plenty of "eureka" moments have been had in the bar at the end of the day that transform the understanding of a site.

- *Equipment*: Major project equipment will usually be provided for you, but every archaeologist should have his or her own basic field kit, together with clothing appropriate to the climate and weather (see the discussion that follows – especially regarding waterproof and sunproof kits). A full list of such suggested equipment is included in Appendix 3 of this book. If nothing else, you need to own your own trowel (in the UK the 4-inch solid-forged WHS pointing trowel is preferred; in the US, the standard is the legendary Marshalltown trowel. Paeans have been written extolling trowels, and they are the most beloved and protectively held of all archaeological equipment – see Flannery 1982). Dig clothing tends to be informal, of the jeans and T-shirt type; most people wear solid boots of some sort, often steel-toecap safety boots (sometimes required; some sites may also require archaeologists to provide additional safety equipment, such as high-visibility jackets and hard hats). It is worth keeping a set of nicer, cleaner clothes to one side for when you head out into the general population – if nothing else, restaurants tend to take a poor view of twenty filthy archaeologists arriving at their premises. Three key tips are: (1) avoid any clothes with political slogans or crude jokes on them; (2) be aware of local sensitivities – so avoid clothes that expose a lot of skin in many countries and be cautious of wearing too much "military" garb in others – make yourself look as harmless and inconspicuous as possible; (3) avoid clothes that, once wet, are uncomfortable and take an age to dry – especially jeans. On some projects you may also be required to provide other accommodation equipment, such as sleeping bags, ground mats, tents, and cooking and other camping equipment – you should be told in advance if you do. Where do you buy all these supplies? Start at your nearest military surplus store and finish up at a camping/outdoor store.

- *Health and safety*: These are taken very seriously. You will be given a briefing on this prior to, and also on arrival at, the project site. There will always be a dedicated, trained first-aider on site, a first aid kit, and a list of emergency services contact details and locations. Many people also bring their own personal first aid kit for minor cuts and grazes; people with particular health issues, such as allergies, should let the project director know well in advance and discuss solutions, such as carrying an EpiPen®. Particular health hazards and risks will be identified and planned for well in advance, so do not worry unduly about these risks. Bear in mind that the climate and weather can have a serious impact when you spend all day outside – even on an apparently cool but sunny day, sunburn, heatstroke, and dehydration are a risk, especially for people unused to doing hard physical labor outside. Plan accordingly and remember: tools are just that – tools, not toys – so do not play around with them.

- *Leisure*: Most projects will usually have one regular day off per week. Sometimes it is entirely up to participants to decide what to do on those days; other times, a trip to a local town or local historic site might be arranged. There can be no doubt that projects based anywhere near the coast tend to see people heading to the beach whenever possible. Above all else, though, remember that projects have clear objectives and you should not expect much free time – this is work, not a vacation. Hours will be long – 6 AM or even earlier starts are not uncommon, with hard labor all day and additional tasks in the evening. There may also be evening lectures and other training events. Bring along a decent alarm clock and get used to those dawn starts, or risk facing the wrath of the project directors; *your* tardiness is slowing down *their* project, on which their careers may depend.

- *Washing*: Cleaning facilities, for both yourself and your equipment, can vary considerably – toilet facilities in particular, especially if your project accommodation is a campsite. If you are squeamish about such things, archaeology really may

Figure 8. The realities of fieldwork, part 2. Field training can mean simple working environments. Here, students from the Marco Gonzalez site, Ambergris Caye, Belize, in July 2010 work in the project lab, a large area under the dig house in San Pedro Town. The students are cleaning the bones from a burial of c. 800–850 CE that they had previously excavated (© Elizabeth Graham 2010, courtesy of the Marco Gonzalez Project).

not be the career for you. Having said that, because accommodations can sometimes be in hotels, motels, and dorms, washing facilities can be pretty good, and if nothing else, someone will eventually make a dash to a laundry. Wet-wipes and antibacterial no-water gel hand-washes are the archaeologist's friend on site.

- *Weather.* Obviously, weather affects your life on site in a manner to which you may never before been accustomed. Except in exceptional circumstances, fieldwork will usually go on no matter what the conditions. Be prepared – the project director will brief you well beforehand on what to expect. If the project director tells you it will be cold and wet, then bring lots of good warm and waterproof clothes and a stout pair of waterproof boots; if, similarly, they say it is going to be incredibly dry and hot, bring along loose, light clothing that covers all your skin – sunburn is no joke. Remember, in particular, that you may be sitting and/or crouching and thus exposing bits of your skin that do not normally see much sun. Even on cloudy days it is possibly to get badly sunburned, be the weather hot or cold – the key is to cover up, and especially to wear a hat of some sort as the prevailing weather necessitates, as well as to wear lots of high-SPF sunscreen.

Pre-university Education and Training

As little as a decade ago, the majority of students studying in an undergraduate degree program in archaeology would have had some previous experience in the discipline. This experience was gained either through their school or college, or through membership of a local or national archaeological society. Such students would have had at least some limited experience of work on an archaeological site that prompted the urge to undertake a formal qualification, some basic appreciation of fundamental archaeological principles, and perhaps even an understanding of the realities of life working as an archaeologist. A smaller number of students would then have had considerably more experience – various now-senior archaeologists received their grounding in the subject as energetic teenage fieldworkers in the 1960s, 1970s, and 1980s, and by the time they arrived at university they were frequently highly skilled field archaeologists in their own right.

The reality now is very different, owing to the tightening of the national school curriculum (particularly in the UK), the relative decline of "local society" field archaeology (especially that involving minors, because child protection and health and safety concerns have made the involvement of children in such fieldwork much harder), and the changes to the nature and public availability of archaeological field-work since the rise of "polluter pays" legislation and the rise of CRM archaeology. As a consequence of all these changes, it is now far harder for volunteers to become involved in fieldwork. Most undergraduate archaeology students arriving for their first year of study therefore have little, if any, experience of the subject beyond that gleaned from TV shows and the Internet. Whether this shift in experience is a good or a bad thing is not an issue that requires discussion here; what does matter is the implication of such a shift for anyone, of any age, who wants to get experiences, and possibly qualifications, in archaeology that are not at the university level.

Some people may want non-university experience of archaeology so they can go on into the university sector and gain a degree in the subject; others may simply wish to formalize a long-held interest in the subject but not spend precious time and money on gaining what may be, for them, a superfluous formal qualification. It is thus important that people considering trying to get experience in archaeology have at least some vague sense of where they see themselves a few years from now – actually studying archaeology somewhere, or simply enjoying the practice and experience of archaeology from a better informed position than before? The former group of individuals could be well served by taking a non-university continuing education course in archaeology, be this at school or college; the latter group of individuals might include this option, but could alternatively be better served through membership of one of the many local, regional, or national archaeological societies that provide an array of opportunities in return for a small annual subscription. Membership in such organizations brings many benefits, most importantly access to an array of events such as lectures and seminars, as well as fieldwork opportunities; many of these are geared toward people who work, with the events held in evenings, weekends, and holiday periods. Many local archaeology societies also have specialist subgroups based around a particular period (e.g., Roman, medieval), subject specialty (e.g., industrial archaeology), or even an individual town, village, district, or neighborhood. Other specialist groups also exist, such as the Nautical Archaeology Society for those interested in maritime and underwater archaeology.

It is relatively easy, and also relatively cheap, to get directly involved in archaeology via organizations like these – to get out from behind the TV or computer and go and learn about archaeology through non-university lectures and classes, do fieldwork, and get specialized training. No one, in the UK and US in particular, lives more than a short journey away from the base of one or another archaeological society. This is the best possible way to become directly involved in archaeology – it is cost-effective, gets you in the field in the shortest possible time, introduces you to like-minded people, and is flexible – it can lead to an entire career in archaeology for some, a lifelong interest and history of involvement for others. Voluntary archaeology is also still an ideal way for children and teenagers (with or without their families) to become involved in archaeology, despite the problems with child protection and heath and safety identified previously, because any excavations will be well planned with regard to health and safety, child protection, and so on. Above all, local community archaeology of this sort is fun – and archaeology ought always to be fun.

Archaeology in the School Curriculum

The constraints of different nations' school curriculums make it extremely hard to study archaeology in school – up until the ages of between 16 and 18, depending on your location – in virtually all countries around the world. These curriculums give little room for innovation to teachers in the classroom and do not include specific archaeological courses. Keen teachers are the only possibility for such content to be integrated into the curriculum (for example, there is sometimes a focus in US and Australian high schools around ancient history, or a primary school focus on social studies), but this is not common and is generally up to the individual teacher rather than part of the curriculum. In the UK, for example, the National Curriculum dictates to a large extent what can (and cannot) be taught in history lessons, the only format for archaeological data and materials until the age of 16 (see Henson 2004a, 2004b).

As Moshenska (2009: 56) notes, this situation is exacerbated by the lack of archaeological training of schoolteachers: "Archaeology graduates usually find it difficult if not impossible to get accepted on to teacher training courses, as archaeology is not a curriculum subject and is generally not taught in schools. The paucity of archaeological knowledge amongst schoolteachers thereby becomes a self-perpetuating problem" (citing Corbishley 1999: 77). This is a similar situation to that in the US and Australia. The easiest way to become involved in archaeology up to the age of 16 in the UK, and up to the age of 18 in the US, is, therefore, to join a local or national archaeological society and learn about archaeology in one's spare time rather than as part of everyday schooling; in the UK, the obvious choice is the Young Archaeologists' Club (for 8- to 16-year-olds) run by the UK's national body for archaeology, the Council for British Archaeology. Similar events are run in the US through the National Park Service's Federal Archaeology Program (as well as by individual state level organizations), and by various state level organizations in Australia (Figure 9).

In the UK at least, things improve after the age of 16, because archaeology can be studied in post-16 education through a variety of qualifications:

- AS and A levels in archaeology and classical civilization exist, and are run at many schools and colleges (England and Wales only).
- Scottish Highers in history and classical civilization (Scotland only).
- BTECs in Countryside Management, available at National Award, National Certificate, and National Diploma levels.
- City and Guilds Advanced National Certificate in Countryside Management.
- Diplomas in Construction and the Built Environment and Environmental and Land-based Studies; after September 2011 there will also be a new Diploma in Humanities and Social Sciences (vocation qualifications available for students aged 14 to 19).

For those who are no longer in school, there is also the National Vocational Qualification in Archaeological Practice. The qualification is offered at levels 3 (entry level) and 4 (experienced professional), with level 5 (strategic management) in development. Each level consists of core units and a range of options. Sadly, there are no US or Australian equivalents to such types of study.

It should be noted in closing that AS and A levels – and equivalent high school qualifications – in archaeology are relatively uncommon. By no means do all schools or colleges offer such courses, and it may simply prove impossible to find a course offered nearby, even as an optional evening class. The reality is that although experience of archaeology prior to university is no bad thing to gain, such skills are not essential if one hopes to eventually work as an archaeologist. An embryonic career will not be destroyed without such experience, nor will it be ensured with it, and no university entry tutor will hold it against someone who did not study archaeology at the pre-university level.

Academic Pathways in Archaeology

The extremely varied higher education systems of countries around the world make it impossible to sum up all the possible academic pathways into archaeology beyond the high school or A level. The situation is further confused by different terminology, as well as slang, for different types and periods of study. Table 3 provides at least a partial guide to the different systems in the UK, US, and Australia. In particular, this is provided to help explain the different types of terminology used throughout this chapter – supported by the glossary of specialty terms provided in Appendix 2.

Figure 9. Archaeology in the school curriculum. Most children love to be taught about archaeology in a practical format, which appeals to their natural sense of fun, and archaeology can be used to help teach many different school subjects. Here, schoolchildren are taught to identify finds discovered in the course of a nearby CRM excavation (© Archaeology South East UCL 2010, courtesy of Dominic Perring).

It should be noted that across the UK, US, and Australia, at all levels of study, part-time study is usually possible, although this normally doubles – at the least – the total duration of study (reduced fees are also usually charged). Such a program is thus worth considering by someone who must work during the course of study to pay for his or her studies and/or has other financial or family commitments.

At the BA/BSc level, many institutions around the world also offer diplomas and certificates of higher education, which are not degree level but are awarded to students who have successfully completed part of a degree course; these credits may be used to transfer to another institution. Similarly, between the BA/BSc and MA/MSc levels, many universities offer graduate diplomas or graduate certificates that are not degree level but are awarded to students who have successfully completed part of a graduate degree course; these credits may be used either to build credit toward an MA/MSc or to transfer to another institution for graduate/postgraduate study.

TABLE 3. A Guide to the Different Educational Systems of the UK, US, and Australia

	England, Wales, Northern Ireland	Scotland	US	Australia
Pre-University (entry qualifications)	AS and A Levels (A1 and A2) – 2 years; submission of predicted or achieved grades plus application materials to the Universities and Colleges Admissions Service (UCAS)	Highers and Advanced Highers (Scottish Qualifications Certificate) – 2 years; submission of predicted or achieved grades plus application materials to universities via the Universities and Colleges Admissions Service (UCAS)	Completion of high school; submission of scores for the SAT or ACT exams.[1] In some cases also completion of advanced placement (AP) courses	Completion of high school (year 12 results); some universities require the submission of STATs (Special Tertiary Admissions Tests) or equivalent; some universities also/instead assess on a ranking system[2]
Bachelor of Arts/Bachelor of Science (BA/BSc)	Single, combined, or double bachelor's degree – 3 years undergraduate, either with a pass or honors[3]	Single, combined, or double: ordinary degree – 3 years undergraduate; honors degree – 4 years undergraduate	Ordinary or honors degrees with majors and minors in different subjects, based on credit hours – 4 years expected[4] undergraduate	Single, combined, or double: ordinary degree – 3 years undergraduate; honors degree – 4 years undergraduate
Master of Arts/Master of Science (MA/MSc)	Master's degree – 1 year [taught] postgraduate[5]	Master's degree – 1 year [taught] postgraduate	Master's degree – usually a minimum of 1–2 years graduate school[6]	Master's degree – usually 1–2 years graduate school

Master of Philosophy (MPhil)[7]	Minimum 2 years [research] postgraduate – submission of a thesis comprising a body of original research undertaken by the candidate	Minimum 2 years [research] postgraduate – submission of a thesis comprising a body of original research undertaken by the candidate	Degree is awarded to PhD candidates when they complete their required coursework and qualifying examinations, but before the defense of a doctoral dissertation	Minimum 2 years [research] postgraduate – submission of a thesis comprising a body of original research undertaken by the candidate
Doctor of Philosophy (PhD/DPhil)	Doctorate – usually 3–4 years [research] postgraduate, writing thesis of 80,000–100,000 words	Doctorate – usually 3–4 years [research] postgraduate, writing thesis of 80,000–100,000 words	Doctorate – usually 3–4 years minimum (commonly 5+ years) in graduate school, writing thesis of 100,000–250,000 words	Doctorate – usually 3–4 years [research] postgraduate, writing thesis of 80,000–100,000 words

---

[1] Some universities will prefer applicants who have performed well in geography and history courses. If an archeology course is offered, applicants are encouraged to take it.

[2] Each university uses a ranking system that reflects the performance of each student against students of the same age in the academic year. The ranking systems have different names in different locations, such as Melbourne's Equivalent National Tertiary Entrance Rank (ENTER) vs. Sydney's Universities Admissions Index (UAI). Although the names are different, they are all nationally equivalent measures.

[3] Unlike the US, Scotland, and Australia, honors in the UK system are awarded not for the duration of the course of study but for the program chosen, given sufficiently good grades.

[4] The four years is merely an estimate of time it should take to complete the required number of credit hours; a degree can be achieved in less time if a student "overloads," taking more classes than normally expected.

[5] In some of the ancient British universities (and also Dublin University in Ireland), the degree of MA can be claimed for a nominal sum, usually after a fixed time after commencing university or after a certain age is reached. To distinguish such degrees from earned MAs, these are usually followed in text by "Oxon.," "Cantab.," "Dubl.," and so on, and other earned MA/MSc degrees from these universities are then signified through the use of other terms for these qualifications.

[6] Applicants to US graduate schools are also usually required to take the Graduate Record Examination (GRE) test as part of their application process – for both MA and PhD study.

[7] It is common for UK and Australian students admitted into a PhD/DPhil program to be initially registered for the degree of MPhil, and then to transfer to the PhD on successful completion of the first (or sometimes the second) year of study.

Choosing Your Degree Specialty

As outlined in Chapter 1, there are a number of different thematic routes into archaeology – practical as well as theoretical schools of thought. In part, these are a consequence of geography: these approaches or schools of archaeological approach are at least partly drawn along national lines, and are also partly a question of regional environmental specialty – such as African, American, Asian, Australian, Chinese, European, or Indian archaeology. These different approaches do, however, have a direct impact on the types of degrees available at both the undergraduate and postgraduate levels.

As previously noted, the anthropological archaeological school of thought is most dominant in the US. As a consequence of this, most archaeological degree courses in the US are in anthropology departments, and most undergraduate degrees will involve a major or minor in anthropological archaeology or even just in anthropology. Historical archaeology, however, is now almost as important a specialty, so there are also many departments and undergraduate degrees involving a major or minor in historical archaeology, or even just archaeology. As a result, choosing a course of study in the US is a relatively straightforward choice between applying for an anthropological or a historical archaeology department or school, a decision likely to significantly influence future training and specialization.

In contrast, in the UK and Australia anthropology departments rarely offer degrees in archaeology unless directly associated with an archaeology department – there, anthropology is a distinct and separate subject from archaeology. In these locations, pure archaeology departments are the norm (although their teaching will usually include a similar series of themes to those in US anthropology departments). In these locations, the choice of degree type is ostensibly even easier than in the US – archaeology, be this anthropological, prehistorical, or historical, is likely to be offered by, simply, an archaeology department. Further confusing the situation, however, the structure of UK university courses means that students there can usually apply directly for specific types of archaeological/anthropological degrees – selecting before their arrival a dedicated degree program on a period, topic, or theme (e.g., prehistoric or historical archaeology, Roman or medieval archaeology, British or European archaeology). This is the opposite of the situation in the US, where the minor/major structure and broader general requirement courses of the credit-based university system mean that students make such specialization choices much later on once at university and into their studies.

When looking around to pick a university and a degree program, students should be aware that each university might offer archaeology courses in anthropology, archaeology, classics, and even history departments and schools. There may also be specialized departments, such as departments of Egyptology. Some universities even have more than one department that teaches aspects of one or more specialty in archaeology, such as an anthropology department and a history department. Prospective students need to look widely at what is offered across any university in which they are interested, and not be afraid to ask for advice on the various professors. Similarly, when trying to decide what particular degree program or course for which to apply, students should be aware that some universities (especially in the UK and Australia) offer very streamed programs with limited options once study has commenced, often on fairly defined or proscribed topics (e.g., a BA in prehistoric archaeology). In contrast, other programs (especially in the US) will have more general requirements and an ability to pick a major/minor in different subjects, building up credits and allowing flexibility throughout the course of study, with the decision on what type and title of degree to graduate with not being finalized until relatively close to the end of a program of study. Again, prospective students need to look widely at what is offered and not be afraid to ask for advice on what is taught, when it is taught, and how flexible a course or program is.

In addition to the preceding information, for students in the UK, the Council for British Archaeology's "Guide to Studying Archaeology at Undergraduate Level" is very useful.[1] A similar resource in the US is the American Anthropological Association's Student webpage,[2] and in Australia, the Australian Archaeological Association's Study Options webpage.[3]

The following pointers should help the choice of degree specialty at both the undergraduate and postgraduate levels:

- *BA or BSc study (broadly focused on humanities or sciences)*: In many cases, this decision will be made in relation to your A levels, Scottish Highers, or high school test subjects and results – most BSc programs will not accept students without a background in the sciences, whereas BA programs will accept a broader range of entry backgrounds. BSc courses will have a heavier focus on archaeological science – some may even be dedicated programs in archaeological science or a specialty of that. All BA archaeology programs will include at least some of these more scientific aspects too, and normally will allow further specialization once the program is under way, so getting a BA degree does not necessarily stop a student from going on to further study at the graduate level in the sciences – for instance, moving on from a BA to an MSc, or from a BSc to an MA, it is merely a question of whether you wish to specialize slightly earlier on in your career or not.
- *Single or double/combined degrees*: This is really a decision that has to be made only in the UK and Australia: as noted previously, the US major/minor credit-bearing system does not focus so early on specialization. Many UK and Australia universities offer both "single honors" programs in archaeology (or specialties such as classical or historical archaeology), and "double/combined honors" programs in archaeology and many other subjects, most commonly archaeology and history (or art or ancient history), archaeology and Egyptology (or classical archaeology), archaeology and anthropology, archaeology and a language (both ancient and modern), and archaeology and geology or geography. The benefits of single honors study are a deeper focus on "pure" archaeology and also a smaller peer

---

[1] See http://www.britarch.ac.uk/education/study/undergrad.
[2] See http://www.aaanet.org/resources/students/.
[3] See http://www.australianarchaeologicalassociation.com.au/study_options.

group; the benefits of double/combined honors study are a broader appreciation of the place of archaeology and a larger peer group. In truth, this is not a decision that should cause undue worry – it is normally fairly easy to swap between single and combined honors programs within a university during the course of study.

- *"Pass" or honors courses*: This is a decision that has to be made only in the US, Scotland, and Australia, where honors courses are the result of taking a degree program with a longer duration and/or more credit – making this decision (which is usually undertaken during the program of study, not at the start) is thus a commitment to longer, harder, and thus more expensive study overall – but the reward is a more "meritworthy" degree that will better impress future employers; the result is that the majority of students in the US, Scotland, and Australia choose to pursue an honors degree if possible. In contrast, in England, Wales, and Northern Ireland, honors are awarded not for the duration of the course of study, but for the program chosen at the start of study, given sufficiently good overall grades; as a consequence, the vast majority of English, Welsh, and Northern Irish students virtually automatically graduate with an honors degree unless their performance is exceptionally poor, unlike students in the US, Scotland, and Australia, where honors are more closely tied to higher academic endeavors.

Getting into the University of Your Choice

The virtual absence of available "entry-level" pre-university training in archaeology should not be taken as indicative of the lack of need for such qualifications later on; the reality is that without at least a bachelor's degree in archaeology or anthropology, even the most naturally brilliant of archaeologists will find it hard to get work. Prospective professional archaeologists have a fairly clear early career path to follow: they need to do what is required to get in the university archaeology program of their choice. In the UK, this means getting good A levels or Scottish Highers (ideally, all A and B grades) in appropriate subjects; in the US and Australia, good high school SAT scores, along with a log of those all-important extracurricular activities that make an application stand out to college admissions officers.

Few A level or high school subjects will harm an application to an archaeology or anthropology department for undergraduate study (unlike, say, an application to study medicine at university, for which high grades in specific subjects are a must to stand any chance of gaining entry); but good subjects include obviously relevant choices such as history and geography; core subjects such as English, mathematics, and any of the hard sciences; as well as more unusual options such as economics. Languages, both ancient and modern, are also a definite bonus – from the ancient world, Latin being the obvious choice, and for the modern, German (Germany has a long tradition of archaeology and remains a publishing powerhouse in the subject). Italian and Spanish are also other excellent second language choices; the latter is especially valuable in the US. Indeed, a thorough command of at least one other language is arguably the most important skill that any aspiring or indeed active archaeologist should have.

Beyond the undergraduate level, application criteria get much tougher. Applicants for graduate study at the MA, MPhil, or PhD level need to have an excellent undergraduate degree (in the UK at 2.1 level or above, in the US with a GPA of 3.4 or above). A proven ability in two languages is also a common requirement for PhD study in many US universities, along with excellent GRE scores, if one expects to go on to any type of graduate study. International students studying outside their home countries in the US, UK, and Australia are also likely to face stringent English language proficiency tests as part of their applications – together with increasingly stringent, government-enforced immigration procedures.

Beyond formal qualifications, there can be no doubt that various other things can be done to help gain entry onto the course of your choice. These will come up for discussion in the personal statement or interview that some universities require for prospective students (interviews are common only in the UK). The aforementioned experience of archaeology with a voluntary society is obviously an excellent start, if possible – if nothing else, archaeologists like to hear about other people's fieldwork, so discussion of your experiences on that summer dig are an good topic to bring up in personal statements and the like. But archaeologists are, by and large, kindly and generous folk, and rare is the admissions tutor who will hold a lack of formal experience against a potential student; these tutors know how hard it is to get such experience. Enthusiasm for archaeology, shown through evidence of reading around the subject (and I mean here reading actual books, not spurious Internet articles), even your thoughts on the approaches of the latest popular archaeology TV show can go a long way. If nothing else, a bit of background research on the specialties of the department, its staff, and their research and publications can help a lot – being able to briefly discuss the latest book by Professor Y from the department, for example, is a good application or interview icebreaker; even if the admissions tutor thinks that Professor Y is an idiot and the new book an abomination, at least you have shown an interest and are conversant with the subject. The worst possible thing to do is to submit an application or turn up for interview and either be so tongue-tied, or worse still, simply so uninformed, that you have nothing to write or say about archaeology in response to the series of kindly – but probing – questions the interviewer will ask.

Even if you cannot find anything to talk about regarding archaeology, then above all, in a personal statement or an interview situation, you must show enthusiasm for *something*. Archaeologists are people too – they will have opinions on sports, current affairs, and TV as well, and your application is the admission officer's moment to judge not what you currently know but rather your capacity to learn and to develop yourself in the future. An agile and inquiring mind and a willingness to think a question through and provide a logical response are the characteristics that will help win that coveted place in a course. An uncommunicative or unenthusiastic candidate is the one who will not be getting that place – if you cannot summon up serious enthusiasm now, then the admissions officer will have an impression of what your attitude is likely to be if you are accepted and then have to deal with similar disinterest on a rainy morning on site. Project directors will not want to have to rouse people's enthusiasm then, and more importantly, they will not have to, because they will be doing archaeology and you will not be, having never been accepted.

Choosing a University – Courses and Locations

Until the 1960s, choices of location for archaeological training were few and far between; perhaps two dozen universities spread across the globe offered some aspect of the subject, frequently at the postgraduate level only. The archaeologist Mortimer Wheeler was of the opinion that archaeology should be offered only at the postgraduate level, available after students had gained a through grounding in ancient/classical history and languages at the undergraduate level. Fast-forward half a century, and there are hundreds of undergraduate archaeology programs available all over the world, with dozens in the UK and Australia and hundreds in the US, mainland Europe, and Scandinavia. Some of these universities and their archaeology departments, courses, and staff are extensive and world famous; others are far less so. All such programs offer countless opportunities and will bombard interested people with glossy brochures at the earliest opportunity. Deciding between such a rich array of options can be tricky, and there is no perfect way to decide – the department of archaeology/anthropology and the program of study that suits one person will not suit another (Figure 10).

As a prospective student, you should carefully consider the following archaeological and non-archaeological issues, including asking questions about these when they visit the various campuses – and above all, you *must* visit; there is no substitute for your gut instinct of a place in which you could end up spending years. You should also ask to meet current students during your visit: any good university will have prearranged such opportunities during your visit, and some may also arrange for recent graduates of their program to be around as well, to provide a longer-term view.

Non-Archaeological Factors

- *Location*: Does the location suit you and your family? If you grew up in a big city, for example, are you sure that a small rural college will work for you? Similarly, if you are from the countryside, are you ready for inner city life? Try to visit a campus twice – once during the workweek, and once at the weekend – that bustling weekday square lined with shops may be a deserted dustbowl on a Sunday.
- *Student body*: Do at least some of the current students come from a similar social/cultural background to yours? If, for example, you grew up in a multicultural inner-city environment and attended a coeducational state school, how do you feel about going to a college at which the majority of the student body was educated at private, expensive single-sex schools?
- *Size/facilities*: How big is the university and, in particular, how large is the school/department? How large will class sizes be, particularly in comparison to the library and lab facilities? Try to visit the library when teaching is fully

Figure 10. Archaeology in the university curriculum, part 1. Practical training plays a major part in the university archaeology curriculum. Here, a final-year student experiments with spindle whorl creation at UCL Institute of Archaeology's Experimental Archaeology Course, an annual practical training course for undergraduate students (© Charlotte Frearson / UCL Institute of Archaeology 2009).

underway, for example, to see how much competition there is for space and books between students. What about other non-subject facilities, such as leisure and sports facilities, or public transport infrastructure? What are the living accommodations like, and where are they located in relation to the campus? Some dorms are virtually luxury hotels located right next to the campus (with the prices to match); others are of much lower quality and may be a considerable distance from the campus.

- *Costs/finances*: What are the tuition fees of the university, and what can you normally expect to pay on top of that in terms of living costs? Do the university in general, and the department in particular, offer financial aid, general hardship grants, merit-based scholarships, and/or specific allowances for fieldwork? If so, how do you apply for these funds and what, realistically, are your chances of getting such assistance – for instance, one in five, one in fifty, or one in five hundred?

Archaeological Factors

- *Specialty*: Does the department offer particular archaeological specialties that you either know you want to study or think you might be interested in? You do not need to have any strong feelings either way, as plenty of students do not specialize until well into their studies; if you do, however, then this will likely be a deal maker or deal breaker. If the specialty of interest is offered, find out about the facilities supporting it, such as the provision of dedicated lab space, specialist equipment, and the like – offering a specialty is one thing, but actually following through on that offer in a meaningful way is quite another.

- *Fieldwork opportunities*: How much field experience do students gain as a part of their studies? Where and when does this take place, and is such work credit-bearing or not? Does the department arrange such work, or it is up to students to do this? Does the department offer financial assistance for travel and/or living costs? Is related training (e.g., scuba training for underwater work) available, and does this carry an additional cost?
- *Professional experience/training*: Does the university offer work placements with archaeological or related organizations such as CRM archaeology firms or museums? As for fieldwork, does the department arrange such work, or is it up to students to do this? Does the department offer financial assistance for travel and/or living costs?
- *Post-degree pathways*: What do graduates of the school/department go on to do after they graduate? How many graduates remain in the department for postgraduate study, and what are the funding opportunities available to support such studies?

Selecting Courses at University

Congratulations – you have arrived at university! Your career in archaeology has begun, most probably based out of a boxlike dorm room. In addition to a busy social life, a bewildering array of courses awaits, some compulsory and others optional; there are then other opportunities – possibilities of taking courses without credit, public lectures and seminars, discussion and reading groups, fieldtrips, and so on; all this before you have even considered all the other nonspecialist training courses in languages, presentation skills, CV writing, and the like, that the university offers. It can all seem like way too much to take in. Therefore, no matter what you see yourself doing in the future – hardened field archaeologist or pampered industry CEO – some basic planning now will reap untold rewards in the future.

The key thing to remember is this: *You do not need to have your future all planned out at this stage.* Some people may feel on arrival that they are destined to become famous archaeologists; such people tend to talk loudly in the cafeteria and can be wildly intimidating. Perhaps they are right, but it is too early to tell. Getting the right balance of academic and field skills in the midst of all this is by no means impossible, but does require some solid thinking. Everyone should begin with the following simple step: At the *start* of your first academic year of study, and then at the *end* of each subsequent academic year of study, plan out roughly (this can be notepad-while-sitting-on-a-park-bench territory) your coming year and file this plan away somewhere. When drawing up your next year's plan, review the previous year's one and think ahead. Near the start of your final academic year of study, think about your post-degree options – what do you need to achieve these aims?

This planning should, as noted, be simple; it is designed to make sure you get the required number of course credits to gain your degree. Confusingly, virtually every university in the world seems to operate a different credit scheme, so I will not even try to generalize here: find out your own university's particular scheme and apply it to this basic model. It does not help that UK universities tend to work on a more chronological-year model of a set number of courses per term or semester, whereas US and Australian universities are more focused on credits, which can be taken at any time and build up toward a total and which offer more flexibility. However, by mapping out the skills you already have and the skills you would like to get, you will have a clearer picture of your goals.

By the start of their last year of study, most people who go on to become professional archaeologists have probably been bitten by the bug and want to at least try to get a job some time in the not too distant future. The result is then, in many cases, what becomes the most crucial decision of one's career: whether to remain in education and gain a higher, postgraduate degree, or to go out and get field experience of one kind or another.

Compulsory Courses/General Requirements

These are the courses you *must* take. You must take them for a reason – they provide the basic tools of understanding and practicing archaeology (in the US, there will also be other nonspecific general requirements in a broader range of subjects). Do not avoid these courses. Some will be general introductory courses on the history of archaeology, basic field methods, and core archaeological concepts (e.g., material culture) and principles (e.g., the laws of stratigraphy). Others will focus in on particular issues to hone your analytical skills in particular: almost every university requires students to take a core option in archaeological theory, for example. You are also likely to have core courses on basic research skills (Figure 11).

Option/Elective Courses

These are the courses from which you get to choose. The risk here is that you pick only what sounds like fun, or what your friends choose, or what that cute classmate is taking. If you pick courses this way, you risk ending up with an odd range of experience and no clear way forward at the end of your studies.

This is where the planning is important. Definitely take some courses that just sound fun – you are interested in the topic, period, or location they focus on. You always need to have at least one course that you are really excited to be taking, one that gets you up in the morning. But make sure you get a balance of these with some strategic courses – these are ones that might sound less fun but provide useful transferable skills. Examples are particular lab-based courses that introduce you to specific archaeological techniques such as petrology, osteology, or environmental sampling, or particular skills-based courses such as finds drawing, the application of geographic information systems (GIS) or statistics in archaeology, and the like.

Some of those harder lab-based classes might also carry a higher credit than the ostensibly easier lecture-based courses; such harder courses might also have longer dedicated class time but require much less personal study time – there is something to be said for knowing that you are done after four hard hours in a lab, rather than having one hour of a lecture but six more in the library. You also do not have to take a course for credit to get the benefit from it; the lecturers of most courses, except for those that have a lot of lab-based or practical work where you might take time away from students who *are* taking credits, will be happy to have students sit in on lectures and seminars but not be graded. It is important not to take too many of these noncredit options – at most, one or two a year – but this can be a great way to get experience of a specialty that intrigues you but in which you do not ever see yourself actively being involved. This might include courses from outside your own department/faculty – for instance, in anthropology, history, classics, or departments that specialize in particular cultures (the author's university, for example, has a department of Scandinavian studies, and separate schools of Slavonic, Oriental, and African Studies, all of which offer courses that have relevance to archaeology). Find out what is offered at your particular university, find out where the lecturer running a course is based, drop by the lecturer's office, and discuss your options.

Fieldwork

Almost all university archaeology courses require some participation in fieldwork that is at least monitored, and in many cases formally assessed, to gain a degree. The length of time required, forms of monitoring and assessment, and variety of work offered varies considerably among universities; some require only a few weeks of work, others the equivalent of several months; some specify only fieldwork organized by the university itself, and others accept any active work (such as an archaeological survey or excavation but also lab or museum work) organized by a reputable organization.

The reality is that most archaeology students want to get as much field experience as possible – summer digging in glorious weather is generally what people had in mind when they signed up for a degree in archaeology. For many, the fieldwork undertaken in the spring or summer of their first year of study will be their first real exposure to the formal practice of archaeology. Some already knew this was what they had long wanted to do and love it from the first moment; others may be less sure, but fall in love with the process fairly quickly; a minority realize, often painfully, that this is not what they thought it would be – such students frequently switch to another degree program entirely in their second year.

Picking fieldwork is as important as picking courses; find out as much as possible beforehand about what the field project in which you want to participate will be doing, what your role will be, what skills and experiences you will gain, and also what the working and living conditions will be like. Many universities give a lecture on the available fieldwork opportunities some time in their spring term, at which time the various project directors tell people about their proposed work, to help

Figure 11. Archaeology in the university curriculum, part 2. Practical training in the university archaeology curriculum takes many different forms. Here, undergraduate students at UCL's Institute of Archaeology undertake an aerial photography interpretation practical as part of their studies (© UCL Institute of Archaeology 2010, courtesy of Ian Carroll).

students choose; other universities simply have one excavation that all students must attend. If you do have an option, think also how the fieldwork you are considering fits into your overall program of study.

Dissertation/Thesis

Another component of university study that many students face is a dissertation or thesis – a longer piece of independent research work. This is usually begun toward the end of the undergraduate degree program. Again, situations vary among universities: many have a compulsory dissertation, but in a few it is only an option; some require only 5,000 to 10,000 words (approximately 20–40 pages of text), others as much as 15,000 to 20,000 words (60–80 pages of text); some require original or field research, and others require only secondary-source library-based work. Student reactions to the dissertation also tend to vary – the concept is both loved and loathed. But these are useful pieces of work for a variety of reasons:

- The dissertation/thesis helps focus your thinking on a particular topic or specialty that you might want to study as a postgraduate, so it may crystallize your career aspirations.

71

- It is a useful document to bring along to a job interview – for non-archaeological as well as archaeological employment – as it demonstrates your capacity for clear thinking and writing, discipline, and independent working.
- It often carries with it considerable credit – so by taking a dissertation/thesis option, you may considerably reduce your class workload.
- It can be fun – you get to follow through a particular issue, topic, or concern from beginning to end, which is (in theory) what real-world archaeology is like, or at least should be like. If, as an undergraduate, you find that you really like doing this research, this is one indication that you might enjoy postgraduate study.

Non-Specialist Courses

Universities also offer a host of other (usually non–credit-bearing) courses and training; you are well advised to make good use of these, as a portion of your tuition fees is contributing toward these whether you take them or not. Such opportunities are usually offered through campuswide rather than school/departmental facilities, and include the following:

- Computing skills – on particular types of software or particular applications.
- Language skills – languages are incredibly useful for archaeologists, and this may be your last opportunity to pick such skills up at no charge.
- Professional development skills, such as how to create a CV and present yourself well in a job interview.
- Academic skills, such as how to write clearly and effectively. Training in the creation and giving of presentations can be particularly useful, as almost everyone – archaeologist or not – needs to be able to give a good public presentation these days. It is better to learn how to do this now, in the safety of a university in front of your peers, than later in front of your new boss.

Extracurricular Activities

Extracurricular activities at university fall into three broad camps; most people sample a bit from all three, but no one should ever feel under pressure to do any of these. They are as follows:

- *Archaeological*: These are the extra opportunities that most archaeology departments offer not only to their students, but also to their staff – public lectures and seminars, reading groups, fieldtrips, and the like. When chosen carefully, such opportunities are a great way to keep up to date on a subject; find out about new sites, concepts, or methods; and meet other archaeologists from elsewhere (some people have even been known to pick a seminar on the basis of the postevent food and drink offered). A top tip for those interested in archaeology but not studying at a university is that most of these events are also open to the public and are free to attend; you just have to find out when and where they are held, as they tend not to be widely publicized. Why not check out the webpage of your local archaeology department and see what is being offered?

• *Career-oriented*: These are those aspects of life at university that, undoubtedly fun, also have at least some tentative career benefit. Volunteering in the community in different ways is a classic example. Cynically, such things *are* worth doing – in the current economic climate, every little thing you can do to make your CV stand out from the hundreds of others on offer to an employer is worthwhile.

• *Social-oriented*: These are all those remaining aspects of life at university in which many students participate, with varying degrees of benefit and/or success. Social, cultural, sporting, political, and religious organizations of every possible variation exist on every campus in the world. For example, many skills or sports have at least a passing applicability to archaeology – in the author's own career, the knowledge of rock climbing, sailing, and scuba diving he picked up in college has come in handy several times.

Postgraduate Qualifications – Graduate School and the MA/MSc

More and more archaeologists now have a postgraduate qualification; whereas at one time a good BA/BSc (graded overall at 2.1 or above in the UK, GPA of 3.4 or above in the US) was sufficient to get a job as an archaeologist and/or to do well in the non-archaeological job market. Now, though, an MA/MSc is increasingly common and, particularly in archaeology, a virtual requirement. This is particularly so for certain archaeological careers; those intending to go on to get a PhD with the goal of an academic archaeological position, for example, can proceed only if they first get a postgraduate qualification. Even for those who never intend to work as archaeologists, such a higher degree is increasingly common, a means of distinguishing oneself from the mass of other applicants for a job.

A number of issues surround the decision to undertake postgraduate study. Common or not, such a course of study is not to be entered into lightly (Table 4). In the UK, an MA/MSc program will normally last twelve months; elsewhere, especially in the US, they can last much longer, twenty-four months or more. Such courses require extensive coursework commitments and prolonged periods of self-study; in all cases, the costs involved are considerable and the demand for merit-based financial support outstrips supply. Government-secured loans for study are usually available, but this still means committing yourself to many thousands of pounds/dollars/euros worth of debt and years of hard work. Finally, not everyone is suited to the particular pressures of this type of study, even those who did well in their undergraduate studies.

For some students, the choice of what course to study is self-evident; the author's main interest at this point in his life was maritime archaeology, so an MA in that archaeological specialty was the obvious way forward. Others may feel the same way about a variety of period, subject, or regional specialties – this is why there are so many hundreds of specialist MAs being offered. Some students may also know

TABLE 4. The Pros and Cons of Studying Toward a Higher Degree in Archaeology

Pros	Cons
Often the only way to get certain types of specialist training such as in ceramic analysis or environmental or conservation work.	Some employers prefer to hire on the basis of practical experience, and may be dubious of university-based training (but there are programs that offer work placements).
A good way to learn about a specialty before you commit to pursuing a career in it.	Can be costly and time-consuming, with no guaranteed return on your investment such as a guaranteed job or higher pay.
A good way to meet people and network for future jobs – decent courses introduce you to possible employers, and you may well end up working with former classmates.	Fewer and fewer programs offer much practical training experience (except for certain dedicated programs – usually the hardest ones to get into). This lack of practical experience can be a barrier to future employment.
A good way to build up generic transferable skills such as research, report writing, and presentation skills.	Some employers – and some family members – are worried that going to graduate school means you simply didn't know what to do with yourself upon graduation and so decided to spend yet more years in college to avoid settling down.
Many employers like to see a higher degree these days – it is a way to distinguish the mass of potential employees from one another, and is often seen to be evidence of greater maturity and common sense.	
If you're hoping to move into some specific sectors of archaeology (particularly academia, but to a lesser extent government and museums) a higher degree is virtually essential – you're unlikely to get hired without one.	Although an MA or MPhil may be looked on in a kindly light, some employers, both archaeological and non-archaeological, are scared off by a PhD, as they feel that you may be too "ivory tower" to work well in the real world.
If you're already employed, it is always worth asking about taking leave to allow part-time study (any decent employer will be keen to encourage your personal development and maybe able to help –	Sadly, some employers are stuck in the dark ages of their employees' professional development and simply will not help out in any way. Others might like to but are too small or too

Pros	Cons
some organizations even give training stipends or interest-free loans). If you are working and paying your own way you may be able to claim some of the expenses back in tax deduction, and/or apply for government loans at preferential rates. A small number of people also get grants, awards, and other bursaries to pay for study.	poor to be able to help. You may have to quit and move jobs to get this kind of support.

that they want to gain skills in a dedicated field or technical skill, such as remote sensing, osteoarchaeology, and so on. Other prospective postgraduate students, though, may simply know that they would like to study for an MA/MSc to enhance their career prospects, without a driving special interest; for such individuals, the choice of which course to pick can be much harder. All MA/MSc degrees require specialization to a greater or lesser extent, which makes them markedly different from BA/BSc studies. Once one has embarked on a postgraduate qualification there is also usually much less room for maneuvering in terms of course options. A badly chosen course may lead to the painful decision either to study specialties in which you are not particularly interested, or else drop out altogether, neither of which is a particularly appealing option. Therefore, it is important to carefully study the content of an MA/MSc program for which you are considering applying to make sure it is the right program for you.

Assuming that you have made the decision to undertake postgraduate study, the process of picking a university – choosing courses and locations – discussed earlier must be revisited. Entry requirements vary widely among universities, but most require a high first-degree score – at the very least a BA or BSc graded overall at 2.1 or above in the UK, or with a GPA of 3.4 or above in the US; more popular courses will require substantially higher overall grades than this. A proven ability in two languages is also a common requirement for PhD study in many US universities, along with excellent GRE scores for any type of graduate study. Entry will also usually depend on a successful and often fairly intensive interview with two members of staff, as well as two or more supportive letters of reference from your previous/current university (you must know how to ask politely for these letters – give plenty of forewarning to busy staff that you would like them to write you a reference, and be polite in asking for this!). Even if all of these hurdles have been negotiated successfully, some courses remain oversubscribed and entry may come down to timing and luck.

The process of applying for postgraduate study begins for many students during their final year of undergraduate study, another burden during an already busy period of one's life. Getting an attractive package of application forms, references, CV, and supporting documentation together is a major task in itself. Visits and interviews can drain funds and spirit alike. Some students, in fact, wait a year, applying for graduate school after they have graduated from their first degree; such a gap year, if used thoughtfully, is a good period in which to build up finances for the coming study and to gain direct archaeological experience as a volunteer.

Choosing a graduate course comes down to a series of factors – all the issues discussed previously in relation to picking an undergraduate program apply again here. Many students, in fact, choose to return to the same university for postgraduate qualifications; there are obvious benefits to this, such as knowing the university, local area, facilities, and the like. The specialty you wish to study may well not be offered at your old university, however; in addition, you may wish to have a change of scene after several years in the same place. Even more so than for undergraduate courses, many postgraduates pick a university on the basis of cost: the prices charged by different universities for postgraduate study vary markedly, sometimes by many thousands of pounds/dollars/euros, and when added to the varying costs of living in different locations, this can add up to tens of thousands of pounds/dollars/euros over the long term, which is no small consideration.

Studying for a Doctorate

The ultimate form of archaeological qualification remains that of the doctorate (most frequently known as a PhD, sometimes as a DPhil), based around a sustained period of independent and original research and writing that concludes in the submission (and then oral examination, in many countries) of a dissertation/thesis anywhere between 80,000 and 200,000 or more words in length.

The decision to study for a PhD in archaeology should be made only after considerable thought and discussion with your tutors, friends, and family. Doctoral study can be incredibly stimulating, enjoyable, and worthwhile – the production of the dissertation alone can be one of an individual's greatest achievements. A PhD can also lead to a distinguished career at the highest professional levels of archaeology. Such study can also be financially crippling and emotionally destructive, though. The quandary is that the path to a successful PhD is littered with the metaphorical corpses of failed doctoral students and abandoned theses, but equally, almost all people who have completed a PhD consider it to be one of the high points of their lives.

The PhD is not a route that suits everyone, and it is not always the best career path. In particular, unlike BA/BSc and MA/MSc qualifications, which almost all employers will welcome, a PhD can actively harm some careers as much as it helps others. For those who wish to pursue an academic or related career in, say, a museum, a PhD is just about essential; but for many others, both archaeologists and others, the PhD can prove to be a waste of time, money, and effort. Although a few CRM, government, and other archaeologists have PhDs, there is an argument to be made against these in such experience-based job sectors; it may prove better to have spent the time doing the job itself and working up to a position of seniority, rather than doing a PhD. Others have completed a PhD in archaeology only to find themselves unable to find work as archaeologists, outcompeted for the few academic jobs that exist and outskilled for the posts in other sectors of archaeology. Meanwhile, the non-archaeological world is even less understanding of a PhD in archaeology – a few employers may be impressed by the qualification but many more will be actively put off by it, feeling that it represents, at best, an unnecessary luxury and, at worst, an otherworldliness fatal to the successful running of a business. Therefore, a PhD is the best option only for a minority. As with all high-risk pursuits, the outcome is far from assured and the end result can be triumph or tragedy.

If you are still seriously thinking about undertaking a PhD, then bear the following in mind:

- *Topic*: Can you write a coherent, referenced 1,000-word essay on your proposed topic that your parents/partner/best (non-archaeological) friend can understand? After you put it away for a fortnight, when you reread this essay, does it excite and energize you? If none or only some of this is true, then are you sure you want to do a PhD on this topic at least, or even do a PhD at all? Such an essay is often required by universities as part of any PhD application – fewer and fewer departments provide prearranged research projects (unlike the sciences, where such a situation is common), so it is normally up to applicants to come up with their own topic and then to sell their ideas as worthwhile and feasible to their university of choice.
- *Method*: How are you going to actually do the PhD? What data do you need access to in order to produce your thesis? What facilities do you need, and at what cost? How and where will you analyze your data? If you plan on doing any fieldwork, what are the logistics of such work, such as getting to and from the site? What happens if you go into the field to collect your information and it either proves impossible to collect or, worse still, it just isn't there – do you have a "plan B"?
- *Supervisors*: Your supervisors will be your main contact with your university for the majority of your studies. A good working relationship with them is essential – you need to be able to talk to them about your work, trusting them to advise you well and in a timely manner. So choose your supervisors wisely. PhDs regularly come to grief through a breakdown of the supervisory relationship; as any relationship, it requires both parties to work at it. If you know that Professor X is a brilliant researcher but you have never hit it off, find another supervisor – you must be able to work well together from day one. Similarly, think very hard about being supervised by Dr. Y, whom you know socially as the funniest member of the faculty, but who has a reputation for not bothering to read students' work quickly.
- *Timing*: How much time, realistically, can you devote to your studies, and thus, roughly, how long will the PhD take? Remember, a full-time PhD student takes, at the very least, three or four years to submit the dissertation or thesis in the UK and Australia; many double that time (especially in the US), and part-timers may

take even longer. A decade-long period of study is not uncommon, and at peak periods may involve long hours of work into the evenings and weekends. This kind of lifestyle gets tiresome really quickly, and can put a strain on the calmest of individuals and strongest of personal relationships.

- *Family*: How do your family and close friends feel about this? If you are in a long-term relationship, what does your partner in particular think of this in relation to his or her own life goals – say, a work promotion, having children, or simply the desire for you to not work (too many) weekends and otherwise free time?
- *Finance*: How are you going to pay for it? Given that the speediest of doctorates takes at least three or four years, how do your long-term finances stack up? What are your other financial goals in this period, such as getting a mortgage to buy a house? Bear in mind that the competition for any sort of financial aid for a PhD is intense, with dozens of high-caliber applicants for every grant given out.
- *Outcome*: What do you see being the end result of the process, beyond those pretty doctoral robes and the fancy letters after your name – a job? If so, what sort of job – based where, doing what, being paid how much? Speak to people with PhDs who have jobs and ask them how they got their current post and how they feel about it.

Additional Training and Skill Sets

One of the greatest joys of working as an archaeologist is the continual process of learning that is inherent to doing archaeology. A good archaeologist is always learning and, perhaps more important, is driven by the desire to learn – sometimes formally, through training, lectures, symposia, and the like; sometimes informally, through observation and participation. As new sites are discovered, new theories expounded, new techniques developed, and new laws and management structures proposed, so an archaeologist continually refreshes his or her knowledge and expertise.

Although a career in archaeology has many practice-specific training requirements, many other skills can usefully be developed both by practicing archaeologists and also those wishing to enter the career. It is worth it to everyone to take the time to think about the array of skills that archaeology brings; this is especially important to students considering pursuing a career who may have the opportunity to pick up additional skills at no additional cost while still in college. Examples include:

- *Bush craft*: Many of the bush craft or wilderness skills that have become increasingly popular of late have an applicability to archaeology. Some of these come down to good common sense: it is valuable to know to how to safely handle sharp tools (and how to keep them sharp), use a compass, read a map, and move efficiently through the landscape with minimal disturbance. Other skills may be more esoteric or equally mundane: a detailed knowledge of plant species, for example, might be helpful on one site, an ability to tie a secure knot on another. In places such as the US and Australia, at least, as well as in many other countries, a basic ability to handle firearms safely can be useful (for instance, when working in an area with a large bear population) – this is in marked contrast to the UK, where the lack of dangerous species on the one hand, and tight gun controls on the other, mean that such a skill would be looked on oddly.

- *Business/financial*: Do you know how to read/create a budget spreadsheet and associated report? How to do basic financial planning? How to develop and run basic statistical analyses? If the answer is yes to any of these questions, then you are one up on many archaeologists. If you have a formal qualification such as an MBA, you will be even more rare in the industry.

- *Computing*: Business-related information technology (IT) skills, such as a high level of competency in a particular type or product of financial management software, can be extremely useful; expertise in building/maintaining websites, databases, GIS, and the like is also of value. The latter are increasingly important to archaeologists.

- *Drafting and surveying*: Although aspects of these skills are taught to most archae-ologists, shockingly few archaeologists are really adept at these skills. People properly trained in landscape and/or building surveying and drafting are incred-ibly useful in archaeology. So, too, are those who can draw up and/or interpret formal building or architectural plans.

- *Editing*: Here, editing means an ability to write good English on one hand (decent schooling in the basics of grammar and sentence construction is a good start; formal/professional training in how to write effectively even better), and specific word skills on the other – such as knowing how to edit work effectively, how to work as a professional editor (including journalism-specific skills such as copyediting), how to proofread, how to create book indexes, and so on.

- *Environmental*: Archaeologists of many guises increasingly use environmental sam-pling of various types. The broader principles of sampling are also highly relevant to archaeology at heart; the "polluter pays" principle behind CRM archaeology is taken directly from similar principles and funding of environmental work, especially environmental impact analyses. Consequently, specific skills such as knowing how to take soil, water, air, or species (flora/fauna) samples can be useful to archaeology, as can broader analytical modeling skills relating to the calculation of statistics, such as species density, threat, and the like.

- *Lab*: Core laboratory skills – how to work in a lab without breaking things or hurting yourself or people – are one thing; more specialized skills in particular biological or chemical sampling, processing, and analysis are another.

- *Languages*: I have said it before and I will say it again: language skills are incredibly useful to archaeologists – the more numerous and extensive, the better.

- *Mechanics*: A host of skills can prove useful under this banner – mechanical skills such as engine maintenance of various forms on the one hand, craft skills such as carpentry and metalworking on the other. If you can get a generator working, make up a serviceable wooden storage box, or undertake similar tasks, you are likely to be welcome on most archaeological sites.

- *Media*: This does not mean the ability to present a TV show; it means the ability to design, produce, write for, and edit different types of media – websites, videos, books, and so on. This encompasses a wide array of practical skills, including computer skills such as website design and maintenance as well as film/video media production, direction, editing, and postproduction.
- *Teaching*: This can comprise basic teaching competencies – can you create a decent presentation in PowerPoint or similar software, and then give a clear, enjoyable presentation to an audience of between five and five hundred people aged anywhere between eight and eighty? This is something that most archaeologists, especially academics, should be able to do but surprisingly, many cannot. More specialized competencies – up to and including formal teaching qualifications – can be even more useful.
- *Transport*: A valid driver's license, plus experience of using different types of vehicles (manual and automatic transmissions, two- and four-wheel drive, the latter especially off-road), is always useful; a driver's license for larger vehicles such as trucks, buses, and the like is even more valuable, and everyone ought at least know how to do basic maintenance tasks such as changing a car tire and checking oil levels. Many maritime archaeologists also have various boat-handling qualifications, from basic leisure boat-handling skills right up to formal merchant navy ship-handling ratings; even more have commercial/industrial rather than sports diving qualifications. In a different light, a few archaeologists even have private pilot's licenses.

Interviewee: Marcy

How did you first become involved in archaeology?

I've loved history for as long as I can remember – probably starting with the *Little House on the Prairie* books, then watching historical reenactments in my hometown and then in Colonial Williamsburg. I did a field school in Williamsburg after my sophomore year at the College of William and Mary (even though I was a geology major). However, my real dive into archaeology started in grad school. I was already in the anthropology program at the University of Arizona, but was working on the Garbage Project with the intent to create the perfect recycling program. I discussed my interest – better understanding what people thought about the natural resources they were being asked to conserve by recycling – with Bill Rathje, who directed the Garbage Project. He told me that to do this, I needed chronological perspective; in short, I needed full-scale archaeology. And so, off I went.

What is your present job?

I'm currently in a fellowship with the American Association for the Advancement of Science (AAAS) in its Science and Technology Policy Fellowship program. I'm placed (fellowship lingo) with the US Environmental Protection Agency National Homeland Security Research Center (EPA-NHSRC). My work is essentially to serve in the role of a social science advisor and support the EPA-NHSRC's responsibilities with respect to public risk perception and risk communication. I also have the chance to be part of ongoing federal discussions regarding climate change adaptation.

I began planning to apply for this AAAS fellowship about ten years ago; given all that I've had the chance to do and see so far, it's likely this will be high on the list of coolest things I've ever done.

What qualifications do you hold? Where and what did you study?

I've earned a BSc in geology from the College of William and Mary and MA and PhD in anthropology from the University of Arizona.

What are your terms of employment, working conditions, or other job benefits?

My fellowship was initially set as one full year and is in the process of being renewed for a second year. I cannot renew in my current position beyond the second year. I'm expected to work forty hours a week. Somehow I've managed to take on enough outside writing projects that I end up working more than that and on weekends, but that's my own fault. I'm quite lucky in that my duties and work hours and locations are flexible; the overall intent of my fellowship program is that I experience a wide range of policy-making activities that relate to my range of interests while also contributing to my placement office. Frankly, I'm a bit worried that returning to a strictly work setting is going to be a bit of a shock to my system.

How did you get your current job? What do you feel was most helpful to you in gaining this position?

Foremost, I've had a deep passion for using our understanding of our past to improve how we deal with the natural environment in the present since I started working with the recycling program during my undergrad days at William and Mary. My current fellowship is my first effort to bring that interest together with all my archaeological training and work experience and apply it to ongoing policy activities. So, I'd say a take-no-prisoners approach to pursuing my interests has been invaluable!

In addition to this, I think diversity of work experience also has been tremendously useful. Between my PhD and this fellowship, I spent six years working in cultural resource management. These jobs forced me to learn to handle many different types of projects, often very quickly, and think about outcomes and implications in ways I'm sure I wouldn't have if I had been left to my own original research topics. This capacity to see anthropological and archaeological issues in many different contexts was essential in applying and interviewing for my current position.

What is the best thing about being an archaeologist?

I worry that this is a really nerdy answer – no place is boring when you're an archaeologist. I can always entertain myself (and usually others) for at least a while thinking about who lived there before, what they did, how what's there now does or doesn't reflect that, and so on.

What is the worst thing about being an archaeologist?

I absolutely hate being caught in and living the manifestations of current conceptions of what archaeology is worth. I think it's a tremendously important field with even greater potential, but have spent too much time in really undesirable hotel rooms and literally fighting for pay as a graduate student not to get high blood pressure whenever this topic comes up.

What do you consider to be your greatest achievement in or contribution to archaeology so far?

I'm really proud of my first edited volume, completed with James Steele, titled *Colonization of Unfamiliar Landscapes: The Archaeology of Adaptation*. It came out in 2003 and I still get happy chills when people mention to me that they have read it and like it. It's just so cool to have had an idea that other people are still finding useful.

What is the one thing that you would change about archaeology if you could?

Please see my response to the "worst thing" question! I want the field of archaeology and the people who practice it to be seen as utterly valuable and providing a service that is not just interesting and entertaining, but genuinely useful and integral to society at large. I see my current fellowship as part of my own effort to change that.

What is your top tip for pursuing a career in archaeology?

If you want to follow a career in archaeology, find a problem in it that fascinates you. Then work on how to solve it. I know this sounds like an archaeological fortune cookie, but seriously – having that problem or question about which you care deeply in mind will be a mental compass as you put your career together. My experience suggests that there are many more jobs that can use archaeology than you might think – having your problem or question in mind will help you make the most of them and give you more professional options.

What do you see yourself doing in ten years' time?

I'd really like to set up or work in an organization devoted to using a range of social science approaches (such as archaeologists, anthropologists, linguists, psychologists, geographers [including but not limited to folks skilled in GIS], and others) to address modern environmental issues and provide information to policy and other decision makers. My current mental model is the National Science Foundation Science of Learning Centers program. I think the Center for the Science of Environmental Learning has a good ring to it! In ten years I'd like this to exist or be well on its way.

Chapter 3

Cultural Resource Management

Introduction

What is meant here by cultural resource management (sometimes known as cultural heritage management [CHM]) are the archaeological jobs that are paid for directly as a consequence of the "polluter pays" laws and policies of different countries. Although the details, terms, legal status, and format of implementation vary widely (particularly issues of applicability on different types of land and the overlap of national/federal and local/state/county laws and regulations), the core principles of such policies tend to be the same. Ultimately, such principles are derived not from archaeology or even the wider historic environment lobby, but rather are modeled on the policies and principles in much longer use within the natural environment sector.

The principle has become enshrined in both common practice and legal statute in some, but by no means all, countries around the world that when developments such as the construction of houses and commercial buildings, transport, energy and other infrastructure, or extraction of primary resources such as minerals take place, then the *historic* environment, alongside the natural environment (i.e., flora and fauna), should be taken into consideration from the outset. This occurs for both firms undertaking development for profit or government, charity, or other organizations for the communal good – in some cases on all lands and properties irrespective of ownership, in other cases only on government-owned or -controlled lands, or on specific types of land such as Tribal or Indigenous-controlled land.

Consequently, a small percentage of money (usually less than 1 percent of the total costs of a development) is spent:

- Assessing the likelihood of the discovery of an archaeological site.
- Either partially or fully surveying or excavating the site (if the likelihood of archaeological discovery is thought to be low, the latter may simply involve monitoring the development in case of unexpected discoveries).
- Analyzing and publicizing the archaeological materials discovered.

Archaeologists, alongside other specialists such as historic buildings experts, ecologists, biologists and the like, are employed to undertake this work in advance of development. Mostly, they are employed by commercial archaeological organizations; these organizations are businesses just like any other, and generally must bid for an advertised piece of work put out by a developer, competing against other firms to win the job on the basis of their proposed costs, services, timescale, practices, standards, and a host of other factors, in a manner akin to construction firms competing to provide equipment, materials, or specialist construction skills on site. In some cases, a developer may also employ consultant archaeologists who will not undertake the primary archaeological work themselves but rather will act as advisors to and liaisons between the developer and CRM archaeology firms and also to the local/central government officials who advise on the legal responsibilities of developers and who monitor work undertaken on such sites.

The impact of the competitive bidding process on the practice of archaeology has been much discussed within the community. It is one of the most loathed aspects of the modern practice, felt to drive down standards of practice, pay, and conditions alike, as developers will very often choose the lowest bid, not necessarily the bid that will provide the best quality or extent or work or treat the archaeologists undertaking such work well, particularly regarding pay, contracts, and working conditions.

As a result of these circumstances, some academic archaeologists do not take this type of CRM archaeology seriously, because the low funding and quick turnaround times of such work tend to place an emphasis on site identification and preservation rather than intensive study and analysis. In return, some CRM archaeologists counter that few academic archaeologists have the expertise in site survey and excavation that comes from working on so many different types of sites – in other words, what is the point in spending so much time on a site if you're going to dig it badly? The reality is that, as discussed later, CRM archaeology accounts for the majority of archaeological fieldwork in the modern world, and this situation is unlikely to change any time soon, so academics who criticize such work are, to some extent, missing the point: CRM archaeologists would love to spend more time on sites, but market forces usually mean this is impossible; furthermore, in most cases, if CRM fieldwork were not done on the site, then no archaeological work would be done at all, leading to a loss of potentially unique data.

CRM and academic archaeology sit alongside one another and are simply different expressions of a greater archaeology – much like, say, different branches of medicine or the law. What both sides need to do more of, however, is cross-working: shockingly few academic archaeologists have ever visited, let alone worked on, a CRM site, and hardly any more use the reams of data produced from such work in their research. Similarly, it is rare for CRM archaeologists to teach university classes on aspects of their fieldwork (although many do undertake research, usually in their spare time). The situation of mutual misunderstanding – in some cases, outright distrust and even dislike – is only exacerbated by modern insurance and health and safety laws that make it very difficult for noncontractual staff, especially university staff and, more importantly, students, to work on CRM archaeology sites.

Types of Work Undertaken by CRM Archaeologists

The options open to archaeological officers for archaeological consultations include requiring CRM archaeologists to undertake some or all of a broad remit of possible types of archaeological investigation – from simple, noninvasive desk-based assessments (reports on the archaeological significance of a site using existing data) right up to total area excavation of an entire site, and going on into postexcavation work, analysis, and publication. These give a sense of the breadth of employment as well as the array of skills used in CRM archaeology (Figure 12). Most of these different types of work are subject to varying degrees of local and/or national guidance on best practice regarding the precise detail and quality of the work involved; an example is the IfA's voluntary Standards and Guidance in the UK (similar peer-reviewed guidelines exist in the US, Australia, and elsewhere), which includes detailed specifications for the following:

- Archaeological archives.
- Building investigation and recording.
- Collection, documentation, conservation, and research of archaeological materials.
- Desk-based assessments (DBAs).
- Excavation.
- Field evaluation.
- Forensic archaeology.
- Geophysical survey.
- Nautical archaeological recording and reconstruction.
- Stewardship of the historic environment.
- Watching briefs.

General

- Environmental impact assessments (EIAs): including a cultural heritage component.
- DBAs.

Figure 12. The structure and interrelationships of the CRM archaeology sector.

- Fieldwalking and/or field survey: as part of predetermination/EIA or as a stand-alone nonintrusive survey, including in some cases a related or stand-alone geophysical survey (Figure 13).
- Watching brief: monitoring the excavation of foundation and service trenches, landscaping, and any other intrusive work to identify and record any archaeological finds or features (which, if so discovered, might lead to amendments to the project design requiring additional evaluation or full excavation).
- Evaluation: appraisal of the archaeological potential and significance of a site by way of sample area excavated as trial trenches, usually 5 percent to 10 percent of the total area of the site or as negotiated; especially on long survey lines for pipelines, roads, and the like in US and Australia, this might take the form of test pitting – small survey excavations at regular intervals along a route.
- Full excavation.

Specific

- Historic building surveys to varying levels of detail.
- Historic area assessments and appraisals (Figure 14).
- Human burials and remains assessments and excavations (which might include the requirement to leave these totally undisturbed and entirely in situ).
- Environmental sampling.

Figure 13. The realities of fieldwork, part 3. In many parts of the world, CRM archaeology means long working hours in tough conditions. Here, an extremely wet and muddy site in southeast England does not stop the work from continuing (© Archaeology South East UCL 2010, courtesy of Dominic Perring).

Figure 14. The realities of fieldwork, part 4. CRM archaeology involves many different skills and working environments. In this photo, an archaeologist surveys an historic sluice system (dating to the 1930s) in southeast England prior to its refurbishment (© Archaeology South East UCL 2010, courtesy of Dominic Perring).

- Historic environment assessments: such as assessment of historic woodlands and trees, hedgerows, and the like.
- Coastal and marine environment: especially intertidal surveys.

Allied

- Postexcavation work (a broad rule of thumb being that every day site = 1.5 days of postexcavation work).
- Mitigation and preservation of remains in situ.
- Community archaeology and outreach.
- Publication.
- Archiving.

Significance of CRM in the Profession

In the US, UK, Australia, and many other parts of the world, CRM archaeology is the single most important component of professional archaeology, which is why of all the thematic chapters on archaeological careers discussed in this book, it has been placed first. Globally, CRM archaeology arguably employs more archaeologists than any other archaeological sector; it is responsible for more money spent than any other archaeological sector; and its work leads to the discovery, analysis, and understanding of the largest number of archaeological sites. Some estimates suggest that as much as 90 percent of total global archaeological spending comes via CRM archaeology; even more conservative estimates put this sum at somewhere between 70 percent and 80 percent. In the UK, for example, the total funding of archaeology from all sources (central and local government, developers, and others) is estimated to have been around £119.3 million in 1999–2000 (Aitchison 2000: table 1.10), rising to c. £144 million in 2003–04 (Aitchison, personal communication, quoted in Hinton and Jennings 2007). Since 2003–04, assuming a growth of about 10 percent per year (fed largely by the expansion of CRM archaeology in relation to developer funding), and alongside an annual inflation rate that fluctuated over this period between 2 percent and 5 percent, a figure of around £200 million per year can be proposed as a realistic estimate of the total spent on archaeology in the UK across the financial years 2002–07 (Perring, personal communication). From 2008 onward, however, that sum has dropped markedly; the precise figure is yet to be calculated but will have been between 25 percent and 40 percent of the previous years' totals – as the global financial crisis affected CRM archaeology, the building sector declined dramatically, and interest rates hovered at around zero to 0.5 percent. For another example, this time from the US, Altschul and Patterson (2008) comment that:

> Annual expenditures for services by public and private sector clients have been esti-mated between $683 million and $1 billion ... based on actual public expenditures and optional surveys of CRM senior management on the scale of private sector funding.

Quite simply, without CRM archaeology, archaeology could hardly be called a profession at all – there would barely be any jobs to be had for archaeologists. Comparable data for spending on other sectors of archaeology – that is, figures for university and public sector spending on archaeologists – do not exist, but by sheer comparison of the number of archaeologists employed in each sector, the spending is undeniably much smaller. If the number of individuals employed is any indicator of the financial contribution of each sector of archaeology, then the £200 million per year spent by on 48 percent of archaeologists employed in CRM or freelance archaeology must be compared with what can only be assumed to be much smaller sums of money spent on the archaeologists working in all the other sectors of the industry combined.

The polluter pays principle that funds the majority of archaeological activity, especially in CRM archaeology, is a well-established system that works, if not perfectly, then of a fashion, which has at heart a positive objective if not necessarily a positive outcome, and which is accepted both as an economic imperative as well as a social necessity. By any standards, archaeology contributes to society more than it costs, even in terms of pure financial profit/loss. Some of the products of archaeology are tangible: publications and reports, websites, and TV and radio media that people pay for; lectures, seminars, and presentations given to public and private audiences alike, usually in return for a fee of one sort or another; excavated materials that end up on display in or storage at museums and archives that people choose to visit; and even whole historic sites that are open to the public, as well as the archaeological projects that people volunteer, some even pay, to go on. Other products are intangible: the benefits to society of an enhanced understanding of our common past; the transferable skills that students gain from their studies; and the pure economics of the polluter pays system, in which legislation requires industries to pay for work on sites in advance of development. As noted earlier, such forms of regulated capitalism pay for an estimated 90 percent of all archaeology; only some 10 percent of money spent comes from the public purse or private philanthropy. That 90 per cent of industrial funding represents, at most, a very few percent of the total costs, let alone the end profits, of any development, so such environmental regulations are not the burden to or block on development that might be supposed. The broader intangible and purely economic benefits of archaeology and, more broadly, heritage to society are then incalculable – these include the money made through public interest and participatory payment when visiting historic sites, people choosing to pay a premium to live in old houses or historic districts, and people buying themed books, toys, and computer games and watching related TV shows.

A Day in the Life

CRM archaeologists get to do, see, and handle the largest amount of "real" archaeology of all archaeologists. If the thought of spending the greater proportion of every year out of doors doing field archaeology – surveying, digging, drawing, and the like – appeals to you, then realistically CRM archaeology is the way forward. Government archaeologists get to spend only perhaps 5 percent to 10 percent of their time doing field archaeology; academic archaeologists, perhaps 20 percent to 30 percent of their time; but CRM archaeologists, especially in junior and midlevel posts, will regularly spend 80 percent to 90 percent or more of their time in the field.

Trying to briefly sum up an average day in the life of a CRM archaeologist is extremely hard. By the very nature of this type of work, which is reactive, responding to the needs of development, there is little "average" to be drawn. Thankfully, however, a few CRM archaeologists have written down their stories. In particular, the American CRM archaeologist Trent de Boer has produced the marvelous book *Shovelbum* (the nickname some US CRM archaeologists give themselves – the British equivalent term is "digger") that offers an insight into the experiences of himself and his friends (de Boer 2004: see also King 2002 for a more formalized but equally impassioned view of the situation in the US). The British archaeologist Paul Everill has also recently published a more in-depth and formalized study of the similar situation in that country (Everill 2009) (see also Smith and Burke's (2007) *Digging It Up Down Under* for experience of working as a CRM archaeologist in Australia). Everill's and de Boer's books in particular, both the products of archaeologists with wide experience of CRM fieldwork, share many similarities in the highs and lows of this section of the profession (Table 5).

TABLE 5. The Pros and Cons of Working in CRM Archaeology

Pros	Cons
Greatest amount of time actually doing archaeology – fieldwork such as excavation and surveying	Poor pay and conditions, with few benefits, long hours, and limited job security.
	Employers may be unable or unwilling to offer leave for career development or training opportunities.
	Many employers require staff to organize their own accommodations and/or provide some of their own equipment.
Constantly on the move – changeable locations/sites, so you see a lot of places, meet new people, and so on	Projects are often relatively short-term, so you may not get to see the long-term development of a site and its analysis – or indeed, see anything beyond the confines of your small section or trench.
Challenging – working on new sites, new types of archaeology, in face of changing environmental conditions – almost always intellectually stimulating	Being constantly on the move also means you often see nasty neighborhoods and stay in seedy accommodations.
	No stable base makes relationships/family life hard, and can be lonely too – fieldworkers have a particularly hard time if they are in a committed relationship.
	Workers can suffer other problems common to transient employees, such as sporadic access to health care, quality accommodations, and access to credit or loans because of regular changes of address.
Can pick up wide range of skills and get to know the distinctive characteristics of the archaeology of a region, the subtleties of its soil types and features, and so on	Can get stuck in a rut doing only one thing – once you have refined your skills, there can be virtually no skills or career progression.
Sense of community on project – most people doing these jobs are in their twenties and thirties, so it can be a friendly, lively working and social environment	Limited career structure – most people advance by leaving one job and trading up to another post with a different employer on the basis of their CV – which often works but can be risky.

The UK and the US also have websites dedicated to these communities: in the UK, the British Archaeological Jobs and Resources website (BAJR 2009a) and in the US the Shovelbums website (Shovelbums 2009). These are no mere dusty web archives of life on the dig, though – both are actively used by practicing CRM archaeologists to share best practices, search for jobs (both include regularly updated archaeological job sections), and gripe about the realities of their daily grind. See, in particular, the BAJR Site Hut web forum (BAJR 2009b) for a view of what real field archaeologists are talking about, or the Getting Started in Archaeology web forum (BAJR 2009c) for those just beginning, or thinking of beginning, their careers. The BAJR also has a fascinating web archive of the now defunct UK CRM archaeologists' newsletter *The Digger*, which ran between 1998 and 2006 (BAJR 2009d). This provides a fascinating, if at times brutal, insight into the world of CRM archaeology in that period.

Some CRM archaeologists spend the majority of their working lives moving from one site to another within a relatively small area – for example, archaeologists working within major cities such as London, New York, San Francisco, Sydney, or Melbourne, which have a rich history as well as a fast-paced process of near constant of redevelopment. Such an archaeologist is doing CRM archaeology just as much as a colleague who travels hundreds or thousands of miles yearly moving among extensive rural sites in advance of new housing developments, mines, roads, or pipelines (Figure 15); indeed, these two archaeologists might even be employed by the same archaeological firm, as well as by the same developer. However, the realities of the fieldwork that these different archaeologists do would be radically different. Urban CRM archaeologists will often work within the tight footprint of an existing building that has been torn down and is shortly to be replaced; they may work many meters below street level, possibly even under cover in a basement area; they will almost certainly work right alongside ongoing construction, and may excavate and plan a feature only to move on and see the feature be destroyed immediately, covered in concrete or with a foundation pile driven through it. Urban archaeologists may deal with many meters of archaeological stratigraphy (vertical layers of archaeological remains), surveying first early twentieth-century features, then nineteenth-century ones, working their way down systematically century by century to, in cities such as London, the Roman or even prehistoric uses of the site (Figure 16). Urban archaeologists may travel to site using public transport, and eat their lunch in a busy city square, surrounded by suited office workers who probably do not even realize that they are archaeologists (their clothes will be almost identical to those of the construction crews on site, with safety boots, high-visibility jackets, and hard hats required). At the end of their day, the urban archaeologist may return home to a small apartment or house in the suburbs shared with friends or family.

In comparison, rural CRM archaeologists may work on an extensive "green" (undeveloped/farmed) or "brown" (previously lightly developed) field site. Their excavation may cover, in one or a series of large trenches, dozens or even hundreds of square meters or, equally, it may comprise thousands of single, meter-square test pits following the line of a new road or pipeline for hundreds of kilometers. The

Figure 15. The realities of fieldwork, part 5. Many CRM archaeology projects follow the routes of new pipelines, roads, or other long-distance developments, surveying the route in advance of development. Here, CRM archaeologists work along the route of a pipeline in southeast England (© Archaeology South East UCL 2010, courtesy of Dominic Perring).

rural archaeologist is likely to be working at approximate ground level, but that level may be anywhere from a green field in the midst of a bucolic farm by way of a densely wooded hillside, muddy riverbank, or even worse: for example, the archaeological work undertaken in advance of London Heathrow Airport's new Terminal 5 was mostly on the site of a former sewage treatment plant. The work of such archaeologists might comprise deep stratigraphy to rival that of their urban counterparts, but could equally comprise the shallow and fragmentary remains of a prehistoric hunter–gatherer encampment distinguished only by subtle changes in soil color and a few pieces of worked flint. Rural archaeologists may travel to sites by car, van, or pickup truck, perhaps driving many miles down tiny roads to reach their site; they may eat their home-packed lunches sitting on top of a hill with a view one day, or crammed into a truck to get away from rain or mosquitoes the next. Their site may be right alongside an ongoing development, similar to that of the urban archaeologist, but might equally be so far away from, or so well in advance of, a development that they never see anyone other than their colleagues (Figure 17). At the end of the day they are most likely to drive back to cheap, short-term rental apartments or motels rather than their own homes.

Figure 16. The realities of fieldwork, part 6. CRM archaeology often works in response to the tight timetables of industry, and extremes of weather must be allowed for within this. Here, archaeologists work on through the winter snows of 2009–10 on the site of a housing development in southeast England (© Archaeology South East UCL 2010, courtesy of Dominic Perring).

For all this generalization, there are certain commonalities of all CRM archaeology, no matter where it takes place. These commonalities are the result of the interplay of circumstances of CRM archaeology, in particular two factors reacting to one another.

Archaeological Factors

CRM archaeology is almost always reactive, responding to construction and other socioeconomic developments. As a result, although the principle of in situ preservation (leaving the site intact, as proposed by many organizations as the preferable option for cultural resources) remains an objective, the reality is often that in situ preservation is simply not possible – an archaeological site will be partially or wholly destroyed by development, and the archaeologists must mitigate for this by following the complementary principle of preservation by record – creating as comprehensive a documentary record of the site as possible, through detailed survey, excavation, and recording. The impact of this principle on CRM archaeology sites can mean that detailed and comprehensive recording takes place; however, the impact of industry-focused factors can also, or instead, mean that this recording is less than ideally detailed and/or partial – for instance, fully excavating and recording only certain selected features, not all features.

The priority to record effectively has also seen the rise of a system known as *single context recording* – that is, ascribing to every significant feature (be it a stratigraphic or nonstratified layer, pit, posthole, or other) a unique reference number, and then recording the details of each feature on preprinted/pro forma record sheets to ensure accuracy and consistency of the type and extent of recording. Alongside feature records a host of other specialized records will also be maintained, each with its own dedicated record sheet – for instance, for different types of archaeological finds and environmental samples, as well as broader logs of all survey information and photos taken on site, drawings and diagrams, site plans, and so on. Together, these documents comprise the site archive that can be worked on after the end of the fieldwork component of any project, used first to assist postexcavation analysis, then to assist publication, and finally stored in perpetuity alongside physical samples of material from the site to allow future scholars to analyze the primary data from the project.

Industrial Factors

Clichéd it may be, but this is the principle of "the one who pays the piper picks the tune": CRM archaeologists must make all sorts of compromises on archaeological practices when on such sites. Such compromises are worth making, though, because the alternative would be to not have the funds and the time to be on site at all – it is far better to get some archaeology done than none.

Some of these compromises are shared by all archaeologists, however and wherever they work. These are environmental impacts – problems with site access, adverse weather or staff illness during the dig, and accidents of chance such as trenches inadvertently only partially running across a major feature. Other compromises are not unique to CRM archaeology but are more common on such fieldwork than on other types of projects funded by other means. These usually have to do with the amount of time and money available – operating in advance of multimillion/billion pound/dollar/euro developments, many CRM archaeology projects run on tight timelines and even tighter budgets. Failure to deliver on both these promises can spell disaster for a CRM archaeology firm, and except under exceptional circumstances, an unexpected significant archaeological discovery during a project will not be given extra time or change the mind of a developer about leaving the remains in situ.

Finally, the particular nature of competitive bidding in CRM archaeology also undoubtedly means that corners are often cut on such projects. To win a bid, CRM archaeology firms are known to cut costs in all sorts of ways. Some of these corners will have an impact on the quality and quantity of archaeological work undertaken – choosing, for example, only to survey, excavate, sample, or record a certain percentage of a site, feature, or context; choosing only to use certain remote sensing, sampling, or dating techniques; or choosing to take only digital rather than digital and film photographs. Other corners will affect the nature of

Figure 17. The realities of fieldwork, part 7. Environmental and geographical extremes faced by archaeologists change around the world. Here, Flinders University graduate student Danny Markey undertakes a total station survey of an extensive open Indigenous campsite along the Woolgar River in north Queensland in July 2009 (© Lynley Wallis 2010).

life as one of the archaeologists – the general bad pay, short-term contracts, and few benefits that make CRM archaeology notorious are a wider reflection of this, but on a site-by-site basis this may be seen in other ways – for example, a lack of specialist staff on site, failure of a firm to provide clothing or tools (requiring the archaeologists to bring these along themselves), failure to provide facilities such as a break room or proper toilet/washing facilities on site, and failure to arrange any (appropriate or not) temporary accommodations.

Career Structure and Qualifications

Stuck in an apparently endless cycle of short-term, low-pay contracts but driven by a great love of the practice of archaeology, many CRM archaeologists would laugh at the suggestion that there is *any* career structure in their industry. University graduates who choose to go into CRM archaeology are at a distinct and permanent career disadvantage compared with their peers who go into virtually all other sectors, be these industry, academia, or the professions. Across their careers, CRM archaeologists will consistently find it harder to get, remain in, and advance at work, will consistently be paid less, and will enjoy fewer benefits. Archaeology regularly comes out at or near the bottom of surveys that balance qualifications against pay levels – archaeology is regularly the lowest paid of all graduate careers.

Most CRM archaeologists hold archaeology or anthropology undergraduate degrees. As discussed in Chapters 1 and 2, an increasingly large proportion have postgraduate qualifications as well, usually an MA or MSc. Their careers thus commence similarly to the careers of millions of their peers: during the end of their last year of university study they polish up their CVs and apply for jobs. Before the financial crash and consequent global recession that began in 2007, entry-level CRM archaeology jobs were relatively easy to get – an enthusiastic graduate with an archaeology/anthropology degree who could write a good letter of application and CV, persuade a tutor to provide a good reference, and show some savvy in an interview stood a good chance of being taken on, albeit at the lowest pay grade. Since 2007 the situation has become more difficult, however, and employers are increasingly vociferous about a problem they have long been experiencing: a BA/BSc in archaeology rarely prepares an individual for a career in CRM archaeology adequately, with university training failing to deliver on the following:

- *Pre-excavation work*: Employers note that few students know how to undertake tasks such as collecting and analyzing secondary (published and unpublished) data in relation to the creation of a desk-based assessment, or even what such assessments should look like and contain. In relation to this, many students have not been introduced to the basic laws, principles, and other concepts that underlie not only CRM archaeology but also related aspects of archaeology, such as the existence and role of local and central government archaeologists.
- *General fieldwork skills*: Employers complain that students have limited field experience in general, having rarely been introduced adequately, if at all, to basic skills such as surveying, excavation, recording, and the like. Employers also note a lack of related core skills such as an inability to read maps/grid coordinates, to know how to lay out trenches with right angles (i.e., basic competencies in mathematics), and so forth.
- *Specific fieldwork skills*: Employers note that students lack familiarity with specialized fieldwork skills, such as the correct handling and use of survey or geophysical equipment such as total stations and resistivity meters.
- *Post-excavation work*: Employers note that students lack familiarity with post-excavation skills, both generic skills such as the construction, writing, and editing of reports and the particular application of specific scientific techniques.

This is a classic "catch-22": although the vast majority of students have worked on some sort of excavation, many have been on only a few types of sites, and may not have had the time to build up these fundamentally time-based competencies. The universities involved are not to blame; indeed many academics take such accusations from CRM archaeology firms very badly: they argue in return that the point of an archaeology degree is to enable students to think broadly about the concepts and processes of archaeology, not to turn out generically skilled CRM "worker bees." The argument goes that it is up to the firms to provide such skill-specific training, just as, for example, law firms expect to teach new employees about the practical realities of working in a commercial law environment. Equally, the CRM archaeology firms do have a point: archaeology students come away with less and less field experience, a result of universities cutting costs on one hand and being fearful of fieldwork for legal and health and safety implications on the other; in addition, students themselves have less free time to go on fieldwork, as so many now need to spend some or all of their vacations earning money. This situation is exacerbated by similar legal/environmental implications making voluntary work on CRM archaeology sites difficult. Consequently, even though it is no one's "fault," it is an undeniable fact that most recent graduates of archaeology programs have less field experience than comparable graduates would have had ten years ago, and those graduates of ten years ago have less experience than those of twenty years ago had.

The question that obviously arises is: Is an archaeology degree necessary to pursue a career in archaeology? Despite what the preceding discussion might seem to indicate, the irony is that it *is* necessary. CRM archaeology firms expect their employees to have university degrees in the subject not so much because they feel that these degrees adequately prepare students for life as CRM archaeologists, but more because there is no other real indicator of experience or expertise.

Lifestyle

Given these facts, one can see why CRM archaeology is harder to break into than ever before: it requires applicants to get a degree that will not adequately prepare them for life in the sector, and it is almost impossible to get voluntary experience of the sector because of legal and health and safety restrictions. Once one starts working within CRM archaeology, there is no clear career structure – advancement is possible, but usually requires a mixture of tenacity and luck.

The lack of formal career structure, however, does not suggest that CRM archaeology itself is unstructured. There are clear hierarchies at work – based on experience on one hand, and expertise on the other – and these hierarchies affect pay, job security, and working conditions. Very few archaeologists proceed all the way through the model laid out here; in part, this is because reality is much less clear-cut – there is much more gray area between the levels discussed here than this model suggests, much more blurring of responsibility and, consequently, of working conditions. It does not help that the levels of experience and expertise needed to progress from one level to another are less than clear. In an industry such as commercial legal practice, for example, seniority is fairly clearly linked to different levels of experience and expertise, which in turn are linked to clear pay and contractual levels. This is not so in archaeology, in which this relationship is very murky indeed, and in which there is also no formally required professional association (and also little union representation) to demand barriers to entry and clearly defined promotional rungs. Finally, plenty of people do not progress all the way through this hierarchical model because they cannot do so – because there are more good people than jobs, because what at first seems a fun lifestyle moving from job to job can become boring, because people get tired of the low pay and tough conditions. CRM archaeology has a high entry rate but also a high turnover/dropout rate: once people hit their late twenties and early thirties, archaeologists who remain in the industry will have seen many friends and colleagues leave.

Junior Field Tech Posts

These are the entry-level positions open to recent archaeology graduates. Similar to such positions all over the world and in every industry, they have their good points. Junior CRM archaeologists get to do the most active archaeology – although this can be tough and tiring, and sometimes very boring, it can also be incredibly interesting and fun, moving from site to site, seeing new places and new types of archaeology, surveying and digging new features, working out contexts and relationships, and physically finding new archaeology.

Such positions also have their benefits in the lack of responsibility that comes along with them – many such position holders will have responsibility only for their immediate area and will not have to manage others or think about the big issues of the project. In such circumstances someone can turn up, do a day's hard work, finish up with a cold drink in the evening, and repeat this cycle for weeks, months, and in some cases years at a time. One can get to become an incredibly capable field archaeologist, visit many sites, and meet many archaeologists. The physical rigors and professional/personal insecurities of this life mean that it tends to attract a young and lively crowd, mostly single people in their twenties or thirties; the consequence can be an active social life, and given the low pay and generally constrained living circumstances, the result can seem like college without the classes, essays, and exams.

Although this may seem seductive for a while, however, most people get fed up with this after a time; responsibility, both professional and personal, can begin to appeal, as can better job security and a larger pay packet. Furthermore, such positions offer little follow-through – archaeologists move from dig to dig, rarely getting to opportunity to stick with a site from discovery through investigation, analysis, and publication. This can be very frustrating.

Mid-Level Posts – Managing a Section of a Site

If the junior field techs are the privates and other entry-level ranks in the military of an archaeological site, then these individuals are the corporals and sergeants, the NCOs of archaeological life. Found mostly in charge of a section of a site, or possibly all of a smaller site, such individuals will most often have been promoted from junior field positions and will be of a similar age and background – the only difference will be their levels of experience as CRM archaeologists. Their responsibility remains relatively low – to manage the crew on their section of the site and the work there only, not to make any broader decisions or take charge of issues such as timescale or logistics. But such individuals nonetheless wield considerable indirect power, for they are effectively the ultimate arbiters of the quality of the physical archaeological work in their section; sloppy digging, surveying, or recording techniques can be theirs to fix or let slide.

Such positions bring with them many of the pros and cons of junior positions – the difference is that the pay will be slightly better (although not by much, and job security is unlikely to be any better at all), and in such a position one can begin to gain at least some vague overall appreciation of the site and its archaeological significance.

Senior Field Tech/Junior Management Posts – Managing a Site or Project

Continuing with the military analogy, these are the battle-hardened lieutenants and junior captains of the archaeological army; just as in the military, they must trust their NCOs to keep the detail of things running on the ground, and again just as in the military, whereas some will be good and experienced souls promoted from the trenches, so others will either have been overpromoted beyond their ability or else parachuted in from above by management. The result can be very mixed in terms of both the quality of the person as well as the person's age and experience – brilliant young managers no older than many of their crew may work alongside tired, older managers in their forties who have spent a long time getting to where they are.

The responsibility for managing an entire site or project, even a small project, is a big one for any archaeologist, but this responsibility is particularly acute for CRM archaeology site managers, with a fine balance to be maintained between archaeological sensibility on the one hand and industrial sensibility on the other (how to do good archaeology within the time and financial constraints that apply), over which, at this level, they have no control; a site manager will be given a timescale and a budget and told pretty much to get on with the job within those constraints.

Going back to the military analogy, such individuals also face a potentially difficult professional and personal series of challenges akin to those of junior military officers. Promotion and responsibility are appealing, especially advances in pay and conditions, but this is the stage at which an individual is literally drawn further and further away from the trenches – doing less and less of the physical fieldwork that so often attracted him or her to this career in the first place.

A manager may be physically based on site but is unlikely to do much, if any, real digging; rather, the manager will be focused on overseeing the program and timetable, monitoring the quality and speed of work, managing the site paperwork archive, and, at heart, thinking about, rather than doing, archaeology – piecing together the three-dimensional jigsaw puzzle that is the site, both in the manager's head and on paper. Individuals at this level may also be asked to make tough decisions regarding the aforementioned balance between archaeological and industrial sensibilities, such as the amount of time to be spent working on a particular component of a site, the techniques, and even field crews to be employed. Many archaeologists promoted to this level have balked at what they see to be impossible compromises to their integrity as archaeologists in the face of demands to dig faster, cheaper, or differently. Similarly, on a personal level, such responsibility may prove very hard if an individual has been promoted up the ranks – friends who have not enjoyed similar promotion may choke at taking orders from them.

On the other hand, being responsible for a site or project can be incredibly rewarding – to make all the decisions, lead the project from beginning to end, actually link method and theory on the investigation, analysis, and reporting of a site is very fulfilling. It sounds hackneyed, but responsibility at this level ensures a bit of immortality – a project director will have been primarily responsible for a project of both individual and communal significance to the understanding of the past. This significance might be immediately apparent – a unique find or an unexpected date – or might become clear only months or years later when compared with other data.

Middle-Management Positions – Managing Multiple Sites/Projects

Archaeologists working at this level in CRM archaeology are unlikely to fit the stereotype of the "make-work" middle manager who costs a lot but does very little. Yes, pay and job security are better at this level than in more junior positions; so too are the fringe benefits – if nothing else, these managers do not have the time or the need to be standing in a freezing muddy trench on a wet November afternoon, which is a big deal for most people once they are in their mid-thirties. The responsibility for managing a number of projects simultaneously, however – thinking again about both the archaeological and industrial sensibilities only on a larger, multiple scale – is not a responsibility to make light of; the financial commitments alone may run to hundreds of thousands or even millions of pounds/dollars/euros from multiple clients, and the personal commitments to the well-being of dozens of field crew are significant as well.

Archaeologists who reach this level are never going to be dumb or lazy: the competition for posts, the demands of the job, the need to multitask and be ruthless with their time and priorities, all mean that managers at this level will be the cream of the crop. Consequently, such middle managers are likely to be relatively young – in their thirties or perhaps early forties – and to be experienced field archaeologists with years of work on dozens or even hundreds of different sites under their belts. They will often have postgraduate degrees in archaeology, some will have PhDs, and they may well publish and lecture on archaeology alongside their main responsibilities. Such a lifestyle clearly is not for everyone – the professional demands placed on such individuals on one hand, and the lack of doing archaeology in the field on the other, put many people off from ever wishing to reach this level.

Many managers at this level also end up with the unenviable role of having to write up different projects – taking the site archive of notes, plans, maps, and photographs produced by a field crew perhaps weeks or even months earlier and piecing it together in a report for the employer and local government archaeologists alike. This can be a very tough and unappealing thing to do, and although it is very common, it is generally frowned on as an archaeological practice.

Senior Management Positions – Managing Sections of or an Entire Organization

The top of the CRM archaeology tree is, frankly, an odd place. Until the mid-1990s, CRM archaeology firms were traditionally fairly small businesses, employing perhaps a few dozen staff at most. This meant that the hierarchical structure tended to be relatively flat – many people did many different jobs, and everyone was on direct speaking terms with the senior managers. Under such circumstances, many managers were originally diggers themselves, who had started off as enthusiastic field archaeologists in their twenties and slowly been given more and more responsibility, until becoming managers in their forties or fifties; in some cases, the firms had been created by old friends joining to form a small private company, of which they were the directors. This structure still exists in a few places, for many archaeology firms remain fairly small (some very small indeed), and even the larger firms that now exist may well have been created from the merger of smaller firms, with their senior management at least partly intact. Under such circumstances, managers at this level will have the skills, as well as the desire, to physically go out on site at least some of the time to keep a direct eye on a project, to talk directly to clients about their needs, and even simply to feel dirt under their boots and do some real archaeology to keep their old field skills up to date.

As the profession expanded and "professionalized" in the 1990s, however, there was also the emergence of a new breed of managers, with either limited, or no, direct field experience. These were purely and simply managers, people with the business/industry skills to manage what, in some cases, have become considerable firms employing hundreds of staff based at multiple locations and with annual budgets that run into tens of millions of pounds/dollars/euros. Working in archaeology at this level is, clearly, not something to which many people might aspire. It is also obviously not something that is easy to achieve – there are really not all that many archaeological firms in existence around the world, so the number of managers is correspondingly small. The benefits, although not commensurate in any way with those of other industries, can nonetheless be considerable in comparison with the pay and contractual conditions of most other CRM archaeologists – a point of some contention.

Specialists

Every organization has specialists who do not fall into a clear hierarchical structure. Archaeology, with its demands for so much specialist knowledge and so much new information, theories, and methodologies being developed, is particularly prone to such circumstances. Some specialists may be dedicated field crew: examples are landscape/topographical and/or building surveyors and geophysical survey experts, people who use very specific tools, requiring very specific expertise, at a key point in most projects, sufficient to keep them solely employed in this one task (Figure 18). Others may have expertise in a particular analytical technique, and so spend time both on site and in the lab when required: examples are environmental sampling, dating, and other specialists on the one hand, or those with particular material experience on the other, say, in osteoarchaeology, ceramics, or waterlogged wood. Finally, there are specialists who play a particular role at certain times in a project – for example, conservators who will take care of any finds recovered from the site or who will stabilize any standing archaeological remains to be left on site.

Bigger archaeological units may also have dedicated photographers (although many archaeologists will take this responsibility on themselves as part of their broader duties on site). More and more CRM archaeology firms also have dedicated education/outreach teams to engage with the local community – such people may have a background in schoolteaching along with their archaeological knowledge. The pros and cons of such specialization are obvious: what happens if you get bored with the specialization you used to love? Once pigeon-holed as the specialist, it can be incredibly hard to move into another specialty or into a general field role. On the other hand, if you really, really like what you do – and many specialists do – this can be an incredibly stimulating life. Such specialists are often world-renowned experts, many with a PhD or equivalent experience and publications in their area of specialty.

Consultants and Specialists within Larger Non-archaeological Organizations

As archaeology has become increasingly professionalized over the past twenty years, not only have CRM archaeology firms increased in number and size, but other organizations have also begun to appear in relation to this process. Some specialized consultancy firms have sprung up, many with their origins in CRM archaeology or local government, providing industry clients with advice on development-led archaeological responsibilities, laws, and strategies. Such firms will often not undertake archaeological mitigation work in advance of development themselves; rather, they will act on a developer's behalf in arranging all the necessary paperwork, liaising with the local and central government officials who oversee the process, finding their clients a CRM archaeology firm to actually do the work, monitoring their output, and so on – "hand-holding" their clients through what may often be an unfamiliar process in return for payment.

Archaeologists who work for such firms come from local government or CRM archaeology. They tend to be attracted into this sector by the traditionally higher pay, better conditions, and improved job security it offers. As with any form of consultancy, this is a relatively risky and high-energy enterprise, particularly when dealing with something as unpredictable as archaeology. Deals need to be struck with clients and archaeologists alike, often in advance of the actual work to be done – unexpected archaeological finds that raise costs and cause delays to a construction program can be most unwelcome, and in such circumstances a client is likely

Figure 18. The realities of fieldwork, part 8. Fieldwork in remote and arid environments such as many parts of Australia requires extensive planning. Here, Flinders University technical officer Louise Holt uses a drawing frame to construct detailed feature plans of Indigenous heat retainer fireplaces along the Woolgar River in north Queensland in July 2009 (© Lynley Wallis 2010).

to blame a consultant. Clients, CRM archaeology firms, and government alike frequently distrust such consultants, all secretly (or not so secretly) fearing that they are being taken advantage of in some way. So the rewards can be considerable, but the risks can be considerable as well.

The step beyond dedicated CRM archaeology-related consultancy is the inclusion of archaeologists into much larger firms, either environmental assessment firms or major industries. On one hand, a number of firms that were already doing natural environment consultancy noted the rise in cultural environment work and so began to hire single archaeologists at first, and then entire teams, to work alongside their existing staffers and so offer industry clients a package of advice covering all the necessary predevelopment advice and work that might be needed – from lawyers to archaeologists through architects, botanists, engineers, groundwater specialists, and so on. On the other hand, some larger industry clients have taken such impact assessment teams into their own organizations – cutting out the consultant intermediaries altogether to have dedicated teams and sections just as they have dedicated teams of structural engineers, architects, and the like. Archaeologists working in such organizations can, on one hand, expect many more benefits than their friends working in CRM archaeology – far more generous pay and benefits such as leave entitlement, pensions, and work-based professional as well as leisure facilities.

On the other hand, archaeologists working in such firms sometimes report that they feel isolated – the archaeological team will often be the smallest and least important in the building, struggling to have its voice heard and respected in meetings alongside the big guns of other, larger teams with more of the project's overall costs/profits riding on them.

Freelance Archaeology

A large – but, by definition, hard to calculate or define – group of archaeologists are freelancers: self-employed and/or working for different archaeological organizations on a case-by-case basis. The motivation behind being a freelancer is varied: in some cases it is simply the best way for an archaeologist to earn the maximum income; in other cases, it may be a decision based on personal or family circumstances, even simply a preference for working quietly on one's own, often in one's own home, rather than in an office environment with all the politics that can entail. Others may have been driven into this position by necessity – in some cases, through being laid off by a previous employer but realizing that they had sufficient skills to branch out, providing the same service as before on their own terms. As can be imagined, there tends to be considerable competition both between them and also between nonfreelance specialists based in archaeological organizations such as CRM firms.

Freelancers in archaeology tend to fall into one of four inherently specialized groups:

- *Technical specialists*: in pottery, dating, environmental sampling, and the like.
- *Thematic or site-specific specialists*: in landscapes, parks and gardens, and so on.
- *Education and outreach specialists*: those leading education and training workshops, public archaeology events, and contributing to media online and in print, TV, and radio.
- *Consultants*: such as individuals specializing, in particular, on advising industry on major infrastructure projects such as new airports, port installations, and road networks.

There are, even more than in other aspects of archaeology, distinct pros and cons about being a freelancer. A major long-term pro/con is financial: by being your own boss no one can fire you, but equally it is up to you to run the business, make the decisions, and, above all, make a profit from which you can live – and there is no one else to blame if things go wrong. Many people also dislike the idea of becoming a freelancer because of the management responsibility that this inevitably entails – running a business, dealing with tax and other related issues, and so forth.

A more day-to-day concern is the reality of the daily schedule. Some people like working on their own, absorbed by a particular task; for other people, this would be the worst possible working environment. A surprising number of people who become freelancers return to a larger organization after a short period realizing that, after all, they did not like working on their own as much as they thought they would.

People choosing to become freelance archaeologists, therefore, must make a series of very hard-headed decisions in advance of going freelance, about what they can offer clients – in a highly competitive marketplace for archaeological services – that will ensure a steady stream of work and so a solid income, perhaps a higher-quality or more specialized service than those offered by other existing providers. Such individuals also must take a long hard look at their own characteristics, preferred working environments, and broader skill sets. As can be imagined, this is not a route that suits all people and is certainly not something that people leap into or come to by accident or as junior archaeologists. Most freelancers are highly skilled archaeologists, usually with many years of prior experience, who reach the decision to go freelance after much thought.

Interviewee: Cass

How did you first become involved in archaeology?

I did an undergraduate double major in archaeology and legal studies at university, and volunteered on my first excavation during my second year. I was hooked!

What is your present job?

I am a maritime archaeologist with the state government in Victoria, Australia. My unit of three full-time staff manages historic shipwrecks and other maritime archaeological sites in Victoria. We also teach maritime archaeology to divers and interested members of the public through the avocational AIMA/NAS (Australasian Institute for Maritime Archaeology/Nautical Archaeology Society) maritime archaeology training program.

What qualifications do you hold? Where and what did you study?

I have an honors degree in archaeology from Flinders University in South Australia. I started a PhD investigating the management of maritime archaeological landscapes in 2000, but after suspending, then going part-time, in 2003, I withdrew due to work commitments.

What are your terms of employment, working conditions, or other job benefits?

My job is ongoing full-time, with flextime and time-in-lieu for work outside of normal office hours. Also the usual four weeks annual leave, sick leave, and other standard government conditions.

How did you get your current job? What do you feel was most helpful to you in gaining this position?

I applied for the job in 2001, but was unsuccessful; six months later, they contacted me and offered me the position, as the other candidate did not work out.

An excellent honors degree, ability to do independent research, good written and interpersonal skills, and, most importantly, vast amounts of volunteer fieldwork experience were imperative to obtaining the role.

What is the best thing about being an archaeologist?

The great combination of fieldwork and office/heritage management tasks, and working with enthusiastic volunteers who have a genuine passion for history and heritage are definitely some of the best things about being a government archaeologist. The public is very interested and inspired by what we do, so getting publicity is usually very easy. Of course, diving and playing with artifacts is also a lot of fun.

What is the worst thing about being an archaeologist?

A lot of weekend work and travel away from family, and the heritage field is notoriously underpaid. Sometimes balancing the political aspects of working in government with trying to save an important site from development can be difficult, although often rewarding.

What do you consider to be your greatest achievement in or contribution to archaeology so far?

I think I have regenerated enthusiasm from divers and the public in the work that we do at Heritage Victoria. I have renewed or formed new relationships with many private individuals and this assists in the ongoing preservation of maritime heritage places in this state. I have also been active in relation to treasure hunting and ethical standards in maritime archaeology in Victoria and Australia. In particular, I have advocated the UNESCO Convention on the Protection of the Underwater Cultural Heritage to bring it to the attention of the state and commonwealth governments in Australia. Whether this is really a great achievement remains to be seen!

What is the one thing that you would change about archaeology if you could?

I would make the public see that the cultural environment is just as important to our health, well-being, survival, and progress in contemporary society as the natural environment.

What is your top tip for pursuing a career in archaeology?

Spend your spare time and holidays getting field experience on surveys and excavations, and being part of your local archaeological community group. This is an invaluable way to build your expertise, mix with people who have a lot of experience and can mentor you, and build a network of contacts. It is the most effective way to demonstrate that you have real passion for your chosen career. As long as your academic record is reasonable, it is these pursuits that will land you the job that you want.

What do you see yourself doing in ten years' time?

I have never been very good at planning that far ahead! But I suspect I will be doing one of two things: managing a maritime heritage program, or working as a maritime heritage consultant. I'd be very happy either way.

Chapter 4

Academia

Introduction

In the public eye, the academic is the archetypal archaeologist who springs to mind when the career is mentioned – this is the path most people assume archaeologists take, either because there are thought to be the most jobs in this sector (wrong) or the best pay (partly right and partly wrong) or the best working conditions and status (again, both right and wrong). Ever since Professor Henry "Indiana" Jones Jr.'s academic credentials were highlighted in the movies of that franchise, the general perception is that at the end of the day, however dirty and tired the archaeologist may be, she or he will be stopping off at campus to drop off his kit and pick up mail on his way back from the field. As discussed in Chapter 1, for a very long time all the above assumptions would, in fact, have been correct. The first professional archaeologists were, arguably, academics – people with a formal educational background in classical, ancient, or medieval history who were employed by major academic-oriented organizations to work as archaeologists. This career is thus the origin of professional archaeology and thus also of the popular modern misconception of the definitive archaeologist.

Chapter 3 made clear, though, that the CRM archaeology world accounts for the vast majority of archaeological jobs these days, and also handles most of the money. Those in these academic posts are thus a lucky – I would emphasize that this does not necessarily equate with "elite" – few. There can be no doubt that when this career sector works out for an individual, such a career can be one of the best in archaeology, both personally and professionally rewarding in terms of lifestyle, pay, conditions, and status (Figure 19).

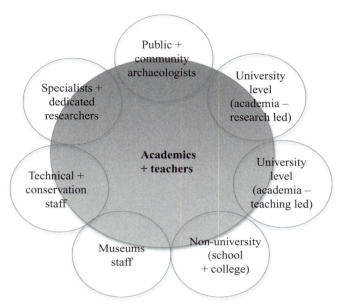

Figure 19. The structure and interrelationships of the academic archaeology sector.

A Day in the Life

The average day in the life of an academic archaeologist is likely to be driven by two things: the time of year and the individual's seniority. Taking time of year first (for it is undoubtedly the more important factor), the year splits roughly into two portions, commencing anew at the start of each academic year. The first (two-thirds) share of the academic year is more or less focused on teaching and its administration, management, and examination – I say "more or less" as this depends on an individual's workload, which is in turn associated with the second issue above, seniority. The latter, one-third share of the academic year is, at least by intent if not outcome, broadly focused on research, which often includes physical fieldwork on archaeological sites but may also mean work in a library, lab, or archive undertaking both pre- and post-fieldwork study, or writing up publications. Some time is also likely to be spent attending conferences and symposia, presenting new data and learning about the work of others, even visiting new sites and museums; other time might be spent being involved in various different types of public and community archaeology, sharing results with the wider community. In the gaps in this busy schedule then fits, hopefully, at least a little time off, although plenty of archaeologists – both within and outside academia – never take a real holiday, and some even maintain a perverse pride in this fact (Table 6).

As a relatively junior and part-time academic, the author has a fairly heavy teaching load, including the administration of several courses (that is, preparing handbooks and assessments, teaching classes and giving lectures, advising students and

TABLE 6. The Pros and Cons of Working in Academic Archaeology

Pros	Cons
Prestigious – university academics are still seen as one of the professions, and you are part of a generic organization that employs many thousands of people and provides associated benefits such as cultural/sports/social facilities on campus.	Poor pay and often surprisingly poor conditions – fewer and fewer posts are permanent/tenured, many are fixed-term with heavy workloads.
Academic books are [generally] held in high regard by the community and general public alike.	You can end up working very long hours – it is hard to turn off when in many ways you are your own boss.
	Hierarchical structure of university system can be frustrating – and stuffy.
	Many women report a glass ceiling based on gender for senior appointments – which, in the twenty-first century, is shocking (and illegal).
Best opportunities to write your own ticket in terms of balance of field/office/lab work, types of sites, or materials studied.	Competition for posts is cutthroat – which the employers know, hence the poor conditions.
Opportunities often exist to do additional consultancy alongside your main job, which can generate additional income.	Once in a post you can get trapped there for lack of other opportunities – which can make it hard if you are in a relationship and your partner wants to move for his or her career.
	Not all university towns are great to live in – for every university in a big and lively city there are half a dozen based either in an older industrial dump or a tiny town with nothing to do on the weekend.
Good research, funding, and other opportunities – stimulating intellectual environment.	Career structure and progression is slight – you often must move to get promoted in any way.
	Once definitely in or out of the academic track, it can be hard to make a move to/from another aspect of archaeology.
Teaching can be rewarding and exciting.	Demands of teaching, administration, research, and grant-winning place constant pressure on academics to produce to meet ever-higher targets. There is consequently a high rate of stress-related problems.

undertaking marking, and so on) and also being responsible for the management of and admission into an MA program (including recruitment to the MA, marketing it, interviewing students, and the like). Other academics are likely to have similar roles, balancing out what are effectively middle-management administrative tasks – such as being admissions or examination tutors on degree programs, chairing various committees (exam, staff-student consultative committee, research, and grants and publications are just some of the internal committees of the author's employer), or acting as the senior tutors for a year or subject group, and so responsible for their overall management. Many staff also have "pastoral" responsibilities, acting as personal tutors to students (advising their studies and professional development); some may also sit on the management panels of internal or external organizations such as archaeological charities and trusts.

More senior staff are likely to undertake broadly similar roles to those described here; what differs may be that they chair the various committees on which others sit and may well have additional management responsibilities, especially if they are the coordinators of large research grants employing specific junior staff. Others may be the chairs, heads, or other type of leaders of the structure in which the archaeology section/department/school sits. Senior staff may also have to sit on university-wide committees, or even be a part of the higher administrative team of the university.

From this description, the benefits of the academic archaeologists lifestyle may not seem clear – it sounds like a lot of rushing and administration in return for only a little archaeology. Although this is true in some ways, it depends what is meant by archaeology: for those interested in a career based around fieldwork on archaeological sites, there can be no doubt that academia offers fewer opportunities than, for example, CRM archaeology. Furthermore, the fieldwork that does occur within an academic's remit will usually be very different from that of a CRM archaeologist – and may not be fieldwork in this sense at all, but rather archival research, noninvasive surveys, or lab work. Academic or research work in general, particularly excavations, tends to be proactive, driven by different objectives than CRM archaeology work, usually the fairly single-minded pursuit of a research question or questions. Because the research on academic-led projects takes place on sites selected by the project director and financed privately (by government or private grants), this mean that timescales, both short- and long-term, are also different.

Research fieldwork is undoubtedly more physically leisurely than CRM archaeology work; rarely will the research archaeologist be working on a site discovered as a result of development or industry, have to work to a predetermined deadline in advance of a site's loss, or even work alongside such destruction, plotting features literally days, or perhaps even minutes, prior to their loss. Research archaeologists also generally do – or at least should – get to be involved in the entire archaeological process, starting with the formulation of research questions and objectives, moving on to site identification and discovery, then analysis (perhaps involving excavation, but just as easily taking the form of noninvasive survey), continuing with data interpretation and secondary analysis, through to post-fieldwork conservation, curation, and publication. This level of control over the choice of sites, manner of investigation, and the pace and format of the process, is undoubtedly one of the major appeals of research archaeology.

Another big plus, especially for younger researchers, is the ability to personally lead smaller, self-contained projects. An academic archaeologist in his or her thirties who can write a successful grant application can be placed in charge of an entire project in the format described earlier. Although such a situation is possible for a CRM archaeologist of the same age, it is far less likely, as the CRM archaeologist usually is part of a much larger project team and perhaps has responsibility for only certain aspects of an archaeological investigation or site, ultimately reporting to others. Indeed, this managerial freedom is one thing that most academics in general, including archaeologists, normally cite as a major perk of their jobs.

Although influenced by the shifting cycle of the academic calendar (in term/semester, in particular, affected by the weekly requirements of tutorials, classes and lectures at set times), academics are overall some of the least managed people in modern society: as long as they turn up to teach at the right times and attend essential meetings, the plan for the rest of their day, week, month, or year is usually left up to them, with minimal external interference. There are plenty of deadlines, usually self-set: complete these lecture notes, finish that book chapter, send off that grant application, and so on; but only very rarely does an academic have a line manager setting the priorities, noting when he or she is in the office, or setting a deadline or new urgent priority. As a result of this freedom, most academics spread their time across a number of locations and times when they work best – early-bird archaeologists might well be writing a site report over the first cup of coffee in their kitchen at 5 AM; night owls might equally be sitting in their studies at 2 AM; in between will be a series of different people spread across their homes, offices, labs, libraries, archives, and sites.

This managerial freedom is also, unfortunately, the source of a good deal of misunderstanding about the academic lifestyle in general. A commonly cited complaint is that non-academics may see an academic leaving the office building in the mid-afternoon, apparently on his or her way home, and equate this with a laid-back lifestyle. But in a career in which one never really turns off, supported by a modern world full of broadband Internet connections, mobile phones, and laptops, the "office" is anywhere one can sit down for more than five minutes, and most academics are some of the least laid-back people out there. It is impossible to succeed in modern academia without a work ethic bordering on the obsessive-compulsive. In a discipline such as archaeology, a social science focused on understanding humans and their behavior, inspiration can strike anywhere – most archaeologists have had a moment when they sat bolt upright in bed, woken by an idea their brain had been mulling over for days or weeks, and rushed off to tap it into their laptop before they forget it. Similarly, a discipline with a tradition of living in fairly rough-and-ready fieldwork camps (Figure 20) has no doubt about doing academic work in such conditions – the author once wrote a major grant proposal while sitting cross-legged on the floor of an old house that was functioning as the site HQ, kitchen, and bunkhouse rolled into one, a floor that was so damp that you could feel the moisture

Figure 20. The life of an academic archaeologist, part 1. Research-led academic fieldwork is usually undertaken under very different circumstances than those of CRM archaeology. Here, at tea break during the Priory Field excavation at Caerleon, south Wales, in mid-2010, the entire project is visible. The excavation and its equipment are in the foreground and the project's campsite and site offices (the caravans at extreme top right) are in the background (© Andrew Gardner/UCL Institute of Archaeology 2010).

rising up through the carpet into one's jeans. I balanced the laptop on my knees both to keep me warm and as the only definitely dry location in that old dump.

The career benefits – the sheer pleasure – of teaching archaeology are also not to be overlooked, both preparing to teach and the teaching itself. This, in itself, is a part of the broader research commitments of academics, and when well done, teaching and research intermesh to a considerable degree – what an academic is reading, writing, and researching, whether in the library, lab, or field, influences his or her teaching, and vice versa. Some "general" classes require lecturers to have a very broad knowledge of site types and locations – for example, the author's graduate classes on the topic "global issues in maritime archaeology" comprises twenty, two-hour linked lectures and seminars encompassing sites above, across, and below water from across the entire world, ranging in date from around 10,000 BCE to 2000 CE. The classes include details of project planning and methodology, site discovery and exploration, post-excavation and analysis, as well as legal and management frameworks in global marine archaeology. Keeping on top of the best and latest work for such a broad-reaching class is a job in itself, and an extremely stimulating one at that. Teaching preparation is one thing, however – teaching itself quite another. Any schoolteacher, as well as most academics, will tell you that the buzz one gets from teaching well, to a responsive class, is one of the finest natural highs obtainable (equally, all have horror stories of classes or lectures that just didn't seem to work and classes on the verge of, or even under, revolt).

Career Structure and Qualifications

It goes without saying that most research archaeologists are academic high achievers. Ask almost any academic about his or her childhood and a familiar story normally appears of a kid who liked reading and got good grades. Put bluntly: academics are often the nerds. This is admittedly an exaggeration, but not a gross one. Academic success requires a peculiar form of single-minded dedication, a dogged pursuit of often-intangible goals that are constantly replaced by another set of goals even further away. This is not a lifestyle that suits everyone – people who like to work as part of a noisy, friendly team may make great CRM archaeologists but would rapidly lose their sanity when they have to sit for days or weeks in an archive, and people who are very shy may simply not be able to cope with the thought of teaching large groups of lively students.

Going slightly against the stereotype, however, academic archaeologists are increasingly extroverts – enthusiasts for the subject of archaeology in general and their own specialty in particular. Perhaps the fastest-changing aspect of academia is the balance it increasingly requires of its practitioners to be at once both introverted loners, good at solo research, and extroverted performers capable of giving a lecture to a hundred or more students. This is not an easy mix to find. Although it used to be a joke that many academics were simply hopeless public speakers, this is an image less and less based in fact. As universities pursue ever more external funding as well as come under increasing public scrutiny, an academic who cannot perform is much less welcome. This is not to say, of course, that all academics give lectures so good that they could be filmed as light entertainment, but it is to say that most can give a well structured, as well as decently presented, talk to a mixed audience without falling over the podium or boring everyone to sleep.

Almost uniformly now, a lecturer at a university will have a BA in archaeology, anthropology, or a related subject (e.g., classics or, at a stretch, history); an MA, usually in a subject or period-specific specialty; and a PhD. Up until quite recently the PhD was not nearly as essential, but that time is now just about over – although it is conceivably possible to get a post without a PhD, such positions are infrequent. The real questions are not "Should I get a degree?" but rather, "What programs, where, and what else?" That is – how should prospective academics focus their studies, whether they should travel to different universities for their different degrees, and what additional archaeological skills make people more attractive to prospective academic archaeological employers. The first two questions are discussed in detail in Chapter 2. The last question is simple and can be answered in one straightforward way – *everything*. An archaeologist who has the requisite academic qualifications – and, thus, research credentials – is one thing, and may get jobs; but an individual who brings such qualifications along with other skills is going to stand a better chance. Crudely speaking, however, there is undoubtedly a skills hierarchy of what universities as employers want, and it goes something like this:

- *Publications*: Peer-reviewed journal articles at least; ideally, chapters in or entire books on hard research from major academic presses (university presses and the major well-known independent academic publishers). These are the highest-valued parts of the various research exercises undertaken by government monitors of the university sector. Edited works show signs of commitment to the process of academic endeavor, but do not rate so highly in such research assessments, as most unfairly edited works do not count as "original" work by editors in such assessments, despite the great effort and originality put into them.
- *Grants and awards*: Major research institutions first, others second. The larger the sum, the better! In the UK, this means funding in the tens and hundreds of thousands or millions of pounds from the AHRC, NERC, Leverhulme Trust, and similar organizations – and/or major government funding streams. That being said, it is understood that or young academics cannot be expected to immediately raise very large sums, and that early in one's career, small grants of thousands of pounds from many different sources are perfectly acceptable, showing ability and potential to consistently engage in original research.
- *Field experience*: Academic archaeologists tend to have an extremely wide range of field experience these days; some are highly competent and experienced fieldworkers, others far less so. But field experience does not necessarily have to include being out in the field: it may mean, rather, experience or research in a laboratory, museum, or archive. Such projects tend to be linked to the aforementioned grants and awards, and are a major selling point for universities when making hiring decisions: academics who can bring existing grants tied to a specific project with them, and/or are involved in an ongoing project in which students can get experience, are highly attractive to universities.
- *Teaching and supervisory experience*: Academics increasingly must teach both within and outside their research specialty: the benefits of being a multifaceted lecturer capable of teaching several different subjects and/or general courses and surveys to undergraduates and postgraduates alike cannot be underestimated, especially for younger academics who generally carry a heavy teaching load than more senior colleagues who are likely to have to do more management and administration. Academics also must recruit and supervise research students – candidates for PhDs – an exciting, if at sometimes extremely challenging, process.
- *Administrative and management experience*: Universities require a growing adminis-trative role from academics, from the everyday tasks of logging student attendance in class, recording tutorials, marking in a timely and fair manner, and attending departmental and examiners meetings, to the highly specific, with certain roles in particular taking up a lot of time, especially those of examinations officer and recruitment/admissions tutor, where the decisions they make influence the future lives of hundreds or thousands of students. The latter role, in particular, can be extremely busy, dealing with hundreds of applications a year that need to be assessed.

Lifestyle, Career Progression, and Employability

The availability of jobs and the pay, benefits, and working conditions in academia vary greatly. Partly, this is a question of professional structures drawn up on national lines. In the US, academics of all types – not just archaeologists – work within the tenure system. Many junior US academics are on the tenure track – their performance over a set number of years in terms of teaching, publication, fundraising, administration, outreach, and other factors is monitored and assessed. At the end of a specific period, their tenure position is reviewed; if successful, they are awarded tenure – effectively, the right not to have their contract of employment terminated without just cause. Once tenured at one institution, an individual usually will be granted tenure automatically at another institution if he or she moves there. Tenured – even tenure-track – positions are highly sought-after, but are also highly stressful – the pursuit of tenure takes many years and if an individual fails to be awarded tenure at the end of this process, it can seriously harm his or her career and professional and personal social standing. Tenured positions also cost universities relatively more, as these tend to be more highly paid; as a consequence, more and more positions in US universities are not tenured or tenure-track – archaeologists in such positions can, in theory, be hired or fired at will, although in many cases they may see their contracts last for years or even decades without threat of termination.

Below this level are also an army of what are usually referred to as "TAs" – teaching assistants. Many of these are graduate students – usually PhD students – who undertake a large measure of teaching, and especially grading, of undergraduates on behalf of more senior tenured or tenure-track staff. Being a TA is good professional experience and also provides at least some salary – but the downside is a lowly academic status and comparably poorer pay and conditions. Many TAs are paid only by the hour or class they teach, with little or no paid preparation time; TA contracts usually are renewed only each term or semester, dependent on student demand, so are extremely insecure; and most TA contracts do not accrue additional benefits, such as insurance. The model is that a bright graduate student works as a TA while undertaking work toward a PhD; completes this PhD and moves on to a tenure-track position; and, after many years, is awarded tenure, teaching the next generation of graduate students in a self-sustaining cycle. The increasing reality is a partial breakdown of this system, with fewer tenure-track or tenured positions being chased by more and more TAs. The result is that more and more professional academics, archaeologists, and others alike are trapped working as TAs even after they have their PhDs, caught in a cycle of poor pay and conditions that make it hard for them to find the money and time to research, write, and produce materials that may help them escape this trap.

In the UK and Australia, as well as in many other nations, the situation of academic employment is less clear-cut than in the US. Tenure is not an issue in the UK and Australia in particular; rather, contracts of employment are either permanent (broadly the equivalent of tenure, and with the greatest benefits and job security, including substantial compulsory payments if terminated) or fixed term (for a set number of weeks, months, or years; furthermore, in the UK in particular, if someone has been on a continuous fixed-term contract for more than four years without break, then at the end of those four years he or she is legally entitled to apply to have the position made permanent). As a consequence of this, the worst abuses of the TA system seen in the US are not present in the UK and Australia. On the other hand, just as in the US, there are fewer and fewer permanent positions and more and more fixed-term positions being offered to academics – in some cases for only a few months, or a term of one semester at a time. Thus, the same structure of an underclass of teaching-focused academics without job security or time to do research exists, to a lesser extent, in these nations as well.

Academic archaeologists around the world thus fall broadly into two distinct groups. On one hand are a small group of fully tenured or permanent positions – these are stable, are well-paid for archaeology (tied to standardized university pay grades for all academics, irrespective of their research specialty), and come with benefits such as health care and child care provisions, private pension and life insurance funds, access to campus facilities, training and so on, the many other benefits that can come from working for a large institution. On the other hand is a growing army of untenured staff, TAs and the like, paid either by the hour, day, or period (six-, eight-, or ten-month contracts are growing increasingly common). These individuals may well have the same academic qualifications, teaching, and field experience as their tenured colleagues. Often such post holders are relatively young, making their first steps on the academic career ladder; worryingly, though, more and more are older and have simply been unlucky in their hunt for a permanent or tenured position. The result means that the nice university archaeologist you meet, whom you imagine teaching bright young students from the comfort and security of a job for life and a wood-paneled study, is increasingly likely to be a nervous soul running toward the end of a short-term contract and worrying about how he or she will pay the rent in a couple of months.

Modern academics, whatever their tenure position, also must juggle an increasingly complex workload. Traditionally, academics divided their time roughly 50–50 between teaching and research, the two aspects cross-fertilizing each other. Nowadays, an increasing administrative burden has crept in, and with staff cutbacks the teaching workload has generally risen in association; thus, on average, the balance is now more something along the lines of 50–30–20 spent on teaching, research, and administration, respectively. Some academics may have wildly different balances, with a lucky few having far fewer teaching commitments and thus more time for research, but a worrying majority teaching more and more and researching less and less. To this can also be added the new demands to publish, on one hand, and generate external grant income, on the other.

Although the negatives are numerous, there are also positives in this archaeological career path. As already mentioned, there is a tremendous amount of freedom within academia, a factor that arguably outweighs all other comparable benefits. This freedom is certainly one of time management and prioritization, but is also the even more intangible issue of intellectual freedom and the social environment that comes with such freedom. Under the right circumstances, the sheer joy of working alongside so many different dedicated people thinking along similar, but not proscribed, lines in the pursuit of the wider understanding of the human past can be incredibly pleasurable and stimulating (Figure 21).

Assuming that the longed-for nirvana of a tenured position has been achieved by the academic archaeologist, it is also possible to have a good long-term quality of life with, for archaeology at least, a larger-than-normal semblance of a career and career progression, working through the hierarchies of academic responsibility described previously. Perhaps more important, however, it is also possible for individuals to identify a professional level that they want to achieve and then stay at without penalizing their status, job security, or salary. Plenty of academics, including plenty of tenured academic archaeologists, have no aspiration to rise beyond their current position within the university hierarchy, to become a senior professor or head of department or a dean or head of school, let alone a vice-chancellor; with the higher pay and perks that such positions undoubtedly bring also come a loss of involvement in what first draw individuals into this world – archaeology itself.

The downside of what is undoubtedly an appealing lifestyle is also the relative lack of jobs; just as in the rest of archaeology, demand for jobs exceeds supply, and for every academic position that opens up there are likely to be dozens, if not hundreds, of highly qualified and motivated applicants. Getting a post, especially a tenured post, can be hard enough; shifting jobs because of personal or other professional commitments can be even more difficult. Ask most academic archaeologists why they have a job in institution X rather than Y, and their answer will usually be, "Because X was hiring." Even if X is not the ideal university in the ideal town or even the ideal country, most academics are glad to get whatever job they can and will adapt their lifestyle to suit. But this can mean some painful lifestyle choices – plenty of attached academics, archaeologists or not, live in a different town or even region from their family, commuting daily or weekly; precious few archaeologists live in their absolute location of their, or their family's, choice.

Working Conditions

Another undoubted benefit of academic-based archaeology is undoubtedly the generally pleasant working conditions, both in the office and in the field. Most of these are shared, indeed as much of the wider circumstances of this chapter, with academia as a whole, irrespective of the subject. Albeit with significant on-site variations, most academics, including academic archaeologists, have access to a similar range of different campus facilities; at best, these are among some of the finest working environments to be found in any job, but even at worst they will still usually be comparable to and frequently better than many other jobs. The most immediate of these benefits is access to an on-campus office that can range, much like inner-city apartments, from the sole-occupant and palatial to the multioccupant and cramped. Similarly, most archaeology departments have at least some additional dedicated facilities by way of conservation or computing laboratories, laying out

Figure 21. The life of an academic archaeologist, part 2. Practical teaching plays an important part in university training and in the life of an academic. Here, David Jeffreys of UCL's Institute of Archaeology teaches students object identification and recording techniques at the Petrie Museum of Egyptian Archaeology in London (© Petrie Museum/UCL Institute of Archaeology 2010, courtesy of Ian Carroll).

space, photographic darkrooms, and the like. Every university, by necessity, also always has a reasonably decent library to which staff has access; the common urban setting of many universities and closeness of campuses can also provide access to other external collections of books or materials. Other campus facilities can then come into greater or lesser play in the lifestyle of the academic – the food and shopping outlets on one hand, the sports and leisure facilities on the other – more academic careers than most might be willing to admit have been forged around allegiance to a particular sport or even a specific team.

It is in the field that the biggest difference between academic and other forms of archaeology becomes most apparent, however. It does not take any formal training to differentiate between a CRM and a research archaeological site no matter what the site's location, period, layout, or extent – nearly anywhere in the world, the CRM site will look little different from, and indeed may be a part of, a construction site, with major machinery, portable office facilities, health and safety, and other equipment present all about. A research excavation is unlikely to have much, if any, of these – site offices in particular, which on a CRM archaeology project will frequently be in portable buildings that may include light, heat, and washing facilities, can, on a research dig, be everything and anything from a tarp or tent, caravan or trailer, outhouse or convenient farm building; the associated washing facilities might include access to running water and/or portable toilets, but may be very much less – down to and including a hole in the ground behind a large enough tree or rock. Similarly, CRM archaeologists, as discussed in Chapter 3, usually look almost identical to construction crews in the near-universal wearing of high-visibility jackets, hard hats, and safety boots. Research archaeologists are unlikely to wear any of these except, on occasion, safety boots if they are undertaking toe-threatening digging; the only clothing rule of plenty of research digs is "whatever the weather demands." Thus, a CRM archaeological project is likely to see serried ranks of near-identically dressed crews working at high speed, usually to someone else's paid-for deadline; on occasion, this can mean a crew mapping archaeology at one end of a site that is being ripped up or covered over at the other, a practice that tends to kill off a lot of site chit-chat and banter. In comparison, a research dig is likely to see a much more varied array of clothing on a potentially more varied range of people working at, if not a slower speed than CRM archaeologists, then certainly a different pace – particularly so if the excavation includes an element of teaching, which most do these days; as a result, there will be rather more talking and joking than on a CRM archaeology site. Most of all, the CRM archaeology project will be at work in all but the worst of weather on all but the coldest of days; the research dig is unlikely to take place outside the main summer months. Finally, the CRM archaeology project may be difficult, if not impossible to visit owing to site access restrictions driven by health and safety/insurance liability concerns; the research dig is likely to be open to the public at least some of the time on advertised open days, and may be willing to provide informal tours for all and any who turn up with an interest.

Specialist Archaeological Staff

Alongside academics are arrayed a variety of both more and less specialized staff. This is not to suggest a lack of professionalism among these individuals; rather, it is a question of contractual obligations – many such specialist staff may be as qualified as, if not even more highly qualified than, the academics alongside whom they work; they may even teach classes and undertake research similar to their exclusively academic colleagues. The difference is that these individuals will usually have major commitments to undertake specific dedicated tasks, such as running and managing dedicated conservation laboratories or other technical facilities such as archaeologically focused computing research clusters; undertaking specific, highly skilled, and/or time-consuming related tasks such as environmental, petrological, or osteoarchaeological analyses; or managing and promoting collections of archaeo-logical materials or data such as university museum or library collections. The skills required to manage such facilities, and the amount of time needed to be spent on such work, usually means that if such individuals do undertake teaching or research this will be in addition to their core employment, rather than central to it. The appeal of such work is that it allows individuals to focus more on their research or professional specialty than the average core academic, while still undertaking elements of outreach and enjoying the wider benefits of life within academia. The downside is that, as with specialists in any industry, these specialists run the risk of becoming trapped by their very own abilities, unable to get work in any other area if they become bored or disenchanted with their specialty.

A different common form of specialty is research-only staff. Usually on a contract lasting a set period of months or years, such individuals are usually hired to work on a dedicated research project in relation to an externally provided grant from a major funding organization. Frequently, such individuals will be a part of a larger team of researchers on a particular topic and may bring with them specific skills in a particular time period or archaeological specialty needed to complement other team members' strengths or weaknesses. The pros and cons of such positions are similar to those of the specialists discussed earlier – it is very easy to get trapped in an endless cycle of such short-term contracts, a particular risk for younger staff members who have usually just completed their PhDs and are keen to work; by taking the contract or a series of such contracts, the constant demands of each particular project can make it extremely hard to build up the wider teaching and administrative experience needed to break the cycle and get a more permanent position among the core academic staff.

Interviewee: Andy

How did you first become involved in archaeology?

I got really interested in archaeology in my early teens and joined the YAC [Young Archaeologists Club]. I volunteered on a local dig – at Boxgrove – at the start of my A levels, then went on to study for a BA in archaeology (general) at the Institute of Archaeology, UCL. I did not (could not) do archaeology A level, but did history, chemistry, and classical civilization, plus AS biology.

What is your present job?

I am a senior lecturer in the archaeology of the Roman Empire at the Institute of Archaeology, University College London (UCL).

I teach a mixture of archaeological theory and Roman archaeology, focusing in the former case on post-process archaeology and in the latter on Roman Britain and the Roman military. My main research interest is in exploring themes of identity, structure, time, violence, and imperialism as particularly manifest in the later Roman Empire and the early medieval world. I am also interested in contemporary use and presentation of the past in political and popular culture.

What qualifications do you hold? Where and what did you study?

I hold a BA Archaeology (General), Institute of Archaeology, UCL; MA Archaeology, Institute of Archaeology, UCL; and PhD Archaeology, Institute of Archaeology, UCL.

What are your terms of employment, working conditions, or other job benefits?

I have a permanent academic contract since 2005, and was promoted from lecturer to senior lecturer in 2010.

How did you get your current job? What do you feel was most helpful to you in gaining this position?

After finishing my PhD it took four years to get the job I have now, with a series of progressively longer contracts filling the gap. I did a range of short-term teaching, administrative, and research jobs for a couple of years, then a year with two half-time contracts simultaneously (in Leicester and Reading), then a year with one fixed-term contract in Cardiff, before coming back to UCL. Getting most of these jobs required me to interview and give some kind of presentation. I also completed lots of applications unsuccessfully! I think my range of experience helped me to get my present job, including, as it did, a lot of different teaching, although managing to produce some publications as all this was going on was also very important. A good proportion of my teaching experience was in adult education.

What is the best thing about being an archaeologist?

Definitely the variety, both of activities involved in the job and of subjects that one can legitimately explore. Archaeology is such a diverse field that lots of different topics of interest to me are relevant to my work. My job is also good in terms of the mix of teaching, fieldwork, library research, and admin, although the balance is not ideal at all times. The generally high level of freedom to organize one's own work in an academic job is also pretty satisfying.

What is the worst thing about being an archaeologist?

I'm very conscious of being in a relatively secure and well-paid part of archaeology (especially in the current financial climate). Working in higher education does have its problems, though, including sustaining a reasonable work–life balance, dealing with the creeping marketization of the sector, and, more particularly, facing the pressure that archaeology is under as a discipline. The challenge will be to sustain recruitment to the field within an increasingly competitive environment. Archaeology has a lot to offer potential applicants, and we need to increase recognition of this.

What do you consider to be your greatest achievement in or contribution to archaeology so far?

Starting up new excavations at Caerleon (with Dr. Peter Guest from Cardiff) is a great pleasure and privilege, as it's a site I've loved for many years and on which I wrote my MA dissertation more than ten years ago. Publishing my first monograph (*An Archaeology of Identity*) was also very satisfying, as it took a long time to turn my PhD into a book. I was delighted that this was short-listed for a British Archaeological Award.

What is the one thing that you would change about archaeology if you could?

I would ensure that the pay and conditions in archaeology are more equivalent to other graduate professions by improving the recognition of and respect for archaeology's professional status in government. This requires that heritage in general be accorded more support and funding from government than is currently the case.

The other problem that afflicts academic archaeology – among other disciplines – that I wish could be changed is the lack of clear career progression between PhD completion and first lectureship, and the consequent rather random nature of preparation for an academic job. Part of the problem is the limited time generally available within PhD programs to gain experience in teaching and publishing, although these are the things that will be essential to getting a job. Frequently, teacher training qualifications are built into the first year or two of a lectureship, at which point you will already be doing lots of teaching and plenty of other things as well; it seems to me that these should be more fully integrated into PhD programs as part of academic training. The decline of archaeology as an adult education subject (which is bad news for lots of reasons) will also have a negative impact on opportunities for postgraduates to gain teaching experience. In short, the priorities for the various early stages of an academic career, from PhD to first years of a lectureship, need to be looked at. It is good that there is increasing national debate on this (especially on the role of the PhD) and attention to it within the Higher Education Academy Subject Centre.

What is your top tip for pursuing a career in archaeology?

Get as broad a range of experience as possible. This will help you focus on what you want to do most but also allow you to be prepared for different opportunities.

Commitment is probably the most important quality to cultivate; the path to a successful career in archaeology is unlikely to be quick and easy.

What do you see yourself doing in ten years' time?

The same job as now, but hopefully with some more books and excavations under my belt, and the opportunity to develop some new courses.

Chapter 5

Local Government

Introduction

Mention "local government" to most people and the mental picture conjured up is unlikely to be very archaeological. Local government means, at best, talk of the school system and municipal facilities such as public parks and recreational facilities; at worst, waste collection and petty politics. Indiana Jones it is not. Many people, including many academic archaeologists, remain largely oblivious to the existence and important role of archaeologists and related heritage professionals in the employ of local government. Local laws protect a vast number of archaeological as well as wider historic sites. Local taxes pay directly for a large amount of archaeology to be explored, understood, publicized – and, most important, protected. Local government archaeologists also represent an incredible pool of expert, locally based knowledge that is easy for the general public to call on, a more immediate and often less intimidating face of the archaeological community than CRM and academic archaeologists alike.

Archaeologists are employed at the local government level because various national, regional, and local laws make this a statutory (formally required) or semistatutory (strongly encouraged/recommended by central government) service (Figure 22). The principle has become enshrined in both common practice and legal statute that when developments such as the construction of houses, commercial buildings, transport, energy, and other infrastructure, or extraction of primary resources such as aggregates, take place, the historic environment, alongside the natural environment (i.e., flora and fauna), should be taken into consideration from the

127

outset. This process occurs no matter what, whether by a firm undertaking development for profit or by government, charity, or the like for communal good; the major variations come in relation to whether a project is on government-owned or -controlled land (or under obligation to the government by way of funding or licensing agreements) or on private property, and thus which national/federal and/or local/state/county laws and regulations apply.

Archaeologists, alongside other specialists such as historic buildings experts, ecologists, biologists, and the like, are thus employed to undertake this work in advance of development, usually bidding for such work on a job-by-job basis – CRM archaeologists. Undertaking what is sometimes referred to as *curatorial archaeology*, local government archaeologists also work at this level – advising on, monitoring, and where necessary, enforcing the laws requiring this work in advance of development. Unlike the CRM archaeologists, this role must be more formalized – the archaeologists undertaking such work cannot be hired on a contractual, case-by-case basis through competitive bids; they must be part of the permanent establishment of local government. This, then, is broadly the place, and the status, of local government archaeologists: civil servants embedded within the complex web of the national and regional planning system, enforcing the law when necessary but there to advise all who might ask for their professional opinion, by dint of their salary coming from the government and thus, ultimately, the tax system.

A Day in the Life

At heart, the role of the local government archaeologist is reactive and, honestly, often combative. It does not suit everyone, particularly people such as archaeologists who tend temperamentally to be conciliatory and disliking of confrontation (Table 7). Boil all the different jobs in local government archaeology down to their essence, and it comes down to making people obey heritage laws and established conventions. In this, the archaeologists involved hope (but do not expect, and will take the time to check) that a few people will be scrupulously honest and follow the letter of the law (the golden 15 percent of the population), expect that the majority of people will be reasonably honest and not try to take too much advantage of any situation (a good 70 percent of the population), and with a heavy sigh will deal with the antisocial minority who have to be variously cajoled and outright threatened to do the bare minimum that the law requires of them (the nasty last 15 percent of the population equation). Along the way, the local government archaeologists will try to find the time to add, to both their own jobs and the external projects over which they have oversight, all the extras that make their jobs, and the archaeology they so deeply care about, more interesting to both themselves and their ultimate masters, the local taxpayers. To ensure that they can best provide timely, meaningful, and up-to-date advice, these archaeologists will be joined by a series of related professionals who maintain historic records, undertake particular specialist roles, and so on.

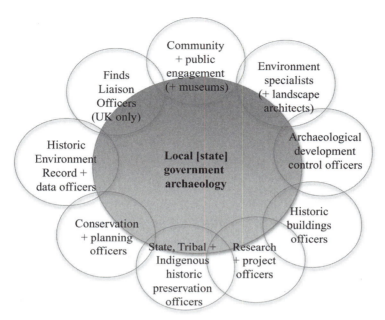

Figure 22. The structure and interrelationships of the local government archaeology sector.

A day in the life of a local government archaeologist, then, varies in relation to a number of dependent issues:

- What precise role within local government they fulfill.
- What time of year it is.
- What their local government area/region/authority is like.

The last, in particular, can have a major impact on what and when work is done, and is worth addressing first. For example, the author works partly for the local government of the English county of Surrey, in southeast England. Surrey is small (covering only about 600 square miles in total), but its northeastern corner abuts the edge of London, meaning that it is a very popular place to build homes and all the facilities and infrastructure (shops, roads, schools, hospitals, and so forth) that come along with a large population crammed into a small space. The result is that the closer in to the edge of London one goes in Surrey, the busier the archaeological workload gets, and vice versa: the farther you go from London the slower the workload, albeit with a few exceptions – various large towns outside this London zone that create a bubble of development. This also means that we know more about the archaeology of the part of the county closest to London than most other parts of Surrey; as a consequence of this fact it can often be harder, not easier, to understand archaeological sites that are discovered in the undeveloped areas, as

TABLE 7. The Pros and Cons of Working in Local Government Archaeology

Pros	Cons
Job security – often permanent, well paid (often the best paid archaeologists of all).	Often very reactive, which can become demoralizing: many working commitments are based on compromise, in which the archaeology rarely comes out best in comparison with the other demands on a site.
Pensions and other benefits provided by government sector, such as sports and family facilities, are common; there is often private health care as well as discounted rates at specific shops and services.	
Can make a real impact on preservation and analysis of sites.	Can be dull, both in types of sites analyzed and types of decisions made.
Stability – usually based out of one office and doing day site visits in a small region. This makes it easier if you are in a relationship/family or have regular personal commitments that tie you to one location.	Limited opportunity to do any field archaeology and/or research. Opportunities for travel outside your area can be few.
Prestige – you're part of local government and so other people (including family) see it as reputable.	Have to put up with corporate, management-heavy structure common in local government.
You can make good contacts for future jobs and it looks good on a CV.	
Good career structure within the archaeological community and government sector itself (often regular pay progression based on performance is common in the first few years of such a job).	The right opportunity can take a long time to appear – people often stay in the same job for many years. There are not many posts in this area.
There are usually good opportunities for internal and external training and professional development; this can include negotiating paid/unpaid leave for further study.	

there are fewer known sites with which to compare new sites. This situation is not helped by a series of other localized environmental factors: for example, the county has a complex and frankly odd geology, which means that forms of remote sensing commonly used in archaeology in advance of fieldwork may simply not work on many sites in Surrey. The county also has heath lands in its northwestern corner that have a sandy, acidic soil that tends to destroy archaeological remains and that have been used by the military for training since the nineteenth century. This training has destroyed many archaeological sites, protected other sites, and rendered still others unexplorable, their inaccessibility owing to military use having led to their settlement by rare flora and fauna now protected by various laws that trump archaeological concerns. The county also has lots of woodland in its southeastern corner (an ancient wooded area known as the Weald that stretches across southeast England) that has never been heavily settled (it has a dense clay geology unsuitable for farming), as well as many thousands of historic houses and gardens across the county (the finest examples of these houses being valued at extraordinary prices thanks to this proximity to London). The county also has relatively limited farming overall, as its proximity to London means that high prices are paid for homes across the county – there is more money to be made there from development than farming.

On the other hand, the county does not have a coastline (so the archaeological teams led by the author do not have to deal with all the marine archaeology that lies up to twelve miles offshore in the territorial sea, as is the case in all coastal counties of the UK); it also has a very even climate than means that archaeologists usually can work outdoors all year round except in the depths of winter. The county also has very little tourism, meaning negatively that there is only a very small "heritage income" to be derived from historic visitor attractions and the like; on the positive side, there is much less pressure to feed this ravenous heritage tourist monster – the local government archaeologists of Surrey can focus far more on doing a good job serving the residents of the county rather than its transitory visitors.

Compare and contrast Surrey, then, with another English county, that of Devon in southwest England. Devon is much larger than Surrey – covering more than 2,500 square miles in total. It has not one, but two coastlines (one each in the north and south of the county, as it is part of the very large peninsula forming southwest England), which means that in comparison with Surrey, Devon has a far larger and more complex physical landscape to manage in terms of heritage, including responsibility for maritime archaeological sites off its coastline; further-more, its geology is totally different from that of Surrey, with the granite landscape of Dartmoor (rich in archaeological sites and a major tourist location in terms of both the natural and historic environment) dominating the central interior of the county and contrasting with the softer sandstone and limestone of the southern coast. Devon also has a large tourist industry, based in part on the county's rich heritage as well as the aforementioned coastline (sections of which are part of a larger UNESCO World Heritage site) that is essential to its economic well-being, alongside a busy farming as well as fishing community. On the other hand, Devon has much less urban development than Surrey, with only one major town (there are two major urban centers within it – Plymouth and Torbay – but these are formally separate and distinct parts, each with its own local government). Both Devon and Surrey are English counties following the same national rules and prin-ciples of heritage management, but they, and thus their archaeologists' priorities, vary enormously – Surrey's local government archaeologists' priorities are driven primarily by the demands of urban and suburban development; Devon's rather by tourism and farming.

Next, compare these two counties with first some US, then some Australian, equivalents. All employ local government archaeologists, but the scope and remit of these archaeologists is defined very differently, by dint of both their laws and their geography. An amusing foreign comparison to the county of Devon, for a start, is the US state of North Carolina, covering more than 53,000 square miles compared with Devon's 2,500 square miles, twenty times the total area of Devon. Comparisons can, however, still be made in terms of Devon and North Carolina's varied geography, important protected historic rural areas, long coastlines, and dependence on tourism and other service industries for a significant proportion of their total income. A similarly laughable, but yet workable, foreign comparison with Surrey is then the Australian state of Victoria, covering more than 91,749 square miles in total, more than 150 times the total area of Surrey. Again, though, comparisons still can be made between Surrey and Victoria, not least in that both see their economies – and thus their archaeological work – driven by a major urban center: in Surrey, London (population about 8.2 million) and in Victoria, Melbourne (population around 3.9 million). These are all examples of local government, but the landscape, work pressures and priorities, and socioeconomic drivers and political structures affect how the work of the archaeologists employed by these governments varies enormously.

It can be understood from these comparisons that ostensibly local government deals with big issues driven by multiple, constantly competing, pressures. To return to the other impacts on a day in the life outlined earlier, the exact job the archaeologist holds and what time of year it is, the first of these is discussed in detail later, and the second of these can be dealt with quickly here: summer (no matter exactly when summer is, wherever one is in the world) is busy, in terms of development (and thus archaeology) as well as outreach such as community archaeology. Autumn and spring are, respectively, the wind-down and build-up periods to the summer rush (complicated in the UK at least by the fact that the British tax year runs from April, meaning that there is always a rush of development and local government spending alike in late February/early March). Winter tends to be quieter – bad weather slows development and access to archaeological sites alike, and the seasonal holidays create a natural gap, although winter is obviously very regionally, even locally, influential.

Career Structure – Development Control Officers

As outlined earlier, if one boils all the different jobs in local government archaeology down to their essence, what it comes down to is making people obey heritage laws and established conventions. The primary laws that make this situation so in the UK are the Ancient Monuments and Archaeological Areas Act (1979) and the Town and Country Planning Act (1990) (see Barber et al. 2008; Hunter and Ralston 2006; McGill 1995); Planning Policy Statement 5 (PPS5): Planning for the Historic

Environment (2010) in England and Wales; Scottish Planning Policy (SPP) (2010) in Scotland; and Planning Policy Statement 6 (PPS6): Planning, Archaeology and the Built Heritage (1999) in Northern Ireland. These laws and regulations are broadly comparable in terms of power and remit to the National Historic Preservation Act (NHPA) (1966, amended 1980 and 1992), the National Environmental Policy Act (1969), the Archaeological Resources and Historic Preservation Act (1974), and the Archaeological Resources Protection Act (1979) in the US (see King 2004) (as well as to many state laws too numerous and varied to list, but following the basic lead of the US federal laws), and to various federal and state heritage laws in Australia, including most notably the federal Environment Protection and Biodiversity Conservation Act (1999) and the Australian Heritage Council Act (2003) (see Smith and Burke 2007: 126–30 and 130–61). Many other nations of the world also have similar federal-level laws: in Canada, for example, the Canadian Environmental Assessment (2003) has stipulations requiring that any impact on archaeological resources be assessed or evaluated, in a manner similar to these British, American, and Australian laws. However, as King (2005: 37) makes clear, for the US in particular:

> the law is seldom so straightforward. There are lots of national, state and provincial, Indian Tribal, and local laws and regulations requiring that some kind of attention be paid to archaeological sites, but there's no universally applicable legal requirement that they be excavated before something destroys them. The federal laws in the US apply only to projects in which there's some kind of federal agency involvement – federal funds, for example, or a federal license, or the use of federal land. State and local laws vary widely in their requirements; some apply pretty specific requirements to a wide range of state and locally regulated or funded projects, while others don't. Many privately funded projects on private land are subject to no archaeological requirements at all. In other countries . . . archaeological sites or at least the stuff they contain are regarded in law as government property, by virtue of being parts of the national patrimony, but that doesn't mean that the government systematically imposes requirements on property owners and developers.

For example, in many US states (and, similarly, Canadian provinces and territories), archaeological sites are protected by state law (above and beyond federal legislation) on both public and private lands under the terms of various archaeological sites and resources acts and public lands acts. In many cases, for example, these laws mean that even on private lands a permit can be required before knowingly disturbing any historic or prehistoric archaeological resource or site (with the property owner or manager agreeing to the issuance of the permit). In addition, many states also have laws protecting Native American burial sites, petroglyphs, and pictographs from intentional disturbance. However, such laws vary widely from state to state: if in doubt, readers should consult local state and/or Tribal authorities for guidance (a useful guide to the US national/federal system is King's [2004] *Cultural Resource Laws and Practice*).

The complexity of the situation is true also in other nations such as Canada and Australia where both the federal system and various Native Title, Tribal, and

Indigenous Communities' legislation and rights (including rights of control of land and cultural resources [especially human remains] and more broadly of self-governance) have an impact on the legislative framework (for a guide to these in Canada, see Denhez 2010; in Australia see Smith and Burke 2007). In terms of archaeology and cultural heritage, there are, in particular, laws such as the federal Aboriginal and Torres Strait Islander Heritage Protection Act (1984) in Australia and the Native American Graves Protection and Repatriation Act (1990) in the US.

There are also many different other national/federal and state/local heritage laws and ordinances regarding particular types of historic sites. For example, many countries have legislation specific to maritime archaeology – primarily submerged archaeological sites. Examples of these include the UK (national) Protection of Wrecks Act (1973), Protection of Military Remains Act (1984), and Merchant Shipping Act (1995); the US federal Abandoned Shipwreck Act (1987) and Sunken Military Craft Act (2005); and the Australian federal Historic Shipwrecks Act (1976). Various Australian and US states and territories also have many state-specific laws pertaining to submerged cultural heritage.

Finally, archaeological development control also increasingly requires an under-standing of related non–heritage-specific legislation. In particular, other local (as well as national) government officials have responsibility for protecting and pro-moting biodiversity and ecology – often under more stringent laws than those protecting heritage. For example, in the UK, there are Section 40 of the Natu-ral Environment and Rural Communities Act (2006), Planning Policy Statement 9 (Biodiversity and Geological Conservation) (2005), and ODPM/Defra Circular ODPM 06/2005 (Defra 01/2005). Local authorities have a duty to protect, man-age, and enhance Sites of Special Scientific Interest (SSSIs). Working closely with natural environment colleagues is a growing component of many local government archaeological officers' roles, as more and more mutual interests are identified – not least in the preparation for, and management and mitigation of, climate change on the landscape, including on historic landscapes, woodlands, park, gardens, and coastlines. This includes working with colleagues in local and national government as well as in the voluntary/amenity sector – such as, for example, the Campaign to Protect Rural England (CPRE), Joint Nature Conservation Committee (JNCC), and Wildlife Trusts in the UK.

Given all these laws and regulations, it can be argued that development control officers are the most important (if not necessarily the most senior or best-paid) local government archaeological officers. In terms of actual people in actual offices, this means:

- *In the UK*: Various archaeological, historic buildings, historic environment record, and other officers based around a county archaeologist with overall responsibility for their region (which, confusingly, might be a UK county – roughly equivalent to a US state in terms of powers but not size – and/or might be an urban borough or unitary authority), under the terms of Planning Policy Statement 5: Planning for the Historic Environment (2010) in England and Wales,

Scottish Planning Policy (2010) in Scotland, and Planning Policy Statement 6: Planning, Archaeology and the Built Heritage (1999) in Northern Ireland, covering all developments on all land irrespective of ownership.

- *In the US*: Various archaeological, historic buildings, record, and other officers, especially State Historic Preservation Officers (SHPOs) and/or Tribal Historic Preservation Officers (THPOs) (performing the same type of preservation planning activities as those performed by SHPOs associated with historic properties located on Tribal Lands), based around a state archaeologist with overall responsibility for the state, primarily under the terms of Section 106 of the National Historic Preservation Act (1966/1980/1992), covering primarily developments in which there is some kind of federal agency involvement, but also other developments dependent on various specific state, Indian Tribal, and local laws and regulations.
- *In Australia*: Various archaeological, historic buildings, record, and other officers, based around a state director (or similarly named official) with overall responsibility for the state, broadly under the terms of the Environment Protection and Biodiversity Conservation Act (1999), but more usually under the terms of various specific state and local laws and regulations, and working closely with various state Aboriginal Heritage Councils.

In addition to the formal planning review process under laws such as PPS5, SPP, and PPS6 in the UK and Section 106 of the NHPA in the US, county/state archaeologists are also usually responsible for:

- Coordinating archaeological research undertaken within their area of remit.
- Advising and assisting the public and local, state (US/Australia)/county (UK), and national (federal) agencies on cultural resource matters.
- Maintaining a preservation plan for their area of remit.
- Engaging in their region's public archaeology endeavors.
- Approving the licensing of professional archaeologists to undertake research on state land (US only).

The primary role, and the majority of the daily life, of such officers are focused on providing reactive advice to, and the management of, archaeological consultations. A site is being developed and the developers have hired an archaeological consultant and/or a CRM archaeology firm to lead them through the heritage-related stages of the planning/development process as laid out in various local and national heritage laws and ordinances; the development control officers receive a consultation pack – consisting of basic information such as the developers', consultants', and/or CRM archaeology firm's details; the site's grid reference, extent, and current usage; and the project's proposed objectives and/or end products. Maps, plans, and other diagrams will usually be included. Together, this package of information is used by the officers to advise on what work regarding the historic environment is required on the site – which may be no work at all, or may be a variety of processes along a sliding scale from a watching brief during development (observing construction work and watching to see whether archaeological features appear, and, if so, intervening to record or preserve these remains) up to the total excavation of some or all of the site, and all the related post-excavation and publication commitments that follow from any work. The decision as to what scale of archaeological work to require is made by the development control officers in liaison with other professional colleagues (such as historic buildings officers, natural environment planning officers such as government ecologists, and the like), as informed by national and local planning policy and guidelines (i.e., meaning that the officers cannot, for example, require all and any projects in their area to undertake total area excavation, and attempting to ensure that approximately the same requirements are enforced nationally on all different sites). Most important, these decisions are guided by existing local heritage records – what are known in the UK as historic environment records (HERs, formerly known as sites and monuments record [SMRs]), a detailed record of all known heritage features (archaeological sites and monuments, historic buildings, parks, gardens, landscapes, wrecks, and so on) in the area, as well as details of the hypothesized archaeological potential of other areas on the basis of this existing knowledge (what are usually known in the UK as "areas of [high] archaeological potential" or the like). HERs are discussed in more detail later. Similar types of records are maintained in the US and Australia by different offices of state archaeology (usually part of larger state historic preservation offices or similar entities).

The options open to archaeological officers in terms of archaeological consultations include requiring some or all of the entire remit of possible types of investigation outlined elsewhere in this book, from predetermination/early discussions and environmental impact assessments, by way of desk-based assessments, fieldwalking, field survey, and watching briefs to partial or full excavations, including, where required, specific types of work such as historic building surveys, human burials, and remains assessments and excavations, environmental sampling and so on, as well as allied post-excavation work, mitigation and preservation of remains in situ, community archaeology, outreach, publication, and archiving. An imprecise management equation is achieved in this decision-making process, weighing the nature of the development proposed, its extent and physical impact on the landscape, other developments in the area that are or have undergone archaeological exploration, and the nature of the known archaeological record – in particular its type, extent, and relative rarity – surrounding the proposed development (Figure 23). This process is inevitably imprecise because, despite popular perception otherwise, we still know shockingly little about the surviving archaeology of many areas, even those subject to massive and constant development, as in the case of the author's own county of Surrey. Consequently, although an estimate can be made of the likely archaeological potential of a site and thus a development's potential impact on the archaeology, surprise discoveries are still made regularly. For example, in 2001 an existing quarry site at North Park Farm, Bletchingley, in east Surrey, planned an extension to the quarry that was subject to a predevelopment archaeological exploration. A range of prehistoric archaeological materials were found, as expected, but within these were a series of unexpected Mesolithic pits associated with buried

Figure 23. Working in local government, part 1. Site visits play a major role in the work of local government archaeologists, to provide advice and check on standards and progress. Here, Tony Howe (on the right-hand side), one of the county archaeological officers of Surrey in southeast England, undertakes a monitoring visit to a partially excavated Saxon burial at Fetcham, Surrey, in August 2010 (© Tony Howe 2010).

soil (intact remnant landscape) containing only material of Mesolithic date within a topographic hollow, occupying an area of almost 1 hectare in extent. Here, in situ evidence was discovered for flintworking at several of the sampled locations, alongside evidence of fires or cooking activities showing that repeated visits were made to the area from around 8000 BCE to around 4500 BCE. This was a most unusual discovery, and was of global significance (Guinness 2009).

Archaeological development control officers' work is not restricted to or completed by preapplication advice; they remain involved throughout the process, in the UK at least until the conditions they place with respect to work on the historic portions of the site have been completed (the technical term is "discharged") to their satisfaction. Site visits to monitor the type and quality of archaeological work and the precise nature of the features under exploration are common; so too are discussions by phone and e-mail with developers about the nature and extent of the work required, the length of time, and thus ultimately the cost of the project. Some of these discussions are good-natured and mutually respectful and useful; a small number will be confrontational, as the development control officer argues for one thing and the consultant or CRM archaeologist for another.

137

Even when actual fieldwork, whatever this may comprise, is complete, the work of the officer is not over; monitoring includes at least reviewing a final project report that must be submitted to the HER or equivalent, a report (commonly known as "gray literature") that must be of a sufficient standard and detail before the officer discharges the archaeological condition, and that will have to show evidence of detailed reporting both of the site's exploration and any post-excavation work required on the site or in relation to it. Such officers will also advise on the final deposition of the archives and any excavated materials of the site in an appropriate publicly accessible location, and also on any formal publication of data from it. Such officers may also write independent reports on the site for internal government as well as public consultation; in situations of legal dispute over the activities undertaken on a site, they may even be required to make formal a written or oral report to a planning inquiry or even, in extreme cases, in court.

Finally, unexpected discoveries of both archaeological and non-archaeological materials may also require officers' attention and even site visits (Figure 24) – for instance, although not a terribly common occurrence, most officers who have been in their positions for any length of time will have had to advise the police at some point on the discovery of human (real or purported – many turn out to be animals) remains that may or may not be ancient/modern and so constitute either an archaeological site or a crime scene.

As can be imagined, it is necessary for such officers to possess a comprehensive understanding of local, national, and international planning law in relation to heritage, and a similarly high level of archaeological knowledge. Although this primary focus on planning development control is the main and most formal component of the development control officers' job, they may also undertake a host of other roles, depending on their workload, temperament, interest, and background. Some or all of this may be within their formal job remit, dependent on their seniority within local government and the structure of that local government authority. In the UK, at least, the majority of the senior archaeological officers (often referred to as county archaeologists – broadly equivalent to US state archaeologists) will, although sufficiently skilled to undertake development control work (and possibly having started off their careers as development control officers), handle some or all of this other, nonstatutory work – which may take up all, or at least the majority, of their time. Such senior officers also usually have management responsibilities within local government, if only the management of their own team, representation on internal budgetary and planning meetings, and so on. These other roles include advising their government employer internally, and many different organizations as well as the media externally, on the archaeology of their area or specialty. Such work will usually be nonstatutory – that is, accepted as important but not formally required under law.

All such officers, irrespective of their seniority, also need to keep up to date on the latest advances in archaeological method and theory, and new sites and discoveries of relevance to their work, to be able to provide the most up-to-date advice. In the UK, at least, they are also increasingly on the receiving end of more and more detailed legal and management advice from central government, both archaeological

Figure 24. Working in local government, part 2. Unexpected archaeological discoveries occur regularly, and local government archaeologists are at hand to advise under such circumstances. Here, a Roman tile kiln is under excavation in a residential garden near Reigate in Surrey. The structure was located less than 20 cm from the surface, yet it missed detection during a prior evaluation carried out to inform a planning decision to redevelop the property (© Tony Howe 2010).

and non-archaeological, that requires detailed reading and then reporting on to their managers, and are asked to advise on central government consultations on the content of such documents. The European Union also has various legal as well as management policies, conventions, and other statutory and nonstatutory management instruments that some European nations have committed to enforce. Consultation and collaboration with a host of other colleagues and contacts is also very important – in some cases mandatory, as well as time-consuming – and may be with:

- Colleagues in other sections of their same local government – natural environment professionals such as ecologists, as well as planning officers and transport, minerals, waste, and other infrastructure colleagues.
- Officials in other sectors of local government – for example, in the UK, many county councils also have subcounty-level administration in the form of district and borough councils, and some towns, cities, and parishes have their own administrations (similarly also in the US and Australia).

- Heritage colleagues from other areas/regions: for example, in the UK there is an organization called the Association of Local Government Archaeological Officers (ALGAO), which has regional, national (England, Wales, Scotland), and transnational (UK-wide) as well as thematic (e.g., marine or countryside) committees that meet regularly; the US equivalent is the National Association of State Archaeologists (NASA). Also included in this can be considered the CRM "cousin" of ALGAO and NASA, the Federation of Archaeological Managers and Employers (FAME), nationally and regionally representing the CRM archaeology lobby (the US equivalent of FAME is the American Cultural Resources Association [ACRA]), and alongside, this organizations like the aforementioned RPA in the US, ACCAI in Australia, and the IfA in the UK – professional organizations that require membership on the basis of demonstrable experience and that enforce codes of conduct and ethical standards.
- Particular sectors of centralized government, most of which, in the UK at least, have both central and regional offices, and that include heritage-focused organizations such as English Heritage, as well as nonheritage but landscape- or resource-focused organizations such as the UK's Department for the Environment, Food and Rural Affairs, and specialized sectors of the government such as the National Park Service and National Oceanographic and Atmospheric Administration in the US and the various decentralized national parks of the UK (most of which, in fact, have their own dedicated heritage management teams). Included within this can also be all the different branches of the military, which remains a significant landowner in most nations of the world.
- Core service/utility and infrastructure organizations such as oil, gas, water, and electricity suppliers; telecommunications companies; road, rail, and airport authorities; strategic resource companies such as the aggregates industry; and representatives at the local and national level of farmers of every type and size.
- Other major heritage stakeholders such as national and local amenity societies (in the UK the National Trust, a heritage-focused charity and major landowner, in particular), local heritage societies, groups, museums, archives, and visitor attractions, and in the UK also the Heritage Lottery Fund, the management organization for heritage-related funding derived from the national lottery scheme.
- Local and national religious organizations, many of which own or care for historic sites, and not just Christian organizations looking after churches and cathedrals. Surrey, for example, is home to the oldest mosque in the UK, an extremely important building that is at the heart of a thriving Islamic community as well as being a highly protected historic site by virtue of its age and cultural significance. Surrey also has a series of large historic graveyards that are not associated with a single religious community and thus are managed communally.

Finally, such officers may also like – although precious few have the formal paid time to do so any more, and tend to do so voluntarily in their own time – to undertake archaeological research into their personal area or specialty, either primary fieldwork surveying or excavating sites or secondary data analysis, comparison, and theorizing.

Career Structure – Historic Environment Records and Their Officers

The work of development control officers is only as good as the information to which they have access – from developers on one hand, and from their own records on the other. If a developer fails to fully advise the development control officers, whether accidentally or deliberately, of the nature or extent of the proposed development or the archaeological fieldwork related to it, then the advice the officers give will suffer for this; the result will be the same if the officers do not have access to the best possible data and sources that local government itself holds. These data and sources are known, in the UK at least, as HERs, and sometimes by their older designation, SMRs. Similar types of records are maintained in the US and Australia by different state and territory offices of state archaeology (usually part of larger state historic preservation offices or similar entities).

HERs are frequently misunderstood – in both their form and their use. This is because all HERs in existence vary in shape, form, and content, and so too do their uses. Their multiple different users worsen this misunderstanding. HERs began life in the UK in the 1960s and 1970s when local government – and, in some cases, local amenity organizations – first began to employ officers to monitor regional heritage. Good management requires understanding of what has gone before; in this case, the extent of the heritage resource, especially the location, date, format, and extent of sites and monuments, mainly archaeological sites. At first these were handwritten or typed lists and catalogs of appropriate data with associated paper maps (some simply marked up by hand) against which officers could check when providing advice. Various forms of indexing, card-record systems, and the like were used to manage more and more data, and after desktop computers came into widespread use in government in the late 1980s, SMRs were increasingly computerized. As computer technology, especially data processing and storage capacity, advanced, so too did these records (SMRs were early adopters of database, spreadsheet, and other similar systems, and also of forms of computer-based mapping, the origins of today's geographic information systems [GIS]). Consequently, by the mid- to late 1990s, SMRs had developed into extremely large and complex electronic datasets comprising thousands of cross-referenced records. This was one of the reasons that SMRs began to be renamed in the early 2000s as HERs, to indicate their broader contents of historic data of all sorts, not just purely archaeological information. However, different types and standards of data, data acquisition, storage, and man-agement were used by different organizations (even within different branches of government), and this situation has only worsened over the past decade. Although attempts have been made to nationally standardize HERs, these have not been comprehensive.

HERs also remain an ambiguous part of government – essential for the smooth running of the planning system but not yet (proposals are currently being made by the UK central government regarding this) a statutory requirement of local government. The varied contents of HERs also often lead to confusion as to their extent; this is not helped by the varied roles that an HER serves. Although originally designed for, and still primarily used by, development control officers, CRM archaeologists and consultants also use HERs; so, too, do a variety of nondevelopment-focused users, in particular members of local heritage societies undertaking research in their area, and more unusually university-based academics or students undertaking research. HERs are best likened to a plant – organic, constantly growing, very different to look at from different perspectives. They are not purely planning- or development-related tools (no matter what some development control officers may imply), nor are these in any sense archives or libraries (HERs are far too current, too constantly evolving, for such a term to apply, and they do not hold original documents, but rather collate copies of useful records held elsewhere).

When first developed, HERs were generally managed and maintained by the development control officers who were their primary users; sometimes these were, in fact, privately managed by local archaeological organizations, many of which were the early employers of county archaeologists, who were then gradually absorbed into the formal structure of local government. As they grew ever larger and more complex, some local authorities began to employ individuals to work specifically on them, usually initially on a part-time basis. This situation has now developed into many dozens of full-time, permanent HER officers whose main responsibility is the management of these HERs, in all their forms. Such employment comprises many different tasks:

- Management, maintenance, and development of the HER, both its physical and electronic components, requiring a sound and diverse expertise in hard and soft data management.
- Assisting and working alongside development control officers in the provision of the best, most pertinent and timely planning advice.
- Advising visitors to the HER on its use, and undertaking paid research into its contents on behalf of consultants, CRM archaeologists, and any clients who would prefer not to visit and consult the HER in person.
- Liaising with the varied series of stakeholders identified earlier in relation to development control officers, and undertaking the same types of continuing professional development in keeping up to date in advances in archaeological method and theory, new sites, and discoveries.
- Undertaking outreach, explaining the contents and uses of the HER to students, and recruiting volunteers willing to work on data input and refining.

As can be imagined, HER officers need a broad range of skills. On one hand, their job is deeply introspective, quiet, controlled, and desk-based – constantly keeping on top of ever more data in different formats and understanding how to best manage these data. On the other hand, their job can be incredibly public, requiring both enthusiasm and a calm professionalism when dealing with the many different types of individuals or organizations that wish to access the HER. Such officers also require as comprehensive an understanding of local, national, and international planning law in relation to heritage as their development control colleagues, as well as a similarly high level of archaeological knowledge. HER officers need to be optimistic pragmatists – turning their hand to many different tasks, happy to spend one day assisting a commercial client, the next day quietly refining data on their own, the third day working with a lively band of local volunteers to promote the HER as a resource. This is in some contrast to the more single-minded, as well as combative, average week of the development control officers with whom they work so closely – many HER officers would readily agree that they cannot imagine leading the life of a development control officer, and vice versa.

Career Structure – Specialists

A number of other heritage-related roles are nowadays fulfilled in local government, working alongside development control and historic environment record officers. All these career paths are more or less applicable to individuals with a background in archaeology – although many require extensive additional or alternative skills.

Specialists – Historic Buildings Officers

Undoubtedly the most influential of these positions in the UK at least is that of historic buildings officers. Such individuals are effectively development control officers with similar responsibilities and broadly the same priorities and lifestyle as described earlier; the difference is that first, historic buildings officers have expertise in historic buildings rather than in archaeological sites and monuments, and secondly, that because under British law the protection of historic buildings is far more extensive (as well as draconian) for historic buildings as compared with archaeological remains, they have considerably more "on the ground" power and influence than their archaeological colleagues. Relatively few people ever end up in court for damaging archaeological sites; fewer still end up with any of the possible forms of sanction that can ultimately be applied, such as fines, a criminal record, and even a custodial sentence. But relatively more people (although still a tiny proportion of the population and the criminal justice system's workload) are pursued in such a manner for offenses related to the damage or destruction of historic buildings.

Beyond the difference in legal circumstances outlined previously, it should be clear from the outset that although a background in archaeology can be useful to a historic buildings officer, this is not essential; such an officer needs, in addition, a considerable, and very different, alternative skill set. The study of historic buildings, although related to archaeology, is a discipline in its own right, requiring years of study and experience if it is to be done well – and, ironically, there are few professional training courses in this. Most of the officers currently in post around the UK have learned their skills on the job, usually in the company of the then-holder of their position; many have spent many years, often decades, getting to know their particular "patch," quite often as district/borough/municipal conservation officers (this role is explained later). The dedication and commitment required, the lack of training courses, and, above all, the distinct lack of jobs mean that the UK at least is facing something of a skills crisis in this area in the next generation – many of the current post holders are now in their forties or fifties, and will retire within twenty-odd years, but there are relatively few new, younger officers in their twenties and thirties currently learning the ropes and getting ready to replace them. The full scope of skills and experience needed from historic buildings specialists is outside the scope of this book. An excellent starting point for those interested in this particular specialty, however, is various UK-based organizations, including the Institute of Historic Building Conservation (IHBC) and the Society for the Protection of Ancient Buildings (SPAB), whose details are listed in Appendix 1.

Historic buildings officers tend also to have a very different lifestyle from that of their archaeological development control colleagues. Although often based in the same teams and/or offices, they will tend in particular to travel around their area of responsibility far more often than archaeological officers, undertaking site visits for advice, consultation, and, more occasionally, confrontation. The nature of developer-led archaeological work, in the UK at least, increasingly means that a relatively small number of industry clients are served by a similarly small number of CRM archaeology firms, and that the impacts on and solutions for archaeological sites are relatively straightforward. Consequently, archaeological development control officers are, in general, spending more and more time these days working by phone and e-mail rather than by on-site visits. In contrast, the nature of the impacts on the UK's historic building stock is far more varied, and requires vastly more on-site work. Many different people are involved (often private owners of single properties rather than industrial developers, who are, consequently, far less familiar with the applicable laws, and who also tend to have far less money to spend on professional legal or management advice). Many different types of changes are also proposed to historic buildings, from small alterations that may still have dramatic consequences for a building's historic identity (replacement of traditional-style windows with modern wooden, plastic, or metal ones being the most common example of this) right up to the partial or even total demolition of a building, or the transformation of a building from one use to another.

The nature of the historic building stock also varies massively from county to county, even within individual counties, with variations in construction and roofing materials traditionally used, in internal layout and external appearance, and so on – and on which even apparently subtle changes can have great impacts. An officer may thus spend a morning advising on the proposed changes to a humble, but (formally protected under law) nineteenth-century cottage, move on to a meeting about the conversion of a rare seventeenth-century barn by lunch, and spend the afternoon at a grand manor house, before returning to the office to write up notes and download digital pictures. The meetings may have been with individual owners who care very much about, and deeply value, the historic nature of their property; with hard-nosed and unscrupulous property developers; or with public and private organizations responsible for large premises for which the proposed changes may cost hundreds of thousands, even millions, of pounds. And an officer will often need to spend many hours at a single location, not only discussing plans with the owner and the architect, builder, and other personnel, but also touring the property, even climbing up into the loft, roof space, basement or outhouses, taking photos, writing notes, and so on. The visit may be in the middle of a town or at a muddy, rutted farmer's track, and the historic buildings officer may be wearing a fine suit for one visit only to have to pull on overalls and work boots for the next.

Specialists – Finds Liaison Officers

One particular type of specialist unique to the UK is the finds liaison officer (FLO) of the Portable Antiquities Scheme (PAS). The PAS is a voluntary program begun in 1997 to record the increasing numbers of "small finds" of archaeological interest discovered by members of the public – in particular, objects (especially but not exclusively metal) found by metal detectorists, although the scheme's officers take pains to make clear that they are there to help all members of the public record finds of any type or period. Funded by the central government, the scheme is managed nationally at a central office based in the British Museum in London, but is most visible through the regional/county-based FLOs, the majority of whom are based within local government or local museums, archives, or university archaeology departments. The scheme is particularly interested in recording materials that do not legally constitute "treasure" (i.e., mainly precious metals) that must by law be reported and dealt with through the Treasure Act of 1996 – without the PAS, such materials would go largely unrecorded.

FLOs undertake a variety of roles in relation to their job. Most important, they examine finds and provide their finders with more information such as the likely material, age, and cultural significance of the materials discovered. With the finders' permission, the FLOs will record such information – including taking photos and/or making detailed scaled drawings – together with the location of the discovery. These data are then stored on the national PAS database, offering professional and amateur archaeologists alike access to the data, helping to highlight previously undiscovered archaeological sites, producing distribution patterns of particular materials such as specific coins or other materials, and so on. As a consequence of this role, FLOs need to be extremely experienced and familiar with a wide range and age of different archaeological materials; they also tend to find themselves traveling widely across their region, often in evenings or on weekends, visiting metal detecting, archaeology, and other local clubs and societies to identify materials or give talks on the scheme, as well as being present at metal-detecting "rallies," often held on weekends, at which metal detecting clubs will meet to systematically record the finds from a particular site.

The politics of work as a FLO are not to be underestimated. Many archaeologists and metal detectorists alike remain dubious of the scheme, some outright hostile to it. Some archaeologists consider the PAS to be anti-archaeology, pandering to an archaeologically destructive hobby that ought to be banned, like egg collecting. Similarly, some metal detectorists consider the PAS to be the "thin end" of the wedge of government control, the first steps in a long-term plan to monitor and eventually ban all metal detecting. Passions concerning the PAS run high, so FLOs often encounter individuals who are hostile to the scheme and to their role. Individuals opposed to the scheme for whatever reason do not tend to hold back on their opinions. Consequently, FLOs must have a thick skin. The working and conditions hours of FLOs can also be quite antisocial: many clubs and societies visited meet in the evenings in village halls, libraries, and community centers, so there can be a lot of travel involved. On the other hand, the up side of the job is that it can be trmendously good fun, working with many enthusiastic people and seeing an extraordinary range of archaeological marterials.

Specialists – Project-Based Officers

Most local government heritage teams regularly employ project-based specialists. Some of these individuals may be permanent, full-time employees; unfortunately, though, the majority are usually fixed-term workers hired for the duration of a specific project, and are often paid for by third-party grants, such as the UK Heritage Lottery Fund, as well as by funding partnerships, such as those between the local government and a local heritage amenity society. Such officers and their jobs tend, broadly, to fall into one of two groups:

- *Data-based positions*: These are projects that have been commissioned to fill gaps in existing data, to expand on specific research themes/topics, or to coordinate wider research; examples in southeast England, where the author works, include officers employed to work on the South East Historic Research Framework (SEHRF), an English Heritage-funded project that has funded both regional resource assessments and research agendas across the country to better under-stand the extent of the historic resource of England as well as gaps in knowl-edge of this. At the county level, the county of Surrey has been undertaking a somewhat similar project collating data on areas of high archaeological potential (AHAPs) – detailed analyses of specific regions, towns, and villages of the county with particular high historic significance and remains, building on a series of projects previously completed, the extensive urban survey and historic landscape characterization of the county that gave broader-brush analyses of the county's historic sites (and for which similar surveys have been undertaken in many other counties).
- *Outreach-based positions*: These are projects designed to promote access to and engagement in the historic environment of a county. For example, Surrey has the Exploring Surrey's Past project,[1] funded jointly by the HLF and the county council, which has placed a modified version of the HER onto a user-friendly website, alongside undertaking outreach activities within the community to both

[1] See http://www.exploringsurreyspast.org.uk/.

encourage use of the website and, perhaps more important, find volunteers to contribute new data to the website on their own area or period of specialty.

Career Structure – Conservation Officers and Other Planning Officers

A number of other local government employees also influence the management of archaeological sites and historic buildings and landscapes. Some of these individuals have extensive training and background in heritage; others have come into contact with heritage from very different origins. Briefly and broadly, the three most important of these groups are:

- *Conservation officers*: Part of local planning departments, usually at the district/borough (US county) level, such officers help to protect and enhance historic buildings, reporting and advising on buildings and areas of special historic or architectural interest and securing the improvement of such places for the benefit of communities. Conservation officers work with heritage specialists and planning officers to guide new developments to maintain the distinctive character of an area – up to a third of planning applications submitted in the UK involve conservation issues. They may also be involved in regeneration projects that have community, economic, and environmental benefits.
- *Planning officers*: Based both at the UK county (US state) as well as the UK borough/district (US county) level, such officers make both long- and short-term decisions about the management and development of towns and the countryside, balancing the sometimes conflicting demands of housing, industrial development, agriculture, recreation, transport, and the environment to allow appropriate development to take place. It is up to them to ensure that any development has permission and that planning requirements are adhered to. Ultimately, when planning permission is breached, they will then negotiate a solution, and in extreme cases gather evidence to present to a formal planning committee, which can include councilors and magistrates. This means, for example, that if the laws applying to the management of an archaeological site discovered before or during an development have not been adhered to, the planning officer will liaise with the heritage specialists to guide the process of mitigation of the damage to the heritage features and either protect these or map out what is left.
- *Landscape architects*: Again, similar to planners, based both at the UK county (US state) as well as UK borough/district (US county) level, such officers help to create landscapes – planning, designing, and managing open spaces, including both natural and built environments. They work to provide innovative and aesthetically pleasing environments for people to enjoy, while ensuring that changes to this environment are appropriate, sensitive, and sustainable. Landscape architects work closely with heritage specialists to guide the development of historic landscapes, finding ways to make the best use of distinctive historic features while modifying landscapes for new uses – for instance, finding the most sympathetic means of inserting new homes into an existing historic parkland

landscape. Some landscape architects are also specialists in historic parks and gardens, an particularly noteworthy specialty that requires highly specialized skills and knowledge, overlapping historic and natural environment knowledge in the understanding, protection, and management of living historic designed landscapes that may be hundreds of years old. Organizations in the UK such as the Association of Gardens Trusts (AGT) and the Garden History Society (GHS) provide specialist support on such matters.

Such types of local government employees enjoy all the same benefits and career structure of the other dedicated heritage professionals discussed elsewhere in this section. The major difference is that they tend to come from a wider range of backgrounds, many having studied planning policy, law, and wider conservation (including both historic and natural conservation) issues at university rather than solely heritage issues.

Lifestyle

The lifestyle of the local government archaeologist is not for everyone. Above all else, although such people get to spend a lot of time reading, advising, and thinking about archaeology, they spend very little time actually doing archaeology in terms of its physical practice – surveying, excavating, and so on. Opportunities to go out, to participate in, or at least physically monitor archaeology as it happens need largely to be generated by the archaeologists in question; such opportunities do not naturally arise in the course of their jobs. This is increasingly so as workloads get heavier and heavier and developers grow ever more wary of the legal problems and health and safety risks of having visitors on site.

In a positive light, though, all this can be a good thing. If the majority of such an archaeologist's time is spent reactively advising developers and their hired archaeologists on their responsibilities and practices, collecting and collating data from many different sites, and promoting this new knowledge to all who are interested in it, this time is not wasted. Archaeologists in local government who do their job well get to see, understand, and directly influence the future protection and understanding of the heritage of their region. No one should feel bad about having such an inherently positive role. Even if the majority of their time is spend reactively, some of such archaeologists' time can still be spent proactively doing a small but extremely worthwhile amount of field archaeology. Perhaps they may choose to follow up on a commercial excavation by undertaking a detailed keyhole excavation at the edge of a larger site to clarify a key point of a site's dating or morphology, or survey an area that is unlikely to ever see commercial development but that is surrounded by such developments, clarifying the heritage of that blank space on the map. Alternatively, such archaeologists may choose to focus on public archaeology, organizing and leading projects that can involve their local community. Many distinguished British archaeologists first were introduced to archaeology by participating on such projects in their youth, so such projects can have both immediate and long-term positive impacts on archaeology at the local, national, and even international scale. Finally, such archaeologists may choose to publish on specific subjects or locations with which their role has given them long-term familiarity and expertise.

Every desk job, no matter the sector, has its pros and cons, and archaeology is no different; to this can then be added the undoubtedly peculiar circumstances of local government civil service. Civil servants of all specialties, grades, and experience will admit that the benefits of such employment are, generally, (relative) job security, the generosity of pension schemes, and the more relaxed pace of work compared with work in industry. Compared with an academic archaeologist, however, a local government archaeologist has relatively less personal freedom to decide his or her daily work schedule. On the other hand, the local government archaeologist is also likely to work shorter hours than the academic, and when compared with a CRM archaeologist, a local government archaeologist is likely to be very much better paid and treated, and will enjoy vastly superior job security. The downside is that, as noted, the local government archaeologist will not get to do much practical archaeology.

The overall result is that jobs in local government archaeology are highly sought after, especially by the middle generation of professionals in their thirties, forties, and fifties. The scenario is pretty obvious once laid out: a young and lively archaeology graduate fresh from college starts off in field archaeology; the early–mid twenties are a blur of sites, places, and people – the person does and sees a lot. By the person's late twenties or early thirties, however, the lifestyle begins to pale a bit. The parties are still great and the archaeology even more so, but the knees are starting to hurt a bit more and being out in all different types of weather is starting to lose its appeal. The individual may also have a long-term partner, possibly a non-archaeologist, who, though sympathetic to the archaeologist's devotion to the subject, would also like to see him or her have better job security and a larger monthly paycheck. The result is that the government job suddenly begins to seem much more appealing – there will be less field archaeology, but a chance to still make a difference in archaeology, to still do some field archaeology, and also the refuge of a comfortable chair in an office on a cold winter's day.

Skills, Expertise, and Qualifications

Because jobs in local government archaeology tend to be highly sought after, employers' demands for skills and experience are correspondingly high. For a start, as noted previously, because many such archaeologists are drawn from the middle ranks of the CRM archaeology community, many will have considerable field experience, including not only pure archaeological skills such as in survey, excavation, planning, finds identification, and the like, but also related skills in project management, perhaps in budget management – as well as in time and people management. One of the things that many such people making the move from CRM to government archaeology note after their first few weeks in their new job is that although timelines are often still tight in government, they are not nearly as tight as in industry. Such archaeologists are also likely to have considerable specialist knowledge of one or more particular periods and/or archaeological specialties, meaning that they offer their employer, and the consultants and others whom they will advise, particular specialist skills. Such specialist knowledge may have been developed in a practical professional context, but is also likely to have been honed through postgraduate study.

Together, it can be seen that many local government archaeologists have a formidable array of different skill sets; even thinking about entry into this field can seem wildly intimidating. Entry-level positions do exist, however, for this is local government, and one of the benefits of this sector of archaeology is that career progression and on-the-job training are common and usually encouraged. A significant number of local government archaeologists are not drawn from the CRM archaeology transfer route described earlier, but rather come in as young and often inexperienced graduate archaeology students on short-term, low-level contracts (say, working within an HER on a particular project) who eventually get longer or even permanent contracts and develop their skill sets.

Most university degree courses in archaeology place little emphasis on this aspect of archaeology. Although most students will have to take one or more courses on the principles of heritage law in their respective countries or regions, few will receive detailed (or any) training in the practice and implementation of such laws – how local government archaeologists implement them. Fewer students still will have seen firsthand the types of paperwork and administrative documents and reports handled by these archaeologists, visited an office or HER, or talked to local government heritage staff. What this means is that students who are proactive, who seek out local government archaeologists, volunteer for unpaid work in the offices, write a dissertation or thesis using the data held in such offices, and so on, will not only make themselves known to a small and often underappreciated sector of archaeologists, but will also gain experiences that make themselves stand out in an interview. Pick one hundred archaeology graduates applying for one entry-level post in local government archaeology, and the one who gets the coveted post will be not necessarily the student with the highest grades, but rather the student who demonstrated experience in and enthusiasm for work in this environment. People who go the extra mile, who volunteer, who stand out from their peers – these are the people who get ahead in this world, as in any other. Thus, a good BA in archaeology, matched with some volunteer experience in a local government archaeology office, form a very good start to a career in this sector; some experience of work in the real world of CRM archaeology, even if only a few months' worth, is very useful as well. An MA/MSc in a specialty is certainly very welcome, but is not essential; such a degree that involves a dissertation focused in on heritage law or that uses data from a local government office is a real plus, however. A PhD when entering the sector is then frankly uncommon, although many such officials, once secure in their employment, choose to undertake such study on an aspect of their region or specialist remit.

Interviewee: Hannah

How did you first become involved in archaeology?

Archaeology was something I wanted to do from a very early age – when I was six, I even wrote a poem at school about wanting to be an archaeologist when I grew up. Since then I have sought out every opportunity to be involved in archaeology: joining the Young Archaeologists Club, doing work experience with my local county archaeologist and English Heritage, and participating in excavations whenever I could. Thankfully, although I never had the opportunity to study archaeology at school, I had a few teachers who encouraged me; and my parents always supported me, driving me to excavations and even letting me dig a small trial trench in the back garden.

What is your current job?

My current position is senior archaeologist for Hampshire County Council. I am responsible for advising planning authorities on archaeological matters and ensuring that where archaeological sites might be disturbed, by developments, pipelines, new road schemes, quarrying, and so on, the sites are properly excavated and recorded. Together with my colleagues I offer more general advice and information on the historic environment of the county to ensure that it is protected and promoted.

What qualifications do you hold? Where and what did you study?

I have a BA (Honors) from Oxford University in archaeology and anthropology and an MA in the archaeology of human origins from the University of Southampton. I am currently writing up a PhD in Paleolithic archaeology, also at the University of Southampton.

What are your terms of employment, working conditions, or other job benefits?

I am one of the lucky people who has a permanent job in archaeology. My full-time contract is 37 hours per week, and there are the associated benefits of working for a County Council such as flexible working hours, travel loans, local government pension schemes, and so on.

How did you get your current job? What do you feel was most helpful to you in gaining this position?

I was just two years into a funded PhD when I saw my current job advertised and was a little uncertain about whether to apply, as the timing wasn't ideal. However, good jobs in archaeology don't come up every day, especially on your doorstep.

Prior to my PhD I had worked for three years in a similar role in another county, and I had been worrying about what I was going to do when my PhD funding ran out, so I decided to apply. Undoubtedly the biggest factor in my getting the position was my previous experience, particularly in local government archaeology. Ironically I don't think my PhD research was of any benefit in getting this job, but hopefully it will make a difference in the future.

What is the best thing about being an archaeologist?

For me the best thing about being an archaeologist is the variety. I never know what I am going to be dealing with next: one day it might be Paleolithic stone tools, the next day eighteenth-century military hospitals. As a result, I never stop learning.

Archaeology has also enabled me to travel all around the world, from Papua New Guinea to Patagonia, and I have made some very good friends along the way. There is always something or somewhere new to investigate.

What is the worst thing about being an archaeologist?

The working conditions for many archaeologists can be pretty difficult, working away from home on short contracts and extremely low pay compared with other professions. One of the unfair aspects of archaeology is the inconsistencies in pay across the discipline, although this has begun to improve in the past few years.

I am lucky in my current job that I have a fair wage and secure position, and for me personally the worst thing about being an archaeologist are the questions about dinosaurs and Time Team when people find out what I do!

What do you consider to be your greatest achievement in or contribution to archaeology so far?

In my professional archaeological life I think there have been a number of smaller achievements rather than one big one: each time a new site is discovered or historical features of a site preserved as the result of advice I have given, I feel a sense of achievement. Personally, one of the most rewarding projects I have been involved in is a research excavation in a cave in eastern Spain, where we have discovered some of the earliest evidence for the controlled use of fire in southern Europe.

What is the one thing you would change about archaeology if you could?

I think archaeology has a lot to offer. One of the challenges facing archaeology today is the diversity of groups and individuals involved; communication and collaboration between these groups is not always what it could be. Working together for a common cause is always going to get better results than working in isolation. For me, one of the ways of improving this would be to introduce a licensing scheme, perhaps similar to that seen in some areas of ecology. This would enable amateurs to demonstrate their worth alongside professional archaeologists and form a sound basis for more equal collaborative working.

What is your top tip for pursuing a career in archaeology?

Get out and dig! There is no substitute for practical experience. You'll be amazed at how much you can learn even doing apparently tedious tasks such as pot washing. It can also be a fantastic way to travel and see the world.

What do you see yourself doing in ten years' time?

I'm not sure I can think that far ahead, but hopefully I'll have finished my PhD by then and will still be working in archaeology. At the moment I am torn between pursuing a career in research and academia, and staying with curatorial archaeology. Either way, I would like to stay involved in teaching the subject; I really enjoy sharing my love of archaeology with others and helping people develop their own interest in the subject.

Chapter 6

Central Government

Introduction

Variations in the national format of archaeological employment become most evident at the level of central government. In federal systems such as those of the US, Australia, and Canada, organizations such as these nations' respective national park services (the National Park Service [NPS], Parks Australia, and Parks Canada) are part of a distinct system with many responsibilities, a clear legal remit, central and regional hierarchy, and a large budget. In comparison, centralized but not federalized nations such as the UK have broadly comparable organizations to the NPS, but the responsibilities, legal remit, organizational structure, and budgets involved are much less clear. The situation in the UK is further complicated by the decentralization of government there, particularly the varying responsibilities of the Regional Assemblies of Scotland, Wales, and Northern Ireland. Notwithstanding the above, central governments around the world employ archaeologists alongside allied heritage professionals, and employment in these organizations can be an extremely rewarding career path for those who choose to pursue it, offering a unique vantage point at the intersection of commercial, academic, and local government archaeology (Figure 25).

Central Heritage Organizations in the UK

In Britain (i.e., the United Kingdom of England, Scotland, Wales, and Northern Ireland), working in central government archaeology primarily (but not exclusively)

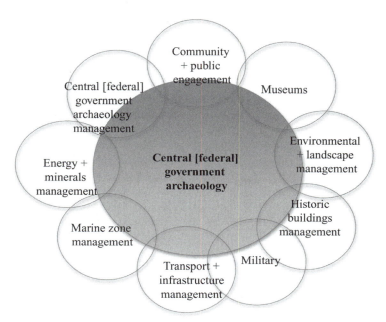

Figure 25. The structure and interrelationships of the central government archaeology sector.

means working for one of four organizations, known in government parlance as *executive nondepartmental public bodies* – part of (and primarily, but not exclusively, funded by) the government and operating on its behalf, but effectively run as independent organizations:

- *England*: English Heritage (EH), sponsored by the Department for Culture, Media, and Sport (DCMS).
- *Scotland*: Historic Scotland (HS), sponsored by the Executive Education Department of the Scottish Parliament.
- *Wales*: Cadw (a Welsh word meaning "to keep"), sponsored by the Welsh Assembly Government.
- *Northern Ireland*: the Northern Ireland Environment Agency (NIEA) of the Northern Ireland Executive, and unlike the other organizations listed here, directly responsible for managing both the cultural and natural environment.

These organizations fulfill a broad remit of managing the historic built environment (including archaeological sites and monuments, historic buildings, parks, gardens, and landscapes, on land and at sea out to the twelve-nautical-mile limit of the territorial sea) of their respective nations/regions. This includes:

- *Managing historic properties for public benefit and access*: EH manages and promotes access to more than 400 sites and HS and Cadw more than 120 sites each (access

155

to which is in some cases free, in other cases charged, either on a pay-per-visit basis or through payment of an annual membership fee that gives unlimited access to all sites, including a reciprocal agreement of visitation rights across the UK). This also includes a significant publication, education, and outreach program.

- *Managing sites of national and international importance that are formally protected by legislation*: This includes, in addition to the hundreds of sites noted previously, "scheduled monuments" (important buried and upstanding archaeological sites and monuments protected under the Ancient Monuments and Archaeological Areas Act of 1979), of which there are currently more than 31,000 in the UK, and "listed buildings" (important historic buildings protected under the Planning (Listed Buildings and Conservation Areas) Act of 1990), of which there are currently more than 373,000 in the UK.

- *Managing central heritage data resources*: In England, the National Monuments Record (NMR), in Scotland the Royal Commission on the Ancient and Historical Monuments of Scotland (RCAHMS), in Wales the National Monuments Record of Wales (NMRW), and in Northern Ireland the NI Sites and Monuments Record (NISMR) and Monuments and Buildings Record (NIMBR). These are the national equivalents to local HERs.

- *Providing specialist services* such as dating, conservation, and the like and providing and promoting guidance and standards on best practice to the heritage profession. EH, in particular, maintains a Centre for Archaeology, comprising a range of specialists including the Central Archaeology Service and the Ancient Monuments Laboratory.

- *Advising the government* on new discoveries of historic sites of national historic significance, on matters of national importance such as attempting to control the international illicit antiquities trade, and advising the government on related matters such as the UK's responsibility to meet European and other international heritage legislation/agreements (e.g., the 1992 European Convention on the Protection of the Archaeological Heritage [known as the Valetta Convention]).

- *Liaison with other government departments* and comparable international heritage management organizations, especially promotion of the UK as a leader in best practice in heritage policy, as well as liaison with national amenity societies and stakeholder groups such as the Council for British Archaeology, Institute of Historic Building Conservation, and Institute for Archaeologists, and including also stakeholders of significant numbers of historic properties, such as the Church of England and the National Trust (Figures 26 and 27).

- *Management of some dedicated heritage-related funding streams*, in particular in England, where EH has had responsibility since 2002 for distributing funds for projects on land and at sea related to the extraction of minerals and aggregates under the terms of the Aggregates Levy Sustainability Fund (ALSF). This also includes the pursuit of new funding streams for heritage projects from industry and other partners, as well as applying for grants from other funding bodies such as the Heritage Lottery Fund.

Figure 26. Working in central government, part 1. Similar to those in local government, archaeologists and related specialists working in central government regularly undertake site visits and inspections to provide advice and check on standards and progress. Here, English Heritage officers visit the historic buildings at Battle Abbey in East Sussex, southeast England (© Jeremy Ashbee / English Heritage 2007).

There is no directly comparable equivalent to EH, HS, and Cadw in the US or Australia. The remit, structure, and responsibilities of the nearest comparable organizations in these nations – in the US, the federal National Park Service and in Australia, the federal Department of the Environment, Water, Heritage, and the Arts, including Parks Australia – are discussed later in this chapter.

Unlike most other nations, the UK divides its central and local government heritage management into distinct "cultural" and "natural" environment sectors. As a consequence, a smaller number of archaeologists also work as part of the management of the latter, again through a series of executive nondepartmental public bodies comparable to EH, HS, and Cadw:

- *The Environment Agency (EA)*: This organization has the primary "natural environment" heritage remit in Britain, employing archaeologists for that purpose. Similar to EH, HS, and Cadw, the EA is responsible to a formal government department – in this case, the Department for the Environment, Food, and Rural Affairs (DEFRA) in England and to the Assembly Government in Wales.

Scotland has a comparable organization based along similar lines, the Scottish Environment Protection Agency (SEPA), accountable to the Scottish Parliament. As noted previously, in Northern Ireland, the NIEA operates on a more collaborative system akin to that of the US.

- *Natural England (NE)*: Established under the Natural Environment and Rural Communities Act of 2006 to "ensure that the natural environment is conserved, enhanced and managed for the benefit of present and future generations, thereby contributing to sustainable development," this organization is similarly responsible to DEFRA in England only.
- *The Forestry Commission (FC)*: accountable in England to DEFRA once again and in Scotland and Wales to the Scottish Parliament and to the Welsh Assembly Government, respectively.

Central Heritage Organizations in the US

The UK is unusual in managing its heritage in the manner described previously, with its archaeological sites and monuments and historic buildings management being divorced from broader issues of the environment. It is far more common, as is the case in the US, for different organizations to take responsibility for the combined management of natural and cultural environments.

The National Environmental Policy Act (NEPA) (1969, amended 1975 and 1982) requires all federal agencies to implement procedures to make environmental consideration a necessary part of that agency's decision-making process. Federal agencies comply with NEPA by, for example, requiring commission licensees and applicants to review their proposed actions for environmental consequences – requiring licensees to consider potential environmental effects and disclose those effects in an environmental assessment that is filed for review. In particular, regarding archaeology and the broader historic environment, the National Historic Preservation Act (NHPA) (1966, amended 1976, 1980 and 1992) is one of the federal environmental statutes implemented in the NEPA rules. Section 106 of the NHPA requires each federal agency to identify and assess the effects of its actions on historic resources. Section 106 applies when two thresholds are met:

- There is a federal or federally licensed action, including grants, licenses, and permits.
- That action has the potential to affect properties listed in or eligible for listing in the National Register of Historic Places.

The responsible federal agency must consult with appropriate state and local officials, Indian tribes, applicants for federal assistance, and members of the public and consider their views and concerns about historic preservation issues when making final project decisions. Effects are resolved by mutual agreement, usually among the affected state's State Historic Preservation Officer (SHPO) or the Tribal Historic Preservation Officer (THPO), the federal agency, and any other involved parties. The Advisory Council on Historic Preservation (ACHP) may participate in

Figure 27. Working in central government, part 2. A key part of the role of English Heritage and similar central government archaeological organizations around the world is work with stakeholders in industry. Here, English Heritage officers talk to visitors about their display at Hillhead 2010, the UK's annual International Quarrying and Recycling Show (© English Heritage National Heritage Protection Commissions 2010).

controversial or precedent-setting situations. The ACHP has also promulgated other regulations that define this process.

A broadly similar management model to that of the US is also deployed at the federal level in Canada, where Parks Canada, the Historic Sites and Monuments Board of Canada, and the Canadian Environmental Assessment Agency have responsibility for heritage management at this level under a variety of laws, most prominently the Canadian Environmental Assessment Act (2003). See Denhez (2010) for more information (the organization Indian and Northern Affairs Canada also has some responsibility for First Nation cultural heritage management at the federal level in Canada).

Advisory Council on Historic Preservation

The ACHP is an independent federal agency that promotes the preservation, enhancement, and productive use of historic resources, and advises the president and Congress on national historic preservation policy. As directed by the NHPA of 1966, the ACHP:

• Serves as the primary federal policy advisor to the president and Congress.

- Recommends administrative and legislative improvements for protecting the nation's heritage.
- Advocates full consideration of historic values in federal decision making.
- Reviews federal programs and policies to promote effectiveness, coordination, and consistency with national preservation policies.

The ACHP's three core program areas are: (1) Preservation Initiatives (focuses on partnerships and program initiatives such as heritage tourism developments); (2) Communications, Education, and Outreach (conveying the ACHP's vision and message to constituents and the general public through information and education programs); and, perhaps most crucially of all, (3) Federal Agency Programs (administration of the NHPA's Section 106 review process, including working with federal agencies to help improve the ways in which they consider historic preservation values in their programs).

Working in relation to the ACHP and the NPS under the terms of the NHPA are a variety of other federal organizations (including archaeologists) involved in historic and cultural preservation initiatives. In particular, the General Services Administration (GSA) Historic Preservation Program provides technical and strategic expertise to promote the viability, reuse, and integrity of historic buildings GSA owns, leases, and has the opportunity to acquire. This includes:

- The Center for Historic Buildings, providing national leadership for compliance with the spirit and substance of the NHPA and other stewardship directives.
- Regional historic preservation officers and technical staff (based in each of the GSA's eleven regions), providing day-to-day consultant support to ensure that regional projects and actions comply with the NHPA and are consistent with GSA policy and national stewardship strategy.

The Historic Preservation Program collaborates with other federal agencies and programs, as well with nonprofit organizations, on developing the following:

- Economical design solutions and building investment strategies to extend the useful life of historic structures and minimize the negative effects of changes needed to keep buildings safe, functional, and efficient.
- Stewardship initiatives to improve the impression buildings make on visitors, to accommodate tenant needs within a preservation framework, and to increase federal use of privately owned historic buildings.
- Strategies to make the most of available legal authorities and partnership opportunities to keep historic buildings occupied and viable – for example, by leasing underutilized federal historic buildings to private entities or transferring ownership of historic buildings no longer needed for federal use to other organizations that can provide better preservation and public access.

The US National Park Service

The NPS has a broad-based remit to study, enhance, and protect archaeological resources above, across, and under the water of the US (Figure 28). The NPS also has a responsibility to enforce extensive laws regarding historic preservation of buildings and monuments, as well as a particular responsibility in relation to the rights and cultural property of Native American communities, primarily as laid out under the Native American Graves Protection and Repatriation Act (1990). Similar to EH, the NPS also has a leadership and advisory role in the management of the historic environment.

The NPS, in particular, maintains the National Register of Historic Places (NRHP), the official list of historic places considered worthy of preservation in the US, as authorized by the NHPA. The NPS's activities in association with the NRHP are part of the much larger national program to coordinate and support public and private efforts to identify, evaluate, and protect America's historic and archaeological resources (Figure 29). There are currently more than 83,500 sites on the register, and more are added annually. Under the terms of the NHPA, the NPS (along with in some circumstances, particularly at sea, the US Bureau of Ocean Energy Management, Regulation, and Enforcement [BOEMRE, formerly known as the Minerals Management Service], discussed later) also has a major archaeological responsibility in ensuring that these rules and regulations are followed on newly discovered historic sites. Just as on state lands (where these laws are enforced by state archaeologists), if a project such as road construction, mining, or property development takes place on federal land, uses federal money, or otherwise must comply with federal regulations, then Section 106 of the NHPA comes into play, requiring identification of significant historic resources or sites (i.e., eligible for the NRHP), consideration of the potential effects of the project on those resources, and preparation of a memorandum of agreement (MOA) among all parties with prime interest in those historic resources.

US National Oceanographic and Atmospheric Administration

The US is distinctive in that the NPS is matched, so to speak, in the marine zone by the other significant federal government organization involved in archaeology and heritage management – the National Oceanic and Atmospheric Administration (NOAA), which has a similar command structure to the NPS with central, decentralized, and regional offices and operates under similar funding and legal structures. Thirteen national marine sanctuaries have been established under the National Marine Sanctuaries Act (1972) – these designate and protect areas of the marine environment with special national significance because of their conservation, recreational, ecological, historical, scientific, cultural, archaeological, educational, or aesthetic qualities as national marine sanctuaries.

The NOAA Maritime Heritage Program is responsible for the management of historic resources in relation to this act, working in partnership with other federal

161

Figure 28. Working in central government, part 3. A major part of the work of central government archaeologists is working with and promoting archaeology to the general public. Here, National Park Service underwater archaeologist Matt Russell demonstrates the use of a full-face communication mask to deaf children during outreach activities at Ellis Island, part of the Statue of Liberty National Monument, New York (© US National Park Service 2010, photograph by Brett Seymour).

Figure 29. Working in central government, part 4. Central government archaeologists undertake site visits in all different types of environments. Here, National Park Service underwater archaeologist Andres Diaz documents the bow of the sunken passenger steamer *America* at Isle Royal National Park, Michigan (© US National Park Service 2010, photograph by Brett Seymour).

management organizations such as BOEMRE and NPS. Federal law requires proper care and preservation of items of significance to the nation's historical, educational, cultural, or artistic endeavors. NOAA's Maritime Heritage Program has been particularly successful in the development of its public archaeology remit, undertaking a wide range of high-profile expeditions across the US, including those outside the formal national marine sanctuaries. Various other federal organizations have a passing role within the management of marine historic resources. Most notable of these is the Naval History and Heritage Command (formerly the Naval Historical Center), the official history program of the Department of the Navy, which includes an underwater archaeology branch operating under similar legislative frameworks to the NPS.

Central Heritage Organizations in Australia

In Australia the national heritage management situation is complicated in comparison with those of the US and UK by the variety of overlapping federal and state laws. Commonwealth (i.e., federal) legislation applies only when commonwealth decisions are required – for example, for matters of national environmental significance, Native Title, World Heritage, foreign investment, and uranium export. The commonwealth's Environment Protection and Biodiversity Conservation Act (1999) is particularly significant, defining the "environment" in an admirably holistic fashion to include the following:

- Ecosystems and their constituent parts, including people and communities.
- Natural and physical resources.
- The qualities and characteristics of locations, places, and area.
- The social, economic, and cultural aspects of a thing mentioned in the preceding three bullet points paragraph a, b, or c – a broad-based definition and law that has no comparable model in current UK law (see Lennon et al. 2001: 8–9).

In addition, under the terms of the National Reserve System Program initiated by the Natural Heritage Trust in 1996 to improve the representation of the Interim Biogeographic Regionalisation for Australia regions in the National Reserve System, there are 153 marine protected areas, including thirteen managed by the commonwealth government, some of which include historic/cultural remains (see Lennon et al. 2001: 27–29). Natural and cultural heritage are inherently and admirably intermeshed in Australia in a manner hard to ever imagine in the UK at either the national or local level, leading to an efficient and thoughtful management of these interlinked worlds.

A detailed guide to specific federal and state legislation in both the terrestrial and marine zone is provided in Smith and Burke (2007: 126–30 and 130–61); see also Lennon et al. (2001: 18–20, 148–51 and 160–62 [appendices 1 and 6]) for a review of such legislation and its operation. Table 26 of Lennon et al. (2001) in particular provides a useful comparative review of funding provided for the protection and management of historic shipwrecks in Australia between 1995 and 2000. Many mining companies and other industries that have an impact on the historic environment of Australia have also established individual or communal codes of conduct for mineral exploration – for example, the Association of Mining and Exploration Companies' Code of Conduct (AMEC 2009). This is particularly significant given the scale of extraction in some regions of Australia by major multinational organizations, such as Rio Tinto, which currently spends around nine million US dollars a year on its Australian exploration program, and which negotiated more than sixty-five Native Title agreements for access over the period 1995–2005 (Lenegan 2005).

The management situation is complicated in Australia through the requirements of native title and other Indigenous ownership/management rights (primarily those established by the Aboriginal and Torres Strait Islander Heritage Protection Act [1984], the Australian equivalent of the US Native American Graves Protection and Repatriation Act [1990]) (see Adams 2001; Greenfield 2003). However, such laws are, in many cases, the best – very often the only – protection of historic terrestrial resources on land that are directly or indirectly affected by industries such as aggregate extraction. For example, in the Australian state of Victoria, Indigenous heritage is protected via either a Cultural Heritage Management Plan (CHMP) or a permit. A CHMP considers the effects of an activity on the known and potential Indigenous sites in any area. It is mandatory if the activity area falls in an area of high cultural sensitivity (an area of known sites or high potential for sites based on predictive modeling) and it is considered a high-impact activity. If approved, a CHMP gives the proponent the go-ahead with the activity under the conditions proposed or outlined in the CHMP. Under the state of Victoria's Aboriginal Heritage Act (2006), mining is considered a high-impact activity, and hence always requires that a CHMP be undertaken. Furthermore, if a CHMP is not required, but a site is discovered inside the activity area during development, then a permit is required to disturb it.

Non-archaeological/Heritage Organizations

A variety of other organizations based within different nations' central governments have varied responsibility for archaeological as well as wider heritage matters. These include, most notably, the military (discussed later), as well as departments associated with specific industries (especially mining and energy production), transport and infrastructure, and, more broadly, various government-related funding bodies – particularly in the UK, where the national Heritage Lottery Fund is a major contributor to heritage protects in a way that the comparable lotteries of many US and Australian states are not.

Transport and Infrastructure

An example of the types of other governmental organizations that employ at least a small number of archaeologists and related heritage professionals is the organization British Waterways (covering England and Wales) and its counterpart, British Waterways Scotland, which together manage 2,200 miles of canals and rivers with more than 11 million visitors a year. Their heritage responsibilities include the management of more than 2,700 listed buildings, more than fifty scheduled monuments, more than 400 miles (640 km) of conservation area, and thousands of archaeological sites, including four World Heritage Sites, fourteen historic battlefields, and thirty-three registered historic parks and gardens.

A very different and uniquely British example is the Crown Estate, which manages land and property owned by the British state (effectively the British equivalent of federal lands in the US and Australia), and which fulfills most of the same management responsibilities shared by the NPS and the Department of the Interior's Bureau of Land Management in the US. The organization was created under the Crown Estate Act (1961) to benefit the taxpayer by paying the revenue from its assets directly to the treasury, and to enhance the value of the estate and the income it generates. The estate's portfolio has a value of more than £6 billion (2009 values) and encompasses many of the UK's cityscapes, ancient forests, farms, parkland, coastline, and communities, including hundreds of scheduled monuments, thousands of archaeological sites, and tens of thousands of listed and historic buildings. The Crown Estate also has a major role as employer, influencer, manager, guardian, facilitator, and revenue creator.

In the US, a variety of distinctive organizations exist that have a varied heritage and/or cultural resources remit. One example is the US Department of Agriculture's Natural Resources Conservation Service (NRCS) Cultural Resources Division. The NRCS considers cultural resources part of its broad-scale conservation planning remit. The stewardship of such nonrenewable cultural and historic resources is an important link in the conservation ethic that underlies the NRCS mission, under the terms of various federal, state, and local laws enacted to preserve cultural resources, most importantly the NHPA.

Another example is the US Department of Transportation's Federal Highway Administration (FHWA) Historic Preservation and Archaeology Program. This program provides guidance and technical assistance to federal, state, and local government staff regarding these federal laws, as well as regulations, executive orders, policy, procedures, and training on topics related to historic preservation and cultural resources. This includes the provision of specific guidance on archaeological sites, historic bridges (particularly encouraging states to incorporate the concepts of context sensitive design in the rehabilitation and reuse of historic bridges), and historic roads.

In a similar context, the US Fish and Wildlife Service (FWS) has an historic preservation remit as part of the National Wildlife Refuge System. These refuges also protect many of important archaeological and historic sites dating from prehistory to the present day, ranging across all of the National Wildlife Refuge System's 96 million acres spanning the diverse landscapes of North America, the Pacific Ocean, and the Caribbean Sea. Many of these cultural resources embody, in particular, values important to communities and Indian tribes that are adjacent to refuges and national fish hatcheries. Alongside the FWS, the US Forest Service similarly undertakes various heritage programs to protect significant heritage resources, share their values, and contribute relevant information and perspectives to natural resource management. To put this in context, the Forest Service is responsible for the management of more than 350,000 recorded cultural resources on national forests and grasslands.

In a rather different context, the US Federal Emergency Management Agency (FEMA) also has an Environmental Planning and Historic Preservation (EHP) Program, as it is FEMA's policy to act with care to ensure that its disaster response and recovery, mitigation, and preparedness responsibilities are carried out in a manner that is consistent with all federal environmental and historic preservation policies and laws, including the NHPA. FEMA uses all practical means and measures to protect, restore, and enhance the quality of the environment and to avoid or minimize adverse impacts to the environment, including the cultural and historic environment. The entails the objectives of:

- Achieving use of the environment without degradation or undesirable and unintended consequences.
- Preserving historic, cultural, and natural aspects of national heritage and maintaining, wherever possible, an environment that supports diversity and variety of individual choice.
- Achieving a balance between resource use and development within the sustained carrying capacity of the ecosystem involved.
- Enhancing the quality of renewable resources and working toward the maximum attainable recycling of depletable resources.

Archaeologists and other heritage professionals working for these types of organizations have a broad professional remit and a highly varied working life, liaising with local and central government authorities (and local heritage volunteer groups) in advance of and during works to heritage features under their care, writing project designs and influencing schemes of work, and in some cases leading or participating in fieldwork, analysis, and public archaeology promotion of sites. In this sense, their jobs are something of a blend of the responsiiblities of local government heritage officers on one hand and CRM archaeologists on the other. They spend the majority of their days in an office environment, but nonetheless will undertake a significant amount of on-site work, doing visits to sites in advance of and during developments, meeting the CRM archaeologists employed, and speaking to the different groups involved. Archaeologists working for the Crown Estate in particular are also responsible for large tracts of seabed within the UK's twelve-nautical-mile territorial sea zone, and so may have, in particular, specialized marine archaeological background and responsibilities, liaising, similar to their BOEMRE colleages in the US, with marine industry representatives and dealing with the distinctive types of survey data that result from seabed search and survey schemes.

Role of the Military

The Ministry of Defence in the UK, Department of Defense in the US, and Department of Defence in Australia all employ a number of archaeologists working across all three branches of the services, and usually collaborating closely with other government, as well as industry, colleagues. As noted earlier, the US Department of the Navy operates the Naval History and Heritage Command, including a dedicated Underwater Archaeology Branch. The UK, meanwhile, manages many hundreds of archaeological sites as well as historic buildings on its property through its Defence Estates section, which has a Built Estate and Heritage subdepartment.

The US similarly undertakes considerable work on military lands under the aegis of the US Army Corps of Engineers (USACE), as well as under the broader remit of the Department of Defense (DoD). In the US in particular, the DoD is the steward of the nation's largest inventory of federally owned or managed historic sites, including 73 national historic landmarks, 694 entries on the NRHP, and more than 19,000 individual historic properties, including more than 16,700 known archaeological sites and 3,200 historic buildings. Under the Office of the Secretary of Defense's (OSD's) Environmental Management Directorate, the Federal Preservation Office functions as the historic preservation policy entity for all DoD historic properties. In addition, OSD's Legacy Resource Management Program has provided millions of dollars in financial assistance to protect and enhance cultural resources on DoD lands while supporting military readiness. In a related context, the US Department of Veterans Affairs (VA) Office of Construction and Facilities Management has a small Historic Preservation Office that keeps information about VA's programs to comply with federal preservation requirements, as well as information about VA history, especially regarding historic building preservation issues (not historical or genealogical research data, such as veterans' military service or patient residency records, which are the responsibility of other organizations).

Even more so than the transport and infrastructure archaeologists and other heritage professionals discussed earlier, individuals working for the different branches of the military have an extremely broad professional remit and a highly varied working life, involving in some circumstances travel to locations anywhere in the world where military units are deployed and need guidance on the management of cultural heritage. This can involve extremely complex negotiations with local communities on one hand, and military authorities on the other, on how to manage historic sites while fitting into often much larger operational demands such as base security. For example, US and British archaeologists faced a tremendous challenge during and after the coalition invasion of Iraq in 2003, when they had to assist in local management of historic sites and museums – often in the face of armed looters – while simultaneously advising their own military authorities on how to avoid damaging historic sites. Some of these coalition bases were on extremely sensitive historic sites, most famously the historic city of Babylon, which suffered considerable damage when sections of the city were turned into a large military base in 2003. As a consequence of such damage, a vociferous lobby within the wider archaeological community (especially in Europe) have argued that archae-ologists fundamentally fail in their professional ethical responsibility if they work with, or for, military authorities either at home or abroad (see Rothfield, 2009). Such debate, however, ignores the more common and mundane experiences of archaeologists working alongside the military at the domestic level, advising the authorities, for instance, on changes to the military bases that cover thousands of square miles in the UK and hundreds of thousands of square miles in the US and Australia, as well as on training every rank of service personnel from all branches on basic good practice to, and the identification of, heritage features.

US Bureau of Ocean Energy Management, Regulation, and Enforcement

In the US, the Bureau of Ocean Energy Management, Regulation and Enforce-ment (BOEMRE) (formerly the Minerals Management Service, part of the US Department of the Interior) plays a significant role in mineral- and mining-related heritage management on land and under the sea. Akin to the NPS on land, the NHPA requires BOEMRE to take into account the effect of a proposed project on any historic property (including archaeological sites and monuments) under the terms of the secretary of the interior's standards for assessing "historical signifi-cance" and to afford the Advisory Council on Historic Preservation (ACHP) an opportunity to comment, including on sites on the outer continental shelf leased by the federal government for oil, gas, and sulfur extraction and related pipelines and infrastructure. In the marine zone in particular, BOEMRE, as a federal bureau, is required to ensure that activities it funds (e.g., environmental studies) and activities it permits, such as lease sales, the drilling of oil and gas wells, and the construction of pipelines, do not adversely affect significant archaeological sites on the federal outer continental shelf.

BOEMRE also undertakes proactive work on historic sites, under auspices of its own archaeological teams and commonly in collaboration with state heritage organ-izations, industry, and academia, both implicitly and explicitly aimed toward public archaeological agendas – and, in some cases, including the specific production of teaching resources. Such work is, in particular, funded under the long-running Environmental Studies Program, initiated in 1973 to gather and synthesize infor-mation to support decision making concerning the offshore oil and gas program under the terms of the Outer Continental Shelf Lands Act and Submerged Lands Act (both of 1953), which set the federal government's title and ownership of submerged lands at three miles from a state's coastline.

The following are examples of recently funded projects:

- Proactive, desk-based resource assessments of areas of high archaeological poten-tial undertaken on the basis of reactive report data submitted by industry.
- Noninvasive fieldwork using remote sensing and divers/remotely operated vehicles (ROVs) on specific identified single or multiple archaeological sites at risk.

169

- Invasive and noninvasive fieldwork on specific archaeological sites that allows methodological experimentation with new tools and techniques (especially deep-water investigation).
- Noninvasive analyses of the impact of specific invasive human activities on archaeological sites.
- Desk-based and remote-sensing modeling of site location probabilities.

A Day in the Life

Although the organizations described earlier manage millions of square miles of land and seabed, and hundreds of thousands of archaeological sites, landscapes, and historic buildings, the reality of daily life for most of the people who work for such organizations is far more localized. Just as a soldier is one small part of the wider military community, so on a daily basis the majority of the archaeologists at work for central government (except for those who are very senior or involved in strategy) generally know or work alongside only a few colleagues, are based in localized offices, and have a fairly focused remit and responsibility. Consequently, making generalizations about a day in the life of a central government archaeologist can be very hard to do. A few generalizations are useful, however, as much as to define what such archaeologists do *not* do, and what in general their working conditions are. Although organizations such as EH and the NPS provide many opportunities, there are no organizations that will suit all comers (Table 8).

Most important of all, it must be made clear that although central government organizations such as those described in this chapter do employ a significant number of archaeologists, extremely few of those archaeologists actually do any regular or extensive archaeological fieldwork. If your desire is to work extensively on excavating actual archaeological sites, then organizations such as these should not be your target – it would be far better to work either for a CRM archaeology firm or to become an academic. Although a significant proportion of such archaeologists will also get to undertake site visits, the majority of central government archaeologists' work is desk- or at least office-based and includes the following:

- Managing a specific site or series of sites; liaising with owners, users, and other stakeholders; identifying impacts to these sites; and devising management regimes, especially to deal with current and future threats.
- Meeting with other heritage professionals and stakeholders to share best practice, policy, and guidance, or meeting with non-heritage communities (including members of government, civil servants, industry, and the like) to explain policy and management principles.
- Analyzing new evidence collected by other archaeologists to inform the understanding of a specific site or series of sites, informing policy and management guidance on a site's local, regional, national, or even international scale.
- Writing reports and other publications and giving presentations on a specific site or series of sites, to promote the public understanding of these locations.

TABLE 8. The Pros and Cons of Working in Central Government Archaeology

Pros	Cons
Job security – often permanent, relatively well paid: central governments do not (generally) go bankrupt.	It can be frustrating to watch decisions being made by other sections of government that contradict what you feel is best for archaeology.
Pensions and other benefits provided by the government sector, such as sports and family facilities, private health care, discounted rates at specific shops and services.	Higher-level political decisions can affect your sector and security – a change in central administration can see funding priorities change and jobs placed under threat.
The right post can be very varied – a mix of site-specific issues and broader objectives.	Can be dull, both in types of sites analyzed and types of decisions made.
Stability – usually based out of one office and doing day site visits. This makes it easier if you are in a relationship/family or have regular personal commitments that tie you to one location.	Limited opportunity to do any "dirt" field archaeology and/or research. Opportunities for travel outside your area can be few.
Can make a real impact on preservation and analysis of sites.	
Prestige – you are part of local government, so other people see it as reputable; some jobs also involve a uniform and clear role of service to your country akin to that of the military.	Have to put up with corporate, management-heavy structure common in central government. Other archaeologists may resent you as being part of the power structure.
You can make good contacts for future jobs and it looks good on a CV.	
Good career structure within the archaeological community and government sector itself (regular pay progression based on performance is common in the first few years of such a job).	The right opportunity can take a long time to appear – people often stay in the same job for many years. There are not many posts.
There are usually good opportunities for internal and external training and professional development; this can include negotiating paid/unpaid leave for further study.	

Alongside this, organizations such as EH in particular employ a growing number of individuals with highly specialized skills, for whom archaeological expertise is not necessarily the most important skill required:

- *Antique and antiquities specialists*: Many of the historic properties under the care of organizations such as EH and the NPS include hundreds of thousands of rare historic items, ranging in scope from clothes, ornaments, and other personal possessions through household goods such as kitchen and cleaning ware, furniture, art, clocks, and other antiques, up to ancient vehicles such as carriages, cars, and even boats, as well as oddities such as garden furniture and statues.
- *Engineers*: On one hand, many historic buildings have a need for specialist maintenance and repair by structural engineers with experience in historic buildings; on the other hand, there are also various engineering features of historic properties – including actual historic engineering equipment and features – that need management.
- *Historic buildings and gardens officers*: Historic buildings need constant maintenance and management, often involving detailed documentary research as well as specialist work on different types of construction and roofing technique and the like. Similarly, many historic properties also include ancient parks, gardens, and other designed or managed landscapes that need specialist knowledge and management.
- *Librarians, archivists, and conservation specialists*: EH's NMR maintains more than 10 million historic documents of virtually every form of media it is possible to archive; many of the historic properties under the care of EH include hundreds of thousands of such items. These materials need constant specialist maintenance and, in some cases, conservation; they also need interpretation and management through resources such as GIS and other computer applications.
- *Planners and lawyers*: Expertise in general planning and planning law is an increasingly necessary skill for a large section of local, as well as central, government heritage professionals.
- *Scientists*: EH's Central Ancient Monuments Laboratory is a international center of expertise in archaeological science, especially in different dating techniques, but also includes specialist skills such as environmental analysis and sampling (including soil and water chemistry and the like), human and animal pathology, and osteology, most of which have a basis in different sectors of the hard sciences of chemistry, biology, or physics.
- *Surveyors*: Specialist skills in detailed surveying of buildings, landscapes, and sites is an important and highly transferable skill, as are related skills in mapping and planning (including digital work and the use of GIS), as well as familiarity with old and new types of data, including air photos and LiDAR survey data. In the marine zone, this can include expertise in hydrographic survey tools such as towed sonar, sub-bottom profilers and magnetometers, and the data that are derived from such tools.

- *Teachers and actors*: EH employs hundreds of staff to undertake different forms of community outreach and involvement, many of whom have some experience or a background in teaching, at every age group from preschool to lifelong learning. Many of these officers may have particular additional expertise, for instance in drama and historic reenactment, arts and crafts, or simply in lively public presentation, or expertise in working with specific groups, such as the mentally or physically handicapped.

Some people simply want to work for the government – the desire to actively serve the country is a very real issue for many government heritage professionals in the US in particular where, for example, members of the NPS have a uniform and an array of insignia. Similarly, NOAA has a selective uniformed branch known as the Commissioned Corps Officers, wearing a uniform similar to that worn by commissioned officers of the US Navy; so too do heritage professionals employed by the USACE. These branches have the most visible evidence of service, but many other nonuniformed heritage professionals in central and local government share a desire to do something worthwhile in the service of their country.

This being government, pay, additional benefits, and conditions in such roles are acceptable if not exceptional – certainly comparable to, and in many cases slightly better than, many other sectors of the heritage profession. A few heritage professionals working for central government also get additional benefits – most notably, in the case of organizations such as EH, a limited number of "tied" houses, the provision of permanent accommodation on site for those individuals working at a specific historic property, especially if that property is particularly remote or in need of a constant professional presence on site. The benefits of such a perk can be great (if nothing else, free or greatly subsidized accommodation costs), alongside benefits such as off-hours access to unique locations and, of course, a commute to work that can usually be measured in minutes. The downsides of such an arrangement are equally obvious, however – the central government heritage officer (and family) lives at work and can never get away from it. But this is a rare situation – most central government heritage officers commute to central offices just as anyone else does; an increasing number are also home-based, logging on to secure central computer networks. Best of all, because governments do not, in general, go bankrupt, job security is usually much better than in the private sector. Government employees also usually benefit from extremely good insurance and pension schemes, again often in positive comparison with the private sector.

Career Structure, Qualifications, and Experience

As with all the other heritage sectors, supply exceeds demand in central government heritage organizations. There are usually dozens, if not hundreds, of applicants for every post that arises, although this is often less so for specialist officers and/or those based at particular historic sites, for whom very defined skills and expertise may be required. Consequently, central government heritage organizations can, and tend to be, extremely choosy about whom they appoint, requiring a high level of demonstrable specialist skills, qualifications, and expertise. The vast majority of archaeologists working in this sector have at least an MA in archaeology or a related subject; a significant percentage of the staff also has a PhD or equivalent. Alongside this usually comes extensive practical experience – there are extremely few entry-level positions for specialists at least, most of whom are recruited from the ranks of existing heritage professionals already working in the CRM archaeology industry or local government, who tend to be lured by better job security on one hand, and new opportunities on the other.

Career structure and progression can also be relatively problematic in this sector; progression, especially so. It is extremely easy to get trapped as a specialist in central government heritage, as much as anything because with so few jobs and so many highly qualified people, the only obvious career path is not sideways but directly up – into the shoes of the existing manager (also normally the manager of many dozens or more colleagues) who may either be perfectly happy where he or she is or else is stymied, at a higher level, by the same problem – the next-level manager will not or cannot move up, and so on.

The above being said, all is not lost for someone who wants to be a central government heritage professional. Two other methods exist:

- *Volunteers*: Many historic sites managed by central government happily accept unpaid volunteers. This may be as low-level as selling entry tickets, but can include, or rapidly lead to promotion to, more interesting roles such as acting as a guide to the site or working on education and outreach programs. Volunteers are well placed to get the jump on those few entry-level job opportunities that arise, and if nothing else, gain a new network of contacts and potential referees.
- *Interns*: Central government offices regularly have opportunities for interns, normally but not always unpaid. This is particularly so for archaeology and other heritage profession students already enrolled in related university courses, especially postgraduate courses. These are no different from mainstream industry and government internships – the employer gets to see what the current crop of students is like, work them hard, and potentially cherry-pick the best for jobs; the interns get insider experience, contacts, and if they work hard and are lucky, the inside track on jobs.

The key in both these cases is that such placements and internships are rarely advertised – they are given to those who ask and who, having asked, work diligently without complaint.

Interviewee: Dave

How did you first become involved in archaeology?

My first experience with archeology (we Yanks spell it without the posh "ae") was with Donny Hamilton's underwater field excavations at Port Royal, Jamaica, in

1987. After that I worked as a volunteer in Bermuda, on projects in Greece, and with the National Park Service in Florida.

What is your present job?

I am currently chief of the National Park Service's Submerged Resources Center (SRC), a division of the United States federal government. Our responsibility includes documenting, interpreting to the public, and protecting submerged cultural resources in 130 national parks, comprising approximately 3.5 million acres of submerged lands and as much coastline as the country of Brazil.

What qualifications do you hold? Where and what did you study?

I have a BA in anthropology from Reed College in Portland Oregon, an MSc in maritime archeology from Oxford University, an MA in anthropology and archeology from Brown University, and a PhD in anthropology and archeology from Brown University. In addition to academic qualifications, I feel it is just as important to seek out and maintain advanced diving qualifications for underwater archeologists. I am a NAUI scuba instructor and hold certifications in multiple types of diving, including deep, technical mixed-gas rebreathers and commercial hard-hat diving. Over the years I have also picked up numerous computer and mechanical skills that I use regularly.

What are your terms of employment, working conditions, or other job benefits?

I am a full-time, career United States government employee.

How did you get your current job? What do you feel was most helpful to you in gaining this position?

I got my current job by taking what I had and building on it both in terms of experience and by networking. I moved upward in my career by accepting the generous assistance of the people I worked for who thought I had done a good job and wanted to help me. I started with the National Park Service as a volunteer and then took whatever opportunities were presented to me or that I could create for myself to gain additional skills or experience.

What is the best thing about being an archaeologist?

The best part of archeology is that it is fundamentally a derivative science in the sense that most of the techniques and ideas we use are derived from other areas of intellectual inquiry. In that regard, as a practicing archeologist you are free to use your imagination to get to an understanding of people's lives in the past via ethnohistory or nuclear physics, depending on your intellectual inclinations and adaptability. Also, by and large although we all serve someone, we are free to exercise our curiosity and imagination in our daily lives.

What is the worst thing about being an archaeologist?

The unfortunate view, on the part of some of my colleagues, is that there is a limited amount of good to go around so that if someone is doing well, it ultimately comes at your expense. This has led to some of the most small-minded and unflattering behavior I have ever seen anywhere – bickering and ugly personal attacks. Part of this is understandable, in the sense that archeological excavations are unrepeatable scientific endeavors and therefore the credibility of some archeological explanations is carried by weight of personality. Building up a personality or tearing one down is therefore a sad part of the field.

What do you consider to be your greatest achievement in or contribution to archaeology so far?

Working with and encouraging my colleagues and seeing how their work complements my own. Contributing to the emerging professionalism of the subdiscipline of underwater archeology. Helping preserve, protect, and share America's underwater history.

What is the one thing that you would change about archaeology if you could?

I would insist on higher standards for underwater archeology – higher standards for methodology, ethics, publishing, and outreach. Some substandard practitioners in the field still try to wrap their shoddy work in the macho of underwater archeology, or insist that because it's hard that somehow makes poor work, meager publishing, and slipshod ethics acceptable.

What is your top tip for pursuing a career in archaeology?

I would never underestimate the power of reputation (good or bad) in a small field such as archeology – play fair and nicely, help out those below you as others have helped you. Don't forget that the ass you kick today may be the ass you have to kiss tomorrow. Celebrate the success of your colleagues, and by giving a little bit, you will get a little bit. Be generous with your time and ideas – others will see and appreciate it. Do not succumb to the myth of the "limited good."

What do you see yourself doing in ten years' time?

I will still be working in the National Park Service, trying to ride herd on a bunch of people who will be much smarter and more talented than I am, doing archeology we can only dream about now and protecting our underwater heritage for the future.

Chapter 7

Public and Community Archaeology

Introduction

For a long time, archaeologists were generally mysterious individuals largely unknown to the general population. Even if on rare occasion someone knew an archaeologist, he or she probably would not know much about that archaeologist's daily life and would be even less likely to read about the archaeologist's work in the media or visit his or her place of work. After a tentative beginning in the 1950s, though, and an exponential expansion from the 1970s, public archaeology has now become a major component of any archaeologist's life. There are entire careers to be forged in the business of this final chapter – the business of telling nonprofessionals about archaeology, getting them involved, and working for and alongside them.

The most distinctive aspect of this sector is undoubtedly the TV archaeologists whose work regularly attracts millions of viewers per episode. Some TV archaeologists are genuine household names, and they are a recognized cause of a rise in university applications for archaeology courses. Such shows, airing around the world (particularly on the hugely popular Discovery Channel), have had a significant impact on popular culture – so much so that one of the most common questions that an archaeologist is likely to get asked these days on meeting someone new is, "Would I have seen you on TV?", a strong indication of how deeply enmeshed into popular culture archaeology has become.

Despite these observations, however, "public" archaeology remains the most difficult part of archaeology to define, not least in terms of professional pathways into a career. All the different archaeological careers outlined in the previous chapters include within them some aspect of public and/or community archaeology – ways of intermeshing archaeology into the daily lives of millions of people around the world, whether they are aware of this or not. Beyond TV, for example, there is a massive public archaeology industry at work, deeply enmeshed within all aspects of the wider archaeological profession. Indeed, the only reason that this particular aspect of the archaeological career path is discussed in a separate chapter rather than blended into the previous chapters is the sheer extent of different opportunities in public archaeology, and the cross-fertilization of skills not only across archaeology, but also with related industries. The key to bear in mind on reading the remainder of this chapter is that *all* archaeologists are (or at least should be) public archaeologists. The broad-ranging skill sets of archaeologists should always include how best to work alongside communities and communicate the value of archaeology to society (Figure 30).

Public Archaeology Organizations

It is useful to begin by outlining the major different groupings discussed in this chapter. Often these overlap, but some distinctive priorities and skills can be identified that help make sense of the situation:

- *Teaching archaeology at the school level*: A small and, sadly, declining number of schoolteachers have archaeological qualifications and teach archaeology, usually (but not exclusively) to students in the 14- to 18-year-old age range. In the UK in particular, the tightening of the national curriculum has made this harder and harder to do, as archaeology is not a core subject and must be integrated into other curriculum aspects, such as history and geography. Those who remain should not be forgotten – they are often the first people to introduce students to the concept of archaeology and are often the cause of a lifelong fascination with or even a career in the subject. A rather larger range of individuals employed by educational and outreach organizations, however, are involved in the creation and delivery of archaeology-themed teaching materials to schoolchildren of all ages, from primary school onward.
- *Archaeological outreach and lobbying organizations*: There are many national archaeology outreach/lobbying organizations: for example, three in the UK are the Council for British Archaeology, Rescue: the British Archaeological Trust, and the Nautical Archaeology Society. Such organizations usually have a small membership fee for dedicated supporters, but also gain financing from public and private sources to make archaeology more visible in, and accessible to, communities; by providing archaeological training and fieldwork courses, publications, talks, and other events; and by lobbying central and local governments to invest more in archaeology. Such organizations are joined by numerous other archaeological organizations, some of whose membership mainly comprises professional archaeologists and that have thousands of members spread across the world, others whose membership is more commonly comprised of avocational archaeologists

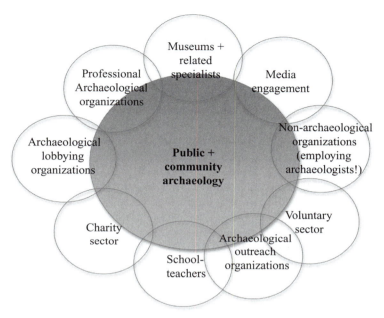

Figure 30. The structure and interrelationships of the public and community archaeology sector.

and whose membership numbers may be rather smaller and more regionally or locally focused. The latter, in particular, are one of the best and most effective ways for people to first become involved in archaeology, as the thousands of such organizations that exist around the world have an enthusiastic local membership offering regular events close to almost everyone's home.

- *Professional archaeological organizations*: Organizations such as the Institute for Archaeologists in the UK, the Register of Professional Archaeologists in the US, and the Australian Association of Consulting Archaeologists in Australia promote professionalism in archaeology through regulation of their membership and creation of and adherence to codes of conduct and standards. Members must demonstrate, through submission of a portfolio and CV, that they have appropriate skills, training, and experience, although "noncorporate" grades of membership are usually available for supporters of the precepts of these organizations who do not have formal qualifications or experience, or who are just starting out in their careers as professional archaeologists. Such organizations also undertake outreach and advocacy, and lobby government and industry for better standards and laws.
- *Heritage organizations*: Organizations such as the National Trust in Britain, the National Trust of Australia, and the National Trust for Historic Preservation in the US are private, nonprofit charitable organizations that manage (and, in many cases, own) hundreds of historic sites and thousands of square miles of land. As a

consequence, these organizations also manage and maintain many archaeological sites and employ archaeologists and related heritage professionals to look after these sites and properties and engage with and involve the community in their understanding and curation.

- *Archaeology and the media*: A very small number of archaeologists make some of their career in the media, primarily presenting TV shows on the subject. As discussed later, the truth is that almost without exception, such individuals also have other jobs, based within CRM archaeology organizations or university archaeology departments, as there is simply not enough constant work in TV alone to generate a regular or reliable income. A much larger number of archaeologists, however, are far more regularly involved in, and in some cases make an entire living from, work in either print or online media, writing and editing for popular archaeology magazines such as *British Archaeology* and *Current Archaeology* in the UK and *Archaeology Magazine* in the US. Some of these individuals also regularly contribute to other mainstream scientific journals such as *Smithsonian Magazine*, *Popular Science*, *Discover Magazine*, *New Scientist*, and the like. Others work wholly in online media, such as the Archaeology Channel or About.com: Archaeology.
- *Museum archaeologists*: As discussed later, a wide variety of museums around the world also employ archaeologists alongside numerous other related heritage and conservation professionals in a complex career path that is too detailed to explore here and that should rather be the subject of another book. Museum-based archaeologists often undertake research and lead fieldwork projects in a manner very similar to (in some cases, identical) their closely related colleagues in university archaeology departments. Such archaeologists also help design and curate both temporary and permanent displays, give talks and lectures to visitors, and write guidebooks to displays and their specialist subject fields.
- *Non-archaeological organizations*: A small number of non-archaeological community organizations also employ archaeologists. Most notably in the UK this means the Church of England, which has a very small team of archaeologists and other heritage professionals (especially buildings historians, architects, and the like) advising a much wider voluntary community involved in the upkeep of the Church of England's tens of thousands of historic properties (ranging from cathedrals to tiny chapels by way of thousands of other properties of all types), including advising on archaeological work within the grounds of such properties.

Lifestyles, Career Structures, and Qualifications

Making generalizations about lifestyles and careers in public archaeology is even harder than for other sectors of the discipline; careers in this sector are not common and follow no regular pattern in terms of lifestyle or structure – most of the practitioners have ended up in their particular post through a mixture of chance and experience. Perhaps the only generalities that can be made come down to attitude and experience (Table 9).

TABLE 9. The Pros and Cons of Working in Public Archaeology

Pros	Cons
Stimulation of meeting/working with people from all walks of life who are excited by archaeology.	Pay is often low, and almost all contracts are fixed-term, with few benefits but long hours.
Ideal if you like meeting people and are enthusiastic; you can get very life-affirming responses of people, especially kids, who catch on to your enthusiasm.	Employers may be unable to offer leave for training opportunities because they do not have the spare capacity or money.
Teaching can be rewarding and exciting.	Can become frustrating after a while to always present entry-level archaeology, not much in-depth work.
	There are rarely opportunities to undertake any higher-level writing/research, or even to get really involved in an excavation or other project – you may always be only scratching the surface all the time to help others progress their skills.
Can involve opportunities for travel.	Money is almost always tight, so projects usually run on a shoestring, costs are cut, and so on. You might end up living pretty rough for weeks on end to keep the project on budget.
	Projects are often relatively short-term, so you may not get to see the long-term development of a site and its analysis.
Can help sites to become better protected/managed/understood, and you can get to meet and influence a wide range of people – from the general public to government officials, even, occasionally, celebrities.	Can be dull and have quite a lot of repetitive office/admin work to do with your organization.
	Can feel like an uphill struggle to get things done or make major changes in the face of public and government disinterest.
Sense of community – people involved in public archaeology are usually very friendly and social; they like people and want to communicate.	Limited career structure – the right opportunity can take a long time to appear.
	Most people advance by leaving one job and trading up to another post with a different employer on the basis of their CV – which often works, but can be risky.

Attitude

More than anything else, those working in public archaeology must have a tremendously positive attitude. When it comes down to it, public archaeology is about sales – selling archaeology. Archaeology is sold through making it accessible, interesting and fun; when challenged with meeting many different people day after day and explaining archaeology to them in an accessible manner, only the most upbeat and enthusiastic individuals cope (Figure 31). There are precious few chances to relax or take downtime under such circumstances – if a party of 45 excited eight-year-olds are turning up at your museum, then even if it is raining and you are worrying about your house insurance, you must be cheery, approachable, and enthusiastic or you will fail in your job at the most fundamental level. You also need to be willing to make a fool of yourself in public, and be ruthless in the pursuit of your organization's ends. Most public archaeology organizations are charities of one form or another and have the tightest of finances; as a result, they must be shameless in pursuing funding and support from the public, industry, and government alike.

Experience

Without exception, those working in public archaeology have previous experience in other types of archaeological work itself, and quite commonly other transferable skills as well, especially formal teaching qualifications or extensive teaching experience (especially among particular ages or skill groups of children). Archaeology is an experience-based profession, so it is very hard to tell others about archaeological sites, finds, or working practices without good personal knowledge and experience of the discipline. There are virtually no entry-level jobs in this sector; most people working full-time in the sector have either moved sideways into it from a related archaeological specialty – for example, working as an archaeologist for a CRM archaeology firm that also has an outreach team, helping out that team at first on odd jobs and moving fully into it when a position opens up – or they get hired directly as public archaeologists on the basis of their previous experience.

As noted earlier, experience might be in archaeological work itself, or experience and training in teaching techniques that enhance the experience of participants in a project. Other useful transferable skills commonly noted among this community are the range of skills that mark professional communicators – on one hand, formal skills such as knowing different languages, being a good artist, or having handiwork or craft skills, and on the other hand more informal skills linked to the previous point about attitude, such as a personable manner; an ability to explain things in a clear, concise, and unpatronizing way; and, above all, confidence in public speaking.

Given this information, the career path for a budding public archaeologist is relatively clear: first, get a degree (or multiple degrees) in archaeology; second, get experience working as an archaeologist; third, if having achieved the first two steps you still feel that you have the right attitude to do well in the business of communicating archaeology, explore the possibilities that present themselves

Figure 31. Public archaeology in action, part 1. Public engagement is one of the most enjoyable parts of any archaeological project. Here, archaeologists from the Thames Discovery Programme and the Portable Antiquities Scheme talk to visitors to their display at the Tower of London, during the Festival of British Archaeology in July 2010 (© Nathalie Cohen / Thames Discovery Programme 2010).

to you – perhaps first volunteering to do site tours for a project on which you are working, getting a placement to work with an existing outreach team of your current employer (or even volunteer to create a new such team if one does not exist), or approaching existing public archaeology organizations to see what opportunities might be available.

Teaching Archaeology at the School Level

The lifestyle and career of those teaching archaeology at the school level is ultimately determined by how such people are employed. Those lucky enough to be formally employed by a school as a teacher (a minority) will benefit from the conditions and salaries of the teaching sector; the downside will be that they will have to teach far more than just archaeology, will be tied to the school calendar cycle, and will have to undertake additional management/administrative duties – all of which means that the actual amount of time doing or thinking about archaeology can be small.

Alternatively, a number of organizations (dedicated outreach organizations such as those discussed in more detail later, and a growing number of museums, CRM archaeology firms, and even national and local government heritage departments) have teams dedicated to producing school-based archaeological outreach materials such as lesson plans, teaching packs, and the like. Such teams also undertake formal teaching – either going into schools to lead a class or event, or providing on-site and evening/out-of-term activities. The upside of this second group is that its members get to think about and do much more archaeology, have a more varied and flexible working day, and do not need to do the kinds of administration and management with which the teaching sector is bedeviled; the downside is that they do not enjoy the same benefits – particularly in terms of length of contract, pay, and conditions – that are fairly standard for teachers. Meanwhile, because of the constraints of the curriculum, there are virtually no jobs for teachers solely specializing in archaeology – all teach other subjects (primarily, but not exclusively, history, as discussed later), and must find their own ways of integrating archaeology into the curriculum.

As already noted, members of the latter group are undoubtedly the more populous school-sector archaeologists, and also have a more distinctive and different "day in the life"; that of the former, the full-time schoolteachers, in all honesty does not vary dramatically from that of any other schoolteacher of any other subject. A day in the life of school-sector archaeologists will generally depend on whether they are preparing materials for outreach or presenting these materials: during the former period, they will be office-based, researching the materials and stories behind their lesson plans and teaching materials and developing these materials, as well as doing administration – contacting partner schools and teachers, and very important, usually chasing new sources of funding or sponsorship. During the latter period, such individuals will be even busier and may be anywhere from a classroom to a beach to the middle of a field – despite the health and safety issues and time demands on the busy modern teaching schedule, parents and teachers alike remain keen on the types of hands-on activities that archaeology-related teaching can provide. Archaeology, being the study of the material remains of the human past, offers room for teaching across the curriculum – if people do something in the present there is usually some analogy for similar activity in the past, so archaeology relates to much more than just history. For instance, archaeology can relate to the following subjects:

- *Biology*: human evolution; the uses and domestication of different plants and animals as resources by humans; the spread of such plants and animals around the world.
- *Chemistry*: the composition of different historical materials, such as ancient metals and ceramics.
- *English*: the development of language and communication skills; the past as a source of inspiration of creative writing exercises.
- *Geography*: the development of the landscape; long- and short-term changes in relative levels of sea and land; human responses to climate change.
- *Mathematics*: ancient counting systems; forms of absolute and relative dating; the development and spread of different forms of currency (relating more tangentially to economics and the history of banking).
- *Physics*: the science behind ancient engineering tools and projects; for instance, how ancient societies built things such as the pyramids without modern machines.
- *Physical education*: ancient sports and related practices; ancient societies' views on mental and physical health and well-being.

Archaeological Outreach Organizations

Lifestyles and careers of individuals employed by archaeological outreach and wider heritage organizations depend on a series of factors outlined in this section. These two related sectors are dealt with in one section here because, at least in terms of public archaeology job opportunities and conditions, they have much in common. Most such organizations that fall into this grouping have a wide range of commitments that mean their staff almost inevitably multitask. For example, the UK's national amenity archaeological society, the Council for British Archaeology (CBA), has the following circumstances:

- *Size and reach of the organization*: a nonprofit educational charity, a national organization founded in 1943, with more than 6,000 members (and more than 3,000 additional members in its youth branch the Young Archaeologists Club).
- *Aims and objectives of the organization*: three strategic objectives: (1) participation (creating new opportunities for participation in and the popular audience of archaeology, promoting the development of skills and learning opportunities at a local level, especially for people under 25); (2) discovery (enabling and supporting research to advance knowledge of archaeology, providing a platform for the archaeological community to communicate and engage with others, and making new thinking in archaeological research accessible to nonspecialist audiences); and (3) advocacy (championing the role of the voluntary sector in

185

archaeological research, campaigning to ensure that archaeology has a place in education and lifelong learning, and promoting care of the historic environment through key partnerships with the private sector, industry, and government).

- *Organization's membership groupings*: drawn from all sectors of society, including professional and avocational archaeologists of all ages and backgrounds; the CBA has fourteen regional groups across the UK, and the YAC has seventy local branches.
- *Funding sources of the organization*: an income and expenditure of around £1 million a year; the majority of expenditure (97 percent) goes directly to the CBA's charitable activities, with only a tiny 1 percent spent on governance/adminstration and the remaining 2 percent on generating income; funding derived from a mix of annual membership subscriptions, donations and bequests, central government funding, and industry sponsorship.
- *Related organizations, events, or other commitment*: has a major commitment to support the YAC, the networks of regional branches of both the CBA and YAC, and publication of the popular magazine *British Archaeology* six times a year and the CBA *Newsletter* three times a year; hosts the Festival of British Archaeology across two weeks in July and August every year, with around 500 excavation open days, guided tours, exhibitions, lectures, ancient art and craft workshops and much more reaching more than 100,000 individuals; CBA staff comprises a total of 28 staff, based mainly in the central offices in York.

Sadly, the opportunities to work for organizations such as the CBA are slim; with tight operating budgets in the best of times, the recent recession has seriously hurt this sector, as on one hand, membership drops as people choose to save money by not renewing their menbership in such organizations, and on the other hand, government and industry support declines as investment income declines and spare capital for supporting community engagement dries up. As a consequence, organizations such as these are, if anything, cutting rather than expanding the number of positions they offer, and increasingly are relying on either part-time or volunteer staff. This is especially so among local archaeological societies, the size of which have meant that they traditionally have extremely small budgets, too small to ever justify or employ full-time staff.

As noted earlier in this section, lifestyles and careers of individuals employed by archaeological outreach and wider heritage organizations are very similar in terms of public archaeology job opportunities and conditions. Organizations such as the National Trust (NT) in Britain, the National Trust of Australia, and the National Trust for Historic Preservation in the US all employ archaeologists along similar terms to those described in relation to the CBA. Perhaps the only significant difference is in the scale of these organizations and thus their relative impact on the job market. For example, the National Trust in Australia owns or manages more than 300 heritage places, has a volunteer workforce of 7,000, and employs about 350 people nationwide. It has more than 50,000 members and more than 1 million annual visitors to its properties; in comparison, the National Trust in the UK owns or manages more than 350 heritage places and more than 623,000 acres

(970 square miles) of land, manages a volunteer workforce of more than 52,000, and employs about 10,000 people nationwide. It has more than 3.5 million members and more than 12 million annual visitors to its properties. Consequently, in the UK in particular, the National Trust is both a major employer of heritage professionals (archaeological and otherwise) and also a major training ground for future such professionals: many people begin their careers as National Trust volunteers before moving on into the professional sector when they have formal qualifications to back up their experience.

Archaeologists and other heritage professionals working for organizations such as the NT have a broad professional remit and a highly varied working life, liaising with local and central government authorities (as well as local heritage volunteer groups) in advance of and during works to heritage features under their care, writing project designs and influencing schemes of work, and in many cases leading or participating in fieldwork, analysis, and public archaeology promotion of sites. The NT also maintains for its own estate a version of the HERs managed by local authorities, so there is a place also for specialists in this type of data management. Furthermore, akin to the archaeologists working for the Crown Estate, those working for the NT are also responsible for large stretches of coastline owned by the NT, and so may have in particular specialized marine archaeological backgrounds and responsibilities. In this sense, their jobs are something of a blend of the responsibilities of local government heritage officers on one hand and CRM archaeologists on the other. They spend the majority of their days in an office environment, but nonetheless will undertake a significant amount of on-site work, doing visits to sites in advance of and during developments, meeting CRM archaeologists employed and speaking to different groups involved. However, archaeologists working for organizations such as the NT will also tend to work extremely closely with natural environment specialists such as biodiversity officers, ecologists, and the like, in the holistic management of all aspects of an environment, both historic and natural.

Professional Archaeological Organizations

A small number of organizations around the world promote professionalism in archaeology through regulation of a corporate membership and creation of and adherence to codes of conduct and standards, with their members having to demonstrate, through submission of a portfolio and CV, that they possess appropriate skills, training, and experience.

Such organizations also undertake outreach and advocacy, and lobby government and industry for better standards and laws. In this light they can be seen as public archaeology organizations. There are, however, extremely few job opportunities in this subsector, as outreach in pure terms is not their main aim. The major UK organization, for example, the Institute for Archaeologists, employs only 14 staff assisting its 2,700 members. The majority of these individuals' time is spent assisting current and potential new members rather than in outreach public archaeology – the closest most such officers come is in their liaison with existing heritage stakeholders, such as government, industry, and the avocational archaeological community, rather than the general public, although organizations such as the IfA are involved in archaeological advocacy alongside organizations such as the CBA.

Archaeology and the Media

The starting point for this section is the following observation: no one goes into professional archaeology with the intention of becoming a media star. Although there are full-time (professional) TV presenters in particular who regularly host archaeologically themed shows, none of these presenters are professional archaeologists – in other words, they could not work as archaeologists for a CRM archaeology firm, university, or government department. Such individuals are professional TV presenters, not archaeologists – an important distinction. The follow-up to this is the other point made earlier in this chapter: although a (very) small number of archaeologists make some of their career in the media, almost without exception such individuals also have other archaeological jobs, as there is not enough constant work in TV alone to generate a regular or reliable income. Such individuals' cachet to a TV audience also comes from their authenticity – these are understood to be professional archaeologists with a wealth of experience to share with the viewers, and their value as presenters lies in that accumulated experience of years of doing archaeology, first as students and then as professionals. This background experience is cited time and time again on the shows themselves and then on associated websites. Thus, the only distinctive thing that differentiates these individuals from other archaeologists who are not on TV is their good luck to get noticed by a TV producer/director, and their ability to be TV-friendly – a combination of charm and charisma, also possibly an appealing distinctive sartorial or personality trait or quirk. Above all else, such individuals must have a genuine ability to explain archaeology in a clear and accessible manner (Figure 32). Those working in TV archaeology generally found their way there by chance: they were either working on a site/project that an existing TV show decided to feature and ended up in that initial show – where if they did well they often got invited to appear on other subsequent shows – or were approached by TV production companies on the basis of either a colleague's recommendation or their biography when the company went talent-hunting. Very occasionally such companies do put out a general call for new talent, but this is rare.

As noted earlier in this chapter, a much larger number of archaeologists are far more regularly involved in, and in some cases make an entire living from, work in either print or online media. Here there are both many more opportunities for individuals to become involved and also rather clearer transferable skills that can be discussed. Above all, good written communication is a skill that *all* archaeologists should have and constantly seek to improve on. Good written skills make the reports, publications, and other documents that go out to not only the general public but also policy makers, government officials, and funding organizations both effective and appealing. Badly written, dull reports do no one a favor and can even harm a site or project – they can lead to a drop in public support or a cessation of funding. Good writing also helps to sell individual archaeologists when

Figure 32. Public archaeology in action, part 2. Archaeology makes good TV! Here, a journalist interviews project directors Andy Gardner and Peter Guest at the Priory Field excavation at Caerleon, south Wales in mid-2010 (© Chris Waite / UCL Institute of Archaeology 2010, courtesy of Andrew Gardner).

they come to apply for new jobs with well-written packages of covering letter, CV, and supporting publications.

Thus, writing for the media in the broadest sense is a sector worth considering and a skill worth acquiring, for entry-level and experienced archaeologists alike. For those already working in the field and with a track record of publication, this is less of a problem: they may well be asked to write a piece of text for a popular publication or choose to write an entire book; they may also be asked to review other people's books in the press, or be interviewed about their work. For entry-level practitioners, there are still opportunities. In particular, many of the archaeological and heritage organizations mentioned in this chapter have their own newsletters, journals, periodicals, and the like, and accept unsolicited submissions for consideration, especially reports of recent projects, book reviews, or reviews of recent events, conferences, or symposia. Such works are a good way to build up experience of writing the types of clear and succinct work in which the mainstream media are interested. Such organizations also inevitably maintain websites where similar such work can be published. In addition, many such organizations have annual essay or report contests – some with financial or other prizes. These are excellent routes for archaeology students to pursue and also offer good things to mention in CVs and job application letters.

Museum Archaeologists

Museum-based archaeologists are in many ways very similar to the types of university-based archaeological specialists discussed in Chapter 4. Indeed, because many museums are affiliated with academic organizations, in some cases these are effectively the same groups. Archaeologists who work in such organizations enjoy the same benefits as those of their university colleagues in terms of pay and conditions (plus, in some cases, additional benefits, such as free entry to their own and other museums), struggle in the same ways to pursue the few and highly sought-after jobs available, and, once in their positions, need to juggle the same types of responsibilities – administration and the pursuit of funding in grants and awards versus the more enjoyable process of research and teaching. Such individuals also tend to need the same high levels of qualification to get positions – the majority of museum-based archaeologists have one, if not several, higher degrees in archaeology, with many having PhDs, alongside extensive experience backed up by a good publication record.

The only significant differences between museum and university archaeologists lie in the audiences and the working environment. In closing this chapter, these are explored here:

- *Audiences*: Such archaeologists help design and curate both temporary and permanent displays, give talks and lectures to visitors, and write guidebooks for displays and their specialist subject fields. In this sense, their audiences and teaching environments are much wider than those of purely academic archaeologists: the latter will generally only be teaching undergraduate and postgraduate archaeology or related students, and so can present their data and arguments at the higher intellectual level that such students are expected to be able to comprehend through supporting reading and research of their own. Academic archaeologists also generally teach through only a relatively narrow range of forms, primarily lectures, seminars, and small practical sessions. In contrast, museum archaeologists must present their work to a much wider range of audiences whose age, experience, and familiarity with archaeology may vary widely. Such archaeologists also must present their work through many different media – through displays of objects and associated texts; talks, gallery guides, and lectures to visitors; and guidebooks.
- *Working conditions*: Many museum-based archaeologists undertake, along with their other duties, research-based fieldwork akin to that of academic archaeologists. However, the primary workplace of most museum archaeologists is, obviously, a museum, so their working environment varies more widely from that of most academic archaeologists, including work in both public and private spaces – from the public galleries and exhibition halls of the museum to its storage, laboratory, and office areas (Figure 33). Museum archaeologists' working schedules also tend to be more flexible than those of academic archaeologists, being less closely tied to the academic calendar. That being said, peak times for museum visits – the school holidays, in particular the main summer holidays – can

Figure 33. Museum archaeology: Archaeological science and conservation play a central role in putting finds on display in museums. Here, Vanessa Saiz Gomez (UCL MSc Conservation of Archaeology and Museums student 2007–09) conducts a conservation assessment of an archaeological collection in a temporary fieldwork laboratory (© Dean Sully / UCL Institute of Archaeology 2008).

cause pressures on workload; these are often the periods when the greatest number of staff are needed in the museum but, paradoxically, are also often the best times to undertake fieldwork, especially in collaboration with university colleagues for whom the summer is the primary research period of each year.

Working alongside museum archaeologists (and often sharing similar backgrounds, training, and skill sets) is a wide array of other museum-based heritage professionals. This sector of the heritage profession is so distinctive, so extensive, and ultimately so different from archaeology that it cannot be addressed in detail here; this is the subject of an entirely different book by a professional with experience in that field, not this author – see Schlatter's (2008) *Museum Careers* for a start. However, to give an indication of some of the skills and so training involved, such jobs include the following issues:

- *Business and marketing*: Modern museums, even small ones, are run like businesses. On one hand, this involves people with a wide variety of business management skills, including financial and personnel management experience. On the other hand, this involves a variety of people with varied marketing skills – including public relations experience promoting museums, as well as production experience producing marketing materials, flyers, posters, websites, and the like.

191

- *Conservation*: The needs of immediate-term stabilization of historic materials (especially newly excavated archaeological materials) and the long-term conservation of these materials are a highly specialized and technical concern requiring years of training at the postgraduate level, extensive practice, and constant professional development as new techniques emerge. Modern heritage conservation facilities include laboratories to match the best of those found in scientific research facilities around the world, and use an incredible array of tools and techniques drawn from dozens of different industries. Equipment includes tools for scanning, monitoring, and analyzing the makeup and stability of different objects (including medical grade scanners), different chemicals and machinery for cleaning, stabilizing, and conserving materials (including special types of drying and freezing facilities), and much else. Such facilities can cost hundreds of thousands or even millions of pounds/dollars/euros a year to run; some of the best facilities are world-renowned, with rare objects being flown in from across the globe to be conserved.

- *Display*: Once materials have been conserved, they need to be displayed. Displays must meet the sometimes conflicting needs of visibility on one hand and long-term object stability on the other. Many objects, for example, are best stored in conditions of very low light and humidity, but those are not the best conditions for the public to view the materials, and these can be difficult and expensive environments to maintain. Display issues also involve questions of providing sufficient supporting information – be this as text or multimedia – to visitors without overwhelming them with data, and are also concerned with even more ostensibly simple issues such as the appropriate use of fonts, color schemes, design layout, and so forth. In a small museum or display this is complex enough – in major international museums with millions of visitors viewing hundreds of thousands of objects, this becomes an entire industry in itself.

- *Interpretation*: Working in relation to the preceding display issues, interpretation issues mean both influencing decisions on the immediate text/media of a display and influencing wider issues of additional interpretation – providing additional information/educational facilities and opportunities for a range of visitors of different ages, backgrounds, experience, and nationality. Interpretation issues vary widely, from dealing with how many directional signs to place in a building and in how many languages, or how many restroom facilities to provide, to how to introduce a complex series of archaeological finds simultaneously to everyone from age eight to eighty-eight.

- *Legal/ethical issues*: Many museums have materials drawn from around the world. In some cases, especially for long-established museums, some materials they hold may have been obtained hundreds of years ago under terms that would never be allowed in the modern world. The most famous example of this is the ongoing claim by Greece for the return of the Parthenon Marbles (sometimes referred to as the Elgin Marbles) taken from the Parthenon in Athens between 1801 and 1812, and on display in the British Museum in London. A less well-known but as emotive an issue is then the example of the thousands of skeletal remains of Indigenous Peoples held in museums around the world that were taken for scientific study in the nineteenth and twentieth centuries, for which numerous communities are now lobbying to have returned. The legal and ethical issues surrounding the ownership and possible return of such materials are a major concern of many modern museum archaeologists. So too are questions of more recent acquisitions, including issues of proving authenticity and the ethical rights and wrongs of materials on sale on the international antiquities market. For example, the second Gulf war that commenced in 2003 has led to thousands of objects stolen from Iraqi museums or looted from archaeological sites in the country coming onto the international antiquities market. Work in this field is undertaken by a variety of specialists – not just archaeologists, but also lawyers and art historians and even scientists involved in the dating and identification of provenance and origin of materials.

Interviewee: Kara

How did you first become involved in archaeology?

I think most archaeologists have followed a calling, so to speak, and I am no different. I have always had a deep fascination with the ancient world, and I've been lucky (or foolish) enough to follow those interests. American primary and secondary education does not include much instruction on the ancient world, and it wasn't until I attended the University of Texas at Austin that I was able to devote myself to the study of ancient cultures, prepare for graduate school, and make a successful transition to serious study.

What is your present job?

I am an assistant professor of Egyptian art and architecture at the University of California, Los Angeles, in the Department of Near Eastern Languages and Cultures, also with an affiliation at the Cotsen Institute of Archaeology. At UCLA, I teach undergraduates and graduate students about ancient Egyptian visual culture, language, and cultural archaeology. I also spend as much time as I can researching and writing. In my previous job, I ran the ancient scholars' program at the Getty Villa in Malibu, California, as part of the Getty Research Institute. At the Getty I administered the scholars' program, but also engaged in significant research activities. Additionally, I'm active in documentary filmmaking as a producer, writer, and host.

What qualifications do you hold? Where and what did you study?

I was a double major at the University of Texas at Austin, resulting in a BA in German as well as a BA in humanities. The humanities degree was an interdepartmental honors program in which I was able to design my course of study with an advisor. I focused on ancient civilizations and took courses in art history, classics, archaeology, and French, culminating with an honors thesis that centered on ancient Egypt. For graduate school, I attended Johns Hopkins University in Baltimore. This was an inclusive MA/PhD program, and I studied there for eight years. I opted for the program in Egyptian art and archaeology, but Hopkins is a multidisciplinary program that requires study of ancient texts for all students. In addition to visual culture, history, and religion courses, I studied Old Egyptian, Middle Egyptian, Late Egyptian, Coptic, and Demotic – the various stages of the ancient Egyptian language. My secondary subject was ancient Near Eastern archaeology.

What are your terms of employment, working conditions, or other job benefits?

At UCLA, I teach "2-2-1," which means that I teach two courses the first quarter, two the second, and one class the third quarter. Teaching graduate students, however, usually means that I teach more than the required number of courses each quarter. I get one quarter's teaching leave for the first two years of my employment at UCLA. Thereafter, I can apply for sabbatical or teaching leaves to complete research and writing essential for tenure and promotions. My position at UCLA is tenure-track, meaning that I am now in a probationary period, lasting from three to six years, during which I need to maintain an active research and teaching schedule to receive tenure. My teaching and research activities will be under periodic review by a tenure committee and the other professors of my department.

How did you get your current job? What do you feel was most helpful to you in gaining this position?

I applied for this position at UCLA after seeing it advertised in one of the online Egyptian lists. I wrote an application letter, explaining my interest and fit for the position. I also submitted teaching evaluations and a selection of publications. I was invited to the university for a day of interviews with various faculty and staff members, and then presented a public "job talk." I was probably successful because of eight years of varied teaching, administrative, and research experience – at Stanford University, the Los Angeles County Museum of Art (LACMA), and the Getty Research Institute. As a cultural archaeologist, I cross many disciplinary boundaries, including art history, social history, economics, religious studies, and philology. My ability to teach both visual studies and Egyptian language was apparently a good fit for the department at UCLA. Finally, I had taught at UCLA for a one-year appointment in 2002–03, so to a large extent I was a known quantity to my colleagues.

What is the best thing about being an archaeologist?

I am privileged to be able to devote my life to the study of ancient people. And I am very aware that I am one of the few people in this world who is paid to follow a dream. Because I am a cultural archaeologist, I integrate visual and philological studies in my Egyptological work. I also try to connect teaching with my museum work, fieldwork, research, and writing. Right now, teaching is one of my main avenues to inspiration and new research ideas.

What is the worst thing about being an archaeologist?

Archaeology in Egypt puts one face to face, on a daily basis, with the depressing fact that Egypt's ancient heritage is being destroyed by the increased population, antiquities theft and smuggling, the expansion of farming into previously unculti-vated desert lands, the rising water table, and high numbers of tourists. And there is not enough economic support for more Egyptologists to record and study as much as we can before these losses become permanent.

What do you consider to be your greatest achievement in or contribution to archaeology so far?

My dissertation topic seems to be the gift that keeps on giving. I specialized in the visual culture of death and funerary ritual in ancient Egypt, and I was able to expand this work significantly for publication. In my recently published book, *The Cost of Death* (published with *Egyptologische Uitgaven*, a series associated with Leiden University), I focus on New Kingdom funerary objects and associated textual material from Thebes. In the first half, I examine the many primary texts (receipts, letters, workshop records, official documents, and legal texts) documenting the purchase and production of funerary goods. The second half of the book includes an analysis of Ramesside funerary arts, particularly coffins, from the perspective of socioeconomic agendas. The book problematizes visual culture from a number of angles (archaeological, socioeconomic, art historical) and uses diverse primary sources (texts and objects) to approach an emic evaluation of death and its visual culture. And this work keeps leading me on to other research avenues. Right now, I'm pushing my research on funerary materiality into the Third Intermediate Period and Late Period, research that I expect to factor heavily into another book.

What is the one thing that you would change about archaeology if you could?

I don't know!

What is your top tip for pursuing a career in archaeology?

First, know your foundations. If your field demands Spanish reading and writing, learn it well. If, as in Egyptology, you need French and German, prepare in advance before you begin graduate studies. It's practically impossible to catch up on these foundational skills while you are also training in your field. Second, engage in

195

complex, nuanced, multidisciplinary research that asks difficult questions that are applicable to other fields of archaeology. Third, push yourself to finish your MA and PhD in eight years or less. Too many graduate students spend a decade or more completing their PhDs.

What do you see yourself doing in ten years' time?

In ten years' time, I hope to still be at UCLA engaged in teaching and research. I hope to be teaching both visual and textual materials. I hope to have seen some of my graduate students finish their PhDs and find gainful employment. I hope to continue my television work in a meaningful way, not as a medium for just entertainment, but as a larger classroom. I hope to have completed my third book. And I hope to have found the time to spend more time with my family, to complement what is already a rich, demanding, and continually surprising career.

Conclusion

Archaeology offers tremendous opportunities for involvement, whether a lifelong interest alongside another career, or a career in itself. It is never too late to become involved in archaeology, and children as young as four or five grasp the inherent pleasures of the subject as well as any adult – who does not like a pursuit that combines mental and physical exercise? Archaeology transcends borders, cultures, languages, and social and economic divisions – anyone, anywhere can become involved in archaeology if they wish, and the opportunities to become involved improve all the time. All that involvement requires is your own decision to become an active participant – and if you are reading this book, you have already taken that decision. Here, then, are some suggested second steps.

Top Ten Tips for Budding Archaeologists

EXPLORE: The best way to get involved in archaeology is to find out what opportunities for participation are available in your own neighborhood, through your local archaeology or history society or club, national organizations or local government, schools or universities. There are talks, walks, guides, and events nearly every week around the world; there are also hundreds of opportunities every year to obtain more formal training in archaeological techniques and become involved in actual fieldwork. Many events are free; even the ones that cost are rarely all that expensive – archaeologists are well aware that people do not have that much money to spare and fight to keep costs of events down. Almost all events are advertised online. Membership in local or national archaeology organizations is similarly cheap and is an extremely good value – membership brings you into contact with like-minded people in your neighborhood and provides access to information and resources such as newsletters and magazines, events, and even library facilities. Some useful Internet links to get you started in your explorations are listed in Appendix 1 of this book.

READ: There are many good popular archaeology magazines now available, often from high-street newsagents rather than specialist vendors. These are a quick and enjoyable way to find out more about archaeology – imagine how much more interesting your daily commute could become if you are reading a magazine about someone exploring a new archaeological site rather than your local newspaper. There are also many excellent introductory books on the basics, origins, and practice of archaeology – mostly published in paperback, cheap to buy, and easily purchased online.

WATCH: The chances are that if you are interested in getting more involved in archaeology, you are already doing this – there are so many good TV shows on archaeology these days, as well as online videos, that these have become the main entry point for budding archaeologists. But just in case you have not been watching these, then start! Not all archaeologists like all these shows, and as your knowledge of archaeology increases then you will rapidly begin to differentiate for yourself between the good and the bad programs in terms of the quality of the archaeology done and the validity of some of the claims. But nonetheless, many of these shows do a great job of introducing key concepts, ideas, and sites that are central to archaeology.

LISTEN: As noted previously, there are talks, walks, guides, and events about archaeology nearly every week around the world and most of these events are free or very cheap – at most, a few pounds/dollars/euros to attend. A great place to look beyond your local archaeology society or club is your local university archaeology, anthropology, or history department: most have weekly talks scheduled by staff and visiting scholars. Although primarily designed for students and staff, visitors are normally welcome by prior arrangement, and such events are usually advertised on departmental homepages. Going to events such as these is a great way to meet real archaeologists and like-minded people.

TALK: Archaeologists are friendly people who love their subject. They want to tell other people about it and help them get involved. Never be afraid to look up archaeologists who work in your neighborhood and ask them for advice on how to participate. They may not be able to help you themselves, but they will know other people who can help you and be able to put you in contact with them. A good starting point is either your local archaeology society or your local government archaeologist – both can be searched for online. If these people cannot help you, then your local university archaeology department should be able to help.

For those of you interested in taking the next step, considering not only becoming involved in archaeology but possibly pursuing a career as an archaeologist, the next five steps are especially for you.

PLAN: Start out by asking yourself what you want out of archaeology – do you really want a career as an archaeologist, to earn a living doing this? Or rather, do you simply want to become more involved in fieldwork? Understand the implications of a career in archaeology from the outset – long years of training, limited job opportunities, low pay, and often short employment contracts – and place this against your other personal aspirations and commitments. Talk about your aspirations with your family and what this lifestyle might mean for them, and be realistic – if you have always wanted a big house and a luxury car in your driveway, then archaeology really is not the career for you. Once you have come to a decision, plan what you need to do to make a start in your career regarding training, experience, and contacts.

TRAIN: Realistically, a professional career in archaeology begins at university. You might not like to hear this, but there it is. Without a university degree in archaeology or anthropology, you are seriously harming your chances of getting any job in the discipline, let alone advancing your career as a professional. So if you are serious about a career, find out what qualifications you need to get into such a university degree course, find out what university you would like to attend, and apply for a place. Remember, in particular, that it is never too late to do this – universities have students with an incredibly diverse array of backgrounds, ages, nationalities, and experience.

SKILL: Archaeologists who do well in their careers have multiple skills and fields of expertise. As Charles Darwin was alleged to have once stated: "It is not the strongest of the species that survives, nor the most intelligent that survives. It is the one that is the most adaptable to change." Multiple skills and specialties make you the most adaptable to change, the most able to apply for the largest number of jobs. This means both archaeological and non-archaeological skills, experience, and expertise. For those already at work who are considering a mid-career move into archaeology in particular, it is well worth making a list of what you do in your current job, what skills you have already, and seeing how these skills might apply to archaeology. Membership in professional organizations such as the IfA, RPA, and AACAI in any case necessitates evidence of continuing professional development throughout a career, evidence of training of your own and as provided by your employer.

VOLUNTEER: There are more archaeologists out there than available jobs – supply exceeds demand. Beyond expanding their training, skills, and expertise, successful archaeologists volunteer to do things that make them, and their CVs, stand out, that provide opportunities for networking, publication, and self-promotion. Early in any career this means volunteering to work, often unpaid (but hopefully with at least some costs covered) on projects – both the exciting fieldwork components of any project and the much less glamorous but equally important pre- and post-excavation phases, planning the project, cleaning, recording, investigating and conserving finds, and writing up notes and reports. More experienced archaeologists who are able to get jobs that perhaps pay them to do these tasks still usually volunteer in other ways – serving on local or national archaeological organizations' committees, editing newsletters and journals, writing conference and book reviews, organizing events and symposia, and so forth. All these different volunteer activities can be seen on the CVs of successful archaeologists, and distinguish them from their peers. By volunteering, such archaeologists have also been busy networking – making informal links and contacts with people, getting known as friendly, efficient, and trustworthy, being the people others want to work with and employ.

PERSEVERE: Finally, do not be afraid or dismayed if at first you do not seem to be getting anywhere. Everyone who has ever ended up with a job in archaeology, from the lowliest digger to the most senior professor, has hit a low at some point, when they wonder if they will ever get work and whether so many struggles are worth it. Struggle and disappointment are part of this lifestyle. If you cannot handle rejection – for jobs, grant applications, or article and book proposals – then get out now. Similarly, learn to accept constructive criticism: archaeology is too big and complex a subject for any one person to know all the answers – there is always something new to learn and some other opinion that can be of significance. When they have a bad day, most archaeologists simply take a deep breath and then get a good night's rest. The next day they get back to work.

Appendix 1

Useful Websites

Chapter 1: What Is – and Isn't – Archaeology?

About.com's Guide to Archaeology: http://archaeology.about.com/ (especially Careers in Archaeology: http://archaeology.about.com/od/careers inarchaeology/Careers_in_Archaeology.htm)

African-American Archaeology, History and Cultures African Diaspora Archaeology Network: http://www.diaspora.uiuc.edu/bookmark3.html

American Anthropological Association: http://www.aaanet.org/

American Archaeological Conservancy: http://www.americanarchaeology.com/

American Society for Amateur Archaeology: http://asaa-persimmonpress.com/

Archaeological Institute of America: http://www.archaeological.org/

Archaeology Scotland: http://www.archaeologyscotland.org.uk/

Australian Archaeological Association: http://www.australianarchaeological association.com.au/

Council for British Archaeology: http://www.britarch.ac.uk/

Council for Independent Archaeology: http://www.independents.org.uk/

Discovering the Archaeologists of Europe: http://discovering-archaeologists.eu/

International Council on Monuments and Sites: http://www.international .icomos.org/home.htm

RESCUE: the British Archaeological Trust: http://www.rescue-archaeology
.org.uk/

Save Britain's Heritage: www.savebritainsheritage.org/

Society for American Archaeology: http://www.saa.org/

Society for Historical Archaeology: http://www.sha.org/

UNESCO: http://www.unesco.org/new/en/unesco/

World Archaeological Congress: http://www.worldarchaeologicalcongress.org/

Chapter 2: Skills and Training

Advisory Council on Underwater Archaeology: http://www.acuaonline.org/

American Anthropological Association student webpage: http://www.aaanet
.org/resources/students/

American Cultural Resources Association: http://acra-crm.org/

Archtools Jobs: http://www.archtools.co.uk/company.asp?ID=69

Archaeological Institute of America Guide to Local Societies: http://www
.archaeological.org/societies

Archaeology Abroad: http://www.britarch.ac.uk/archabroad/

Archaeology Summer Camps: http://www.summercamps.com/cgi-bin/
summercamps/search.cgi?Archaeology=Archaeology

Archaeology Training Forum: http://www.britarch.ac.uk/training/atf.html

Archaeology Volunteer Opportunities: http://www.archaeologyfieldwork.com/
forums/viewforum.php?f=4

Australian Archaeological Association Study Options webpage: http://www
.australianarchaeologicalassociation.com.au/study_options

Australian Association of Consulting Archaeologists Inc.: http://www.aacai.com
.au/

Australasian Institute of Maritime Archaeology: http://aima.iinet.net.au/

British Archaeological Jobs and Resources: http://www.bajr.org/

CBA Community Archaeology Forum: http://www.britarch.ac.uk/caf/

CBA Guide to Post-16 Archaeological Education: http://www.britarch.ac.uk/
education/study

CBA Guide to Professional Development: http://www.britarch.ac.uk/taxo
nomy/term/692

CBA Guide to Regional and Local Archaeology and History Societies:
http://www.britarch.ac.uk/archonline

CBA Guide to Studying Archaeology at Undergraduate Level: http://www
.britarch.ac.uk/education/study/undergrad

I Love the Past Fieldwork Opportunities: http://www.ilovethepast.com/digs

Institute for Archaeologists: http://www.archaeologists.net/

National Occupational Standards in Archaeological Practice: http://www.torc .org.uk/nos/index.asp

Nautical Archaeology Society: http://www.nasportsmouth.org.uk/

Register of Professional Archaeologists: http://www.rpanet.org/

Training Online Resource Centre for Archaeology: http://www.torc.org.uk/

Young Archaeologists' Club: http://www.britarch.ac.uk/yac/

Chapter 3: Cultural Resource Management

Archdiggers Portal: http://www.archdiggers.co.uk/

British Archaeological Jobs and Resources: http://www.bajr.org/

Federation of Archaeological Managers and Employers: http://www.fame archaeology.co.uk/

Kenny Aitchison's archaeology blog: http://kenny.aitchison.typepad.com/

Shovelbums: http://www.shovelbums.org/

Tom King's CRM plus blog: http://crmplus.blogspot.com/

Chapter 4: Academia

The Chronicle of Higher Education: http://chronicle.com/

Higher Education Academy Subject Centre for History, Classics and Archaeology: http://www.heacademy.ac.uk/hca/home

Society for American Archaeology Guide to Academic Programs in Archaeology: http://www.saa.org/careers/ac-progs.html

Society for Historical Archaeology Guide to Graduate Programs in Historical and Underwater Archaeology: http://www.sha.org/students_jobs/higher/default .htm

Times Higher Educational Supplement: http://www.timeshighereducation.co.uk/

Chapter 5: Local Government

Association of Gardens Trusts: http://gardenstrusts.org.uk/new/index.asp

Association of Local Government Archaeological Officers: http://www.algao .org.uk/

Building Conservation Directory: http://www.buildingconservation.com/

Campaign to Protect Rural England: http://www.cpre.org.uk/home

Garden History Society: http://www.gardenhistorysociety.org/

Heritage Gateway (for HERs): http://www.heritage-gateway.org.uk/

Institute of Historic Building Conservation: http://www.ihbc.org.uk/

Jobs Go Public: http://www.jobsgopublic.com

National Association of State Archaeologists: http://www.uiowa.edu/~osa/nasa/

National Association of Tribal Historic Preservation Officers: http://www.nathpo.org/mainpage.html

National Conference of State Historic Preservation Officers: http://www.ncshpo.org/find/index.htm

Portable Antiquities Scheme: http://www.finds.org.uk/

Royal Town Planning Institute: http://www.rtpi.org.uk/

Society for the Protection of Ancient Buildings: http://www.spab.org.uk/

Chapter 6: Central Government

Advisory Council on Historic Preservation: http://www.achp.gov/

Cadw: http://www.cadw.wales.gov.uk/

Canadian Environmental Assessment Agency: http://www.ceaa.gc.ca/

Crown Estate: http://www.thecrownestate.co.uk/

English Heritage: http://www.english-heritage.org.uk/

Historic Scotland: http://www.historic-scotland.gov.uk/

Historic Sites and Monuments Board of Canada: http://www.pc.gc.ca/clmhc-hsmbc/

Jobs Go Public: http://www.jobsgopublic.com

Minerals Management Service: http://www.mms.gov/

National Oceanographic and Atmospheric Administration: http://www.noaa.gov/index.html

National Park Service archaeology program: http://www.nps.gov/archeology/

Naval History and Heritage Command (formerly the Naval Historical Center): http://www.history.navy.mil/

Northern Ireland Environment Agency: http://www.ni-environment.gov.uk/

Parks Canada: http://www.pc.gc.ca/

Royal Commission on the Ancient and Historical Monuments of Scotland: http://www.rcahms.gov.uk/

UNESCO: http://portal.unesco.org

US Army Corps of Engineers: http://www.usace.army.mil

US Bureau of Indian Affairs: http://www.bia.gov

US Department of Agriculture, Natural Resources Conservation Service Cultural Resources Division: http://www.nrcs.usda.gov/technical/cultural.html

US Department of Defense, Cultural Resources Division: https://www.denix.osd.mil/portal/page/portal/denix/environment/CR

US Department of Transportation Federal Highway Administration, Historic Preservation Division: http://environment.fhwa.dot.gov/histpres/index.asp

US Department of Veterans Affairs, Historic Preservation Division: http://www.cfm.va.gov/historic/

US Federal Agency Historic Preservation Programs and Officers Agency Information: http://www.achp.gov/fpoagencyinfo.html

US Federal Emergency Management Agency, Historic Preservation Division: http://www.fema.gov/plan/ehp/index.shtm

US Fish and Wildlife Service, Historic Preservation Division: http://www.fws.gov/historicpreservation/

US Forest Service Heritage Programs: http://www.fs.fed.us/recreation/programs/heritage/

US General Services Administration, Historic Preservation Division: http://www.gsa.gov/Portal/gsa/ep/channelView.do?pageTypeId=17109&channelId=-24361

US Historic Preservation Learning Portal: https://www.historicpreservation.gov/web/guest/5

US National NAGPRA Guidance: http://www.nps.gov/history/nagpra/

Chapter 7: Public and Community Archaeology

American Anthropological Association: http://www.aaanet.org/

The Archaeology Channel: http://www.archaeologychannel.org/

Archaeology Magazine: http://www.archaeology.org/

Association of Preservation Trusts: http://www.ukapt.org.uk/

Australian Archaeological Association: http://www.australianarchaeologicalassociation.com.au/

British Archaeology [magazine]: http://www.britarch.ac.uk/ba/

Council for British Archaeology: http://www.britarch.ac.uk/

Current Archaeology [magazine]: http://www.archaeology.co.uk/

Historic Houses Association: http://www.hha.org.uk/

International Council of Museums: http://icom.museum/

Museum Association: http://www.museumsassociation.org

Museum Jobs: http://www.museumjobs.com

National Geographic [magazine]: http://www.nationalgeographic.com/

National Trust: http://www.nationaltrust.org.uk/

National Trust for Historic Preservation: http://www.preservationnation.org/

National Trust of Australia: http://www.nationaltrust.org.au/

Nautical Archaeology Society: http://www.nasportsmouth.org.uk/

Appendix 1: Useful Websites

Past Horizons [magazine]: http://www.pasthorizons.com/

Portable Antiquities Scheme: http://www.finds.org.uk/

RESCUE: the British Archaeological Trust: http://www.rescue-archaeology.org.uk/

Save Britain's Heritage: www.savebritainsheritage.org/

Sierra Club: http://www.sierraclub.org/

Smithsonian Magazine: http://www.smithsonianmag.com/

Society for American Archaeology: http://www.saa.org/

Society for Historical Archaeology: http://www.sha.org/

University of Leicester Museum Jobs Desk: http://www.le.ac.uk/ms/jobs/jobs/htm

Young Archaeologists' Club: http://www.britarch.ac.uk/yac/

Appendix 2

Glossaries

Official and Unofficial Terminology, Concepts, and Meanings (Including Legal Terms)

ABD	"all but dissertation"; a doctoral student who has completed all the requirements for a PhD but has not written and defended the dissertation (US only)
AL	Aggregates Levy (UK)
A and AS levels	Advanced and Advanced Subsidiary Level exams; national school leaving certificate exams and university entry qualifications (UK – England, Wales, and Northern Ireland)
ACT	commonly used college entry test/exam system (US)
ALSF	Aggregates Levy Sustainability Fund (UK)
AMAAA	Ancient Monuments and Archaeological Areas Act (1979) (UK)
AP	Advanced Placement; secondary school advanced courses that are generally eligible for college credit (US)
ARPA	Archaeological Resources and Protection Act (1979) (US)
ATSIHPA	Aboriginal and Torres Strait Islander Heritage Protection Act (1984) (Australia)
AUV	Autonomous Underwater Vehicle
BA/BSc	Bachelor of Arts/Bachelor of Science; often referred to as a bachelor's degree

Appendix 2: Glossaries

BTEC	Business and Technology Education Council; a form of secondary educational qualification (UK)
CHM	Cultural Heritage Management (see CRM)
Contract archaeology	see CRM
CPD	Continuing Professional Development
CRM	Cultural Resource Management, archaeological work undertaken on a paid for basis for specific clients, usually organizations undertaking developments that affect archaeological sites and for which legal requirements to mitigate the impact of any development exist
Digger	slang term for an archaeologist employed in CRM archaeology (UK) (see also Shovelbum)
Dissertation	commonly used term for a major piece of original written work produced by university-level students. In the UK, the dissertation is normally associated with undergraduate level work of between 5,000 and 15,000 words; in the US and Australia, the dissertation is normally associated instead with master's or PhD level work, anywhere between 50,000 and 250,000 words or even more in some circumstances (see also Thesis)
DPhil	see PhD
EIA	Environmental Impact Assessment (UK)
ESP	Environmental Studies Program
FLO	Finds Liaison Officer (of the Portable Antiquities Scheme) (UK)
GDP	Gross Domestic Product (sometimes referred to as gross domestic income [GDI]); a measure of a country's overall official economic output
GIS	Geographic Information System[s]
GPA	Grade-Point Average
Grad[uate] school	an institution awarding advanced academic degrees (MA/MSc, MPhil, DPhil/PhD), with the general requirement that students must have earned a previous undergraduate (bachelor's) degree; normally a part of or associated with a university
Gray literature	formally unpublished reports on archaeological sites, usually held in HERs and the like, often the product of CRM archaeology
GRE	Graduate Record Examination (US)
HER	Historic Environment Record (also known as an SMR) (UK)
Highers (including Advanced Highers)	the national school-leaving certificate exams and university entrance qualifications of the Scottish Qualifications Certificate (SQC) offered by the Scottish Qualifications Authority (UK – Scotland)

Honors	a term used in association with university-level degree qualifications, signifying a degree with a higher academic standard than a standard pass or ordinary degree
Indigenous Peoples	Peoples, Communities, and Nations who claim a historical continuity and cultural affinity with societies endemic to their original territories that developed prior to exposure to the larger connected civilization associated with Western culture (US and Australia in particular, but not exclusively)
IT	Information Technology
LiDAR	**light detection and ranging**, a form of ground-based and aerial survey, developed primarily by the geological and defense industries, which measures the height of the ground surface and other features in large areas of landscape
Looting	the indiscriminate theft of goods, generally during times of crisis, unrest, or upheaval; in specific reference to archaeology, the theft of archaeological materials under such circumstances or threat of such circumstances, usually with the intention to recover materials for subsequent resale on the international antiquities market and including – in terms of archaeological ethics at least, although not under law – salvage and treasure hunting, in which the primary motive of a program of fieldwork is the recovery of valuable items for resale
MA/MSc	Master of Arts/Master of Science
MBA	Master of Business Administration
MOA	Memorandum of Agreement (sometimes also known as a memorandum of understanding [MOU])
MPhil	Master of Philosophy; intermediate higher-level university degree between an MA and a DPhil/PhD
NAGRPA	Native American Graves Protection and Repatriation Act (1990) (US)
NEPA	National Environmental Policy Act (1969) (US)
NHL	National Historic Landmark (US)
NPG	National Planning Guidance (UK – especially Scotland)
NPP	National Planning Policy
NVQ	National Vocational Qualification; a form of secondary educational qualification, usually associated with practical skills (UK)
PDP	Personal Development Plan (part of CPD)
PhD	Doctor of Philosophy
Postgrad[uate] –	an individual engaged in university study toward advanced degrees (MA/MSc, MPhil, DPhil/PhD), with the general requirement that students must have already earned a

209

	previous undergraduate (bachelor's) degree (see Grad[uate] school)
PPG	Planning Policy Guidance Note (e.g., PPG No. 15 (Planning and the Historic Environment) (1994) and PPG No. 16 (Archaeology and Planning) (1990) (UK)
PPS	Planning Policy Statement (e.g., PPS 5 Planning for the Historic Environment) (2010) (UK)
Rescue archaeology	archaeological research undertaken in a hurry, usually in advance of a site being destroyed; the term is rescue archaeology in the UK and salvage archaeology in the US and Australia
Resistivity meter	a device for undertaking electrical resistance survey (sometimes called earth resistance or resistivity surveys), detecting and mapping subsurface archaeological features and patterns through the analysis of variations in an electrical current run through the earth between the meter and associated electrical probes
ROV	remotely operated vehicle
Salvage archaeology	see Rescue archaeology
Salvage	see Looting
SAT	Scholastic Aptitude Test or Scholastic Assessment Test (now formally known as an SAT Reasoning Test); a standardized test for college admissions (US)
Shovelbum	slang term for an archaeologist employed in CRM archaeology (US) (see also Digger)
SHPO	State Historic Preservation Office (US) (sometimes also used for employees of this office – i.e., state historic preservation officers)
School	an institution for the teaching of students; in the context of this book, generally meant to refer either to secondary-level education (i.e., pre-university high school), or university-level education, including study toward advanced university degrees (i.e., graduate school)
SMR	Sites and Monuments Record (also see HER) (UK)
SSSI	Site of Special Scientific Interest (UK) (official legal site designation for important natural environment sites)
Stratigraphy	layers, generally in the soil or rocks, a sequence of strata (from the geological term *stratum* [plural *strata*], a layer of rock or soil with internally consistent characteristics that distinguishes it from contiguous layers); as a general rule, the deeper the layer the older it is, and vice versa
Thesis	commonly used term for a major piece of original written work produced by university level students. In the UK, the thesis is normally associated with master's or PhD level work anywhere between 50,000 and 250,000 words;

	in the US and Australia, the thesis is normally associated instead with undergraduate level work of between 5,000 and 15,000 words (see also Dissertation)
THPO	Tribal Historic Preservation Office (US) (sometimes also used for employees of this office – i.e., tribal historic preservation officers)
Total station	an optical surveying instrument, mounted on a tripod, that combines a theodolite (an instrument that can measure angles in horizontal and vertical planes) with an electronic distance meter to calculate distances from the machine with extreme accuracy
Treasure hunting	see Looting
UNCLOS	United Nations Convention of the Law of the Sea
Undergrad[uate]	an individual engaged in university study toward a bachelor's degree (i.e., BA/BSc)
WHS	World Heritage Site

NB. For a detailed description of archaeological terms, there are various dictionaries of archaeology available, the most up-to-date being Darvill (2008).

Organizations and Acronyms

AAA	American Anthropological Association (US)
AAA	Australian Archaeological Association
AACAI	Australian Association of Consulting Archaeologists Inc.
ACHP	Advisory Council on Historic Preservation (US)
ACRA	American Cultural Resources Association
ACUA	Advisory Council on Underwater Archaeology
AGT	Association of Gardens Trusts (UK)
AHRC	Arts and Humanities Research Council (UK)
AIATSIS	Australian Institute of Aboriginal and Torres Strait Islander Studies
AIMA	Australasian Institute for Maritime Archaeology
ALGAO	Association of Local Government Archaeological Officers (UK)
ALSF	Aggregates Levy Sustainability Fund (UK)
AMEC	Association of Mining and Exploration Companies (Australia)
AMS	Ancient Monuments Society (UK)
ASHA	Australian Society for Historical Archaeology
BAJR	British Archaeological Jobs and Resources (UK)
BIA	Bureau of Indian Affairs (US)
BOEMRE	Bureau of Ocean Energy Management, Regulation and Enforcement (formerly the MSS) (US)
Cadw	Welsh National Heritage Agency (not an acronym)
CBA	Council for British Archaeology
CE	Crown Estate (UK)
CEQ	Council on Environmental Quality (US)

Appendix 2: Glossaries

CoE	Council of Europe
CPRE	Campaign to Protect Rural England (UK)
DCMS	Department for Culture, Media and Sport (UK)
DEWHA	Department of the Environment, Water, Heritage and the Arts (Australia)
DoD	Department of Defence (US and Australia)
DoE	Department of Energy (US)
DEFRA	Department for the Environment, Food and Rural Affairs (UK)
EA	Environment Agency (UK)
EH	English Heritage
EPA	Environmental Protection Agency (US)
FaHCSIA	Department of Families, Housing, Community Services and Indigenous Affairs (Australia)
FAME	Federation of Archaeological Managers and Employers (UK)
FC	Forestry Commission (UK)
FCC	Federal Communications Commission (US)
FEMA	Federal Emergency Management Agency (US)
FHWA	Department of Transportation Federal Highway Administration (US)
FPI	Federal Preservation Institute (US)
FWS	Fish and Wildlife Service (US)
GHS	Garden History Society (UK)
GSA	General Services Administration (US)
HLF	Heritage Lottery Fund (UK)
HS	Historic Scotland
HSE	Heath and Safety Executive (UK)
HUD	Department of Housing and Urban Development (US)
HWTMA	Hampshire and Isle of Wight Trust for Maritime Archaeology (UK)
ICOM	International Council of Museums
ICOMOS	International Council on Monuments and Sites
IfA	Institute for Archaeologists (UK)
IHBC	Institute of Historic Building Conservation (UK)
JNCC	Joint Nature Conservation Committee (UK)
MCA	Maritime and Coastguard Agency (UK)
MMO	Marine Management Organisation (UK)
MMS	Minerals Management Service (US) (see BOEMRE)
MNTB	Merchant Navy Training Board (UK)
MoD	Ministry of Defence (UK)
NASA	National Association of State Archaeologists (US)
NAS	Nautical Archaeology Society
NE	Natural England (UK)
NERC	Natural Environment Research Council (UK)
NHHC	Naval History and Heritage Command (US) (formerly the Naval Historical Center [NHS])
NHPA	National Historic Preservation Act (1966) (US)
NHS	National Heath Service (UK)

NIE	Northern Ireland Executive
NIEA	Northern Ireland Environment Agency
NMR	National Monuments Record (UK – England)
NMRW	National Monuments Record of Wales
NOAA	National Oceanographic and Atmospheric Administration (US)
NPS	National Parks Service (US)
NRCS	Department of Agriculture – Natural Resources Conservation Service (US)
NRHP	National Register of Historic Places (US)
NT	National Trust (UK and Australia)
NTHP	National Trust for Historic Preservation (US)
OHSA	Occupational Heath and Safety Administration (US)
PADI	Professional Association of Diving Instructors
PAS	Portable Antiquities Scheme (UK)
QAA	Quality Assurance Agency for Higher Education (UK)
RCAHMS	Royal Commission for Ancient and Historic Monuments of Scotland
RPA	Register of Professional Archaeologists (US)
RYA	Royal Yachting Association (UK)
SAA	Society for American Archaeology
SAA	Sub Aqua Association
SEPA	Scottish Environment Protection Agency
SHA	Society for Historical Archaeology
SPAB	Society for the Protection of Ancient Buildings
SRC	Submerged Resources Center (US – part of the NPS)
UCAS	Universities and Colleges Admissions Service (UK)
UNESCO	United Nations Educational, Scientific, and Cultural Organization
USACE	US Army Corps of Engineers
USSA	US Sailing Association
VA	Department of Veterans Affairs (US)
WAC	World Archaeological Congress
WHS	William Hunt and Sons (UK)
YAC	Young Archaeologists Club (UK)

Appendix 3

Suggested Equipment to Take on an Archaeological Project

Please exercise your own judgment in deciding what to take of the following. This is an exhaustive list of things that the author has used in extremely varied circumstances around the world – but if the project you are going on is a fifteen-minute drive from your home, much of this equipment is superfluous. Some of this equipment may also be provided by the project itself, so the golden rule is: *Check first:* do not be afraid to ask what equipment is appropriate to bring. Better to ask before you go than to get there and find that you should have brought some essential equipment.

Things to Do before You Go on Fieldwork

- Speak to the project director and ensure that you have been given specific guidance on any equipment that you might need to bring and/or any special circumstances of the project. This should include details of any vaccinations that you need to get in advance of the project, as well as details of any personal health, equipment, or travel insurance that you might need to take out in relation to the project. Ensure, above all else, that any questions you might have about any aspect of the project are answered.
- Get from the project director details of the project's precise location and address (both of the fieldwork itself and any off-site accommodation), and ensure that you leave a copy with a family member/relative/close personal friend; ensure that this includes emergency contact details such as the project director's mobile

phone number, as well as a contact postal/driving address on or near the site, so that in an emergency a message can be delivered to you and/or someone can come and find you.

- Provide the project director with any medical or other personal information that might have an impact on your participation in the project – such as any underlying health issues that you experience, any allergies you have, and the like.
- Ensure that you have any vaccinations required for the location and duration of the project – and a record of these to take with you.
- Ensure that you have any personal insurance necessary in place – especially medical and/or travel insurance – and a record of this to take with you. This might include ensuring that your home building/contents insurance covers your prolonged absence if no one else will be living there while you are away (some insurers only cover a property being vacant for up to 28 days at a time).
- Ensure that you receive from the project director precise instructions about travel arrangements and timing to and from the project, and your responsibilities in this. If it is your responsibility to arrange travel to and from the site, make sure that you have done so; if the project is taking care of this, be sure to know where you need to be at what times, and ideally also who some of your fellow travelers are in advance. Think in particular about airport transfers – how you will transfer to and from the nearest airport to the site (especially if this is very remote).

General Items

- *Identity information*: passport, driver's license, and other important documents; and store photocopies of these elsewhere.
- *Banking necessities*: credit or debit card, traveler's checks (but check whether you will be able to change them where you are visiting) and cash (if abroad, in particular, include some cash in a commonly accepted and popular denomination, such as euros or US dollars, that can be easily changed into the local currency).
- *Contact essentials*: mobile phone, charger, and charge adaptor (or an external power source like a solar charger) (check that your service provider covers the area you are going to and the costs of calls in and out – some phone companies charge you for receiving a call overseas); also a list of key addresses and phone numbers written down elsewhere (so you have these even if your phone breaks or is stolen). This should include a clearly labeled emergency contacts section listing the contacts you would like notified in an emergency. More prosaically, make sure you have the addresses of people you might want to write or send postcards to.
- *Guidebook and phrase book for the places you will be visiting/working in, and a map of the immediate area of the site*: a little politeness goes a long way, so memorize at least some basic polite phrases before you arrive and also learn about local social conventions of behavior and dress.

Archaeological Equipment

At an absolute minimum, you should bring along the following personal equipment:

- 4-inch solid forged pointing trowel (WHS in UK; Marshalltown in US)
- 1-m folding ruler
- 10-m retracting tape measure
- Notebook
- Drawing kit – pens, pencils, eraser, paper, etc.
- Carry-bag, box, or other container in which to carry this material

Your project director should advise you of any additional personal archaeological equipment that you would be expected to provide.

When advised in advance, you may also need to provide specific health and safety equipment, including:

- Protective boots (with steel or Kevlar toecaps)
- A protective hard hat
- A high-visibility vest, jacket, and/or trousers
- Protective eye and ear covers, also in some cases protective dust masks
- Protective gloves

General Clothing

- Comfortable, flexible, hard-wearing clothes appropriate to the location and climate you will be working in (jeans are fine in many places, but are horribly uncomfortable when they get soaking wet and take a long time to dry, so are to be avoided on some sites; low-cut or short-sleeved tops will cause offense in some countries, and are also not a good idea in very sunny places where you need to protect yourself from sunburn; military sourced or stylized clothing or equipment is also to be avoided in many counties because of political sensitivities; so too are clothes with political slogans or jokes on them). Common choices are simple, plain-colored cotton shirts, T-shirts, and trousers. These are cheap, comfortable, easy to wash, and quick drying.
- Comfortable socks and underwear (bearing in mind that you may have to wash these yourself in a public place: think twice about racy designs or cuts). Women may also wish to bring sports bras as a more comfortable alternative if the project is likely to involve a lot of walking around or very heavy work.
- Smarter casual clothes for the evenings/weekends/travel.
- Swimwear (if anywhere near a beach, pool, and the like) (a cheap diving mask is also a good addition if you are going somewhere on the coast with good visibility or marine life).

Footwear

- Boots for daily wear – steel toecap if advised by the site director, and/or Gore-Tex ankle boots for general use (these support your ankles and also protect against bites, stings, and scratches from animals and plants)
- Sneakers or athletic shoes for off-site wear
- Sandals or flip-flops for evening/beach wear

Some projects in very wet locations – pretty much anywhere in the UK, for one – may also mean that a pair of Wellington or rubber knee-height boots is a good addition.

Outerwear (Situation Dependent)

- The best quality waterproof jacket, overtrousers and hat you can buy – ideally again not in military colors such as camouflage. Good waterproof outerwear is particularly worth investing in – the quality stuff is tough, durable, and breathable and will last for years if you care for it.
- Sun hat, sunglasses, and sunscreen (of a high SPF factor).
- Scarf – warm for cold weather, thin and light for the sun and heat (the keffiyeh/schemagh scarf is popular in many countries, as it can be tied in different configurations and used for many more things than as just a head covering, although it does have political connotations in many locations around the world, and so can be a culturally sensitive thing to wear).
- A light windproof jacket and/or pullover/sweater/jumper/sweatshirt for evenings – a good compromise are synthetic fleeces.
- Gloves and hat – warm and waterproof for the cold, suitably wide-brimmed and secure for the sun. On very rocky/stony/thorny sites, some people also choose to wear lightweight protective gloves of the type that can be purchased at hardware or gardening stores; similarly, wearable knee protectors bought from the same location can be useful on such sites.

Health and Hygiene

All this should be capable of being packed down into a small, portable, waterproof bag, except for the towel.

- Towel (ideally a larger bath towel and also a smaller hand towel).
- Washing and grooming kit including nailbrush, soap, shampoo, deodorant, and so forth, plus a nail file and clippers – dirty and torn fingernails are an occupational hazard. A small mirror, ideally one of the unbreakable sort, is also a useful addition here. Many people – of both genders – also do not bother to shave on projects, but this is a personal choice. If you can't imagine not shaving, then be sure to pack your standard shaving kit – and ensure in particular, if so, that you take a mirror with you.

- Makeup (if that's your thing – but can you really be bothered to wear this, at least on site?).
- Sunscreen with a high SPF factor.
- Travel sickness medications (if necessary).
- Insect repellent (and in some circumstances, a personal mosquito net).
- No-water antibacterial gel hand wash and/or wet wipes.
- Spare/emergency toilet paper/tissue (pocket tissues are a handy and flexible compromise).
- Sanitary products for women.
- Spectacles, contact lenses, and spares of these if you need them, plus cleaning and storage materials (plus a copy of your current prescription that can be used to make you a new pair if your main and spares both get broken/lost/stolen). If you are going somewhere very sunny and do not already own a pair, prescription sunglasses are a worthwhile investment.
- Contraceptive devices (if that's your thing – however, condoms are especially useful in wider circumstances. For example, they can be used in an emergency to provide a waterproof cover for many smaller pieces of electronic equipment!).
- Personal first aid kit (containing disposable gloves and aprons, antibacterial swabs, various sizes of Band-Aids/plasters, tweezers, various sizes of bandage, safety pins, and so on). A useful addition to this pack is an emergency whistle (the no-ball ones that work anywhere, even in the water) and a foil emergency space blanket.
- Personal medications (such as allergy medicines, including EpiPens if required, insulin for diabetics, and so on, as well as things like generic over-the-counter painkillers, throat/cough medications, and the like). *You must clearly label prescription medications in particular as to what the products are, who prescribed them, to whom they belong, and how they are to be administered in any given emergency. You may also need to bring along a letter from the prescribing physician explaining their use, and/or have formal, written permission from the embassy of the nation you are visiting to carry medications into the country.*

Miscellaneous – Serious and Essential

- Rucksack sufficiently big to carry everything in, but not too big that you cannot personally carry it.
- A tough, waterproof day pack – big enough for all of your daily essentials, including for travel to and from the project, but as small as you can make it given what you need to carry.
- Plug adaptor for the location[s] you will be visiting.
- Spare AA and AAA batteries and spare batteries of other sizes for any specific electronic equipment you might be bringing.
- Different sizes of zip-lock bags (useful for spare kit and to keep things dry).
- Disposable cigarette lighter (even if you do not smoke – lighters have many potential uses, not least the "can I offer you a light" icebreaking potential when meeting new people).

- A roll of heavy-duty trash/rubbish bags (useful for spare kit and to keep things dry).
- Waterproof watch with alarm setting.
- Compass (and the knowledge how to use it properly, both with and without the aid of a map) – especially if you will be in a remote location.
- Camera plus spare batteries and film if you are old-school, or spare memory cards if not.
- Unbreakable, lightweight water bottle (i.e., the aluminum ones): in some circumstances also an unbreakable, lightweight mug, plate, bowl, and cutlery may be required. The mug, at least, is an excellent addition no matter what.
- Penknife or multitool (remember to pack this in your check-in luggage, not your carry-on, if you are flying).
- Flashlight plus spare batteries – the types that you can wear on your head may look a bit foolish but are a useful choice on badly lit sites or where there is no power/lighting, allowing you to keep your hands free.
- Ear plugs and eye mask (to enable sound sleeping).
- A ball of strong string (endless uses).
- A roll of duct tape – the strong, usually silver colored, reinforced tape (can be used to mend nearly anything).
- Fun books to read – such as paperback novels that you do not care about and so can swap/sell/trash.

Miscellaneous – Not-So-Serious Possibilities That Are Not Essential

- Tennis ball (or softball, or baseball) for games (plus a baseball glove if you are a fan); a football (British or American style) is also fun to have around if you can spare the space in your luggage.
- Mini kite (great for windy sites).
- Bungee cords – useful for tying things on to other things and tying things on to vehicles.
- Portable music player, MP3 player, or CD player (and CDs) – plus something to power or charge these (solar-powered chargers are now available and are most useful) and headphones. Mini speakers are also a worthwhile addition.
- Laptop and charger – assuming where you are going has electricity, and assuming you want to carry this around and/or risk losing it (and so have a safe enough place to store it).
- Portable global positioning system (GPS) plus spare batteries – once the preserve of the military, these are now fairly affordable, portable, and reliable.
- Binoculars (and a guidebook on the local wildlife if you are interested in that kind of thing).
- Portable games – a pack of cards, dice, mini versions of popular board games such as Scrabble, chess, and the like (but be cautious – some nations ban playing cards and dice on the basis of their use in gambling, which is illegal in some places).
- Photos of friends, family, and home (great talking points with strangers).

- Multipacks of your favorite candy, chocolate, sweets, or gum – to eat and/or give away. Cigarettes, too, if you smoke – although bear in mind local import laws (do not forget a lighter or matches).

Things That You Absolutely Should Not Even Think about Bringing or Doing

As the saying goes, there is no such thing as a stupid question and so no such thing as too obvious a warning. So please, do not even thinking about bringing the following things onto a site:

- Drugs of any kind, including alcohol, except when permission to bring the latter only has been *explicitly given in advance by the project director* (if in doubt, do not bring alcohol).
- Weapons of any kind.
- Pornography.
- Overtly political or religious documents, magazines, books, and the like, including clothes with any related slogans on them, or any rude/crude statements or images on them. This includes copies of any holy or sacred texts. These may well be precious to you, but may cause offense to others, including immigration and other government officials you come across in your travels. Like all precious things, these are thus best kept safely at home.
- Anything that you value too much to want to risk losing – a prized heirloom, piece of jewelry, and so on.

This is also a good place to reiterate Smith and Burke's (2007: 119) guide, "What Not to Do at a Site":

- Do not interfere with the site in any way.
- Do not collect souvenirs.
- Do not leave rubbish behind.
- Do not make details of the site public without obtaining the proper permissions first.

Bear in mind also the sage advice on heath and safety in archaeology by Poirier and Feder (2001).

Camping Equipment (If Instructed to Bring)

- Tent
- Groundsheet
- Sleeping mat
- Sleeping bag (of suitable weight for the advised climate)
- Cooking and eating equipment

References

Adams, R. (ed.). 2001. *Implementing the Native American Graves Protection and Repatriation Act.* Washington, DC: American Association of Museums.

Agbe-Davies, A. S. 2002. Black Scholars, Black Pasts, *SAA Archaeological Record* 2(4): 24–28.

Agbe-Davies, A. S. 2003. Conversations: Archaeology and the Black Experience, *Archaeology* 56(1): 22.

Aitchison, K. 1999. *Profiling the Profession: A Survey of Archaeological Jobs in the UK.* Reading, UK: Institute of Field Archaeologists.

Aitchison, K. 2000. The Funding of Archaeological Practice in England, *Cultural Trends* 39: 2–32.

Aitchison, K. 2006. Forum: What Is the Value of an Archaeology Degree? *Papers from the Institute of Archaeology* 17: 4–12.

Aitchison, K. 2009. After the Gold Rush: Global Archaeology in 2009, *World Archaeology* 41(4): 659–71.

Aitchison, K. 2010. *Job Losses in Archaeology – April 2010: Report for the Institute for Archaeologists and the Federation of Archaeological Managers and Employers,* http://www.archaeologists.net/modules/icontent/inPages/docs/JobLossesApril2010.pdf.

Aitchison, K. and Edwards, R. 2003. *Archaeology Labour Market Intelligence: Profiling the Profession 2002/03.* Reading, UK: Institute of Field Archaeologists.

Aitchison, K. and Edwards, R. 2008. *Archaeology Labour Market Intelligence: Profiling the Profession 2007/08.* Reading, UK: Institute of Field Archaeologists.

All-Party Parliamentary Archaeology Group. 2003. *Current State of Archaeology in the United Kingdom.* London: HMSO, http://www.appag.org.uk/report/report.html.

Altschul, J. H. and Patterson, T. C. 2008. Trends in Employment and Training in American Archaeology, in Ashmore, W., Lippert D., and Mills, B. J. (eds.). *Voices in American Archaeology.* Washington, DC: Society for American Archaeology Press.

221

References

American Anthropological Association. 2009. *Statements on Ethics: Principles of Professional Responsibility*, http://www.aaanet.org/committees/ethics/ethcode.htm.

American Cultural Resources Association. 2010. March 2010 Effects of the Economy Survey, http://acra-crm.org/associations/9221/files/ACRA%20Effects%20of%20the%20Economy%20Results%2C%202005–05-10.pdf.

Association of Local Government Archaeological Officers. 2008. *Local Authority Archaeological Services Report*, http://www.algao.org.uk/Publications/Docs/SurveySummary.pdf.

Association Research, Inc. (ARI). 2005. *Salary Survey Conducted for the Society for American Archaeology and Society for Historical Archaeology*. Rockville, MD: ARI Inc.

ARI. 2006. *Needs Assessment Conducted for the Register of Professional Archaeologists*. Rockville, MD: ARI Inc.

Association of Mining and Exploration Companies. 2009. Interim Code of Conduct, http://www.amec.org.au/index.php?id=72.

Atalay, S. 2006a. Decolonizing Archaeology, *American Indian Quarterly* 30(3&4): 269–79.

Atalay, S. 2006b. Indigenous Archaeology as Decolonizing Practice, *American Indian Quarterly* 30(3&4): 280–310.

Australian Archaeological Association. 2009. *Code of Ethics*, http://www.australianarchaeo logicalassociation.com.au/ethics.

Barber, B., Carver, J., Hinton, P., and Nixon, T. 2008. *Archaeology and Development: A Good Practice Guide to Managing Risk and Maximising Benefit*. London: CIRIA.

Bass, G. F. 1966. *Archaeology Under Water*. London: Thames and Hudson.

Baxter, J. E. 2002. Popular Images and Popular Stereotypes: Images of Archaeologists in Popular and Documentary Film, *SAA Archaeological Record* 2(4): 16–17, 40.

Beck, W. 1994. Women and Archaeology in Australia, in Claassen, C. (ed.). *Women in Archaeology*. Philadelphia: University of Pennsylvania Press, 210–18.

Benjamin, R. P. 2003. Black and Asian Representation in UK Archaeology, *The Archaeologist* 48: 7–8.

Benjamin, R. P. 2004. Building a Black British Identity Through Archaeology, *Archaeological Review from Cambridge* 19(2): 73–83.

Bowens, A. (ed.). 2009. *Underwater Archaeology: The NAS Guide to Principles and Practice*. Oxford: Blackwell.

British Archaeological Jobs and Resources. 2009a. homepage, http://www.bajr.org/.

British Archaeological Jobs and Resources. 2009b. Site Hut web forum, http://www.bajrfed .co.uk/mod/vanillaforum/vanilla/?CategoryID=1.

British Archaeological Jobs and Resources. 2009c. Getting Started in Archaeology web forum, http://www.bajrfed.co.uk/mod/vanillaforum/vanilla/?CategoryID=4.

British Archaeological Jobs and Resources. 2009d. Digger archive, http://www.bajr.org/ DiggerMagazine/default.asp.

Byrne, D. 1991. Western Hegemony in Archaeological Heritage Management, *History and Anthropology* 5: 269–76.

CHL Consulting Co. Ltd. 2002. *The Future Demand for Archaeologists in Ireland*. Dublin: The Heritage Council.

Claassen, C. (ed.). 1994. *Women in Archaeology*. Philadelphia: University of Pennsylvania Press.

Colwell-Chanthaphonh, C. and Ferguson, T. J. (eds.) 2008. *Collaboration in Archaeological Practice: Engaging Descendant Communities*. Walnut Creek, CA: Altamira.

Corbishley, M. 1999. The National Curriculum: Help or Hindrance to the Introduction of Archaeology in Schools?, in Beavis, J. and Hunt, A. (eds.). *Communicating Archaeology*. Oxford: Oxbow, 71–78.

Council of Europe. 1985. *Convention for the Protection of the Architectural Heritage of Europe*, http://conventions.coe.int/treaty/Commun/QueVoulezVous.asp?CL=ENG&CM=0& NT=121.

Council of Europe. 1992. *Convention on the Protection of the Archaeological Heritage*, http:// conventions.coe.int/Treaty/Commun/QueVoulezVous.asp?NT=143&CM=1&CL= ENG.

Council of Europe. 2000. *European Landscape Convention*, http://www.coe.int/t/dg4/ cultureheritage/heritage/Landscape/default_en.asp.

Council of Europe. 2005. *Framework Convention on the Value of Cultural Heritage for Society*, http://conventions.coe.int/Treaty/Commun/QueVoulezVous.asp?NT=199& CM=8&CL=ENG.

Darvill, T. 2008. *Concise Oxford Dictionary of Archaeology*. Oxford: Oxford University Press.

Darvill, T. and Russell, B. 2002. *Archaeology after PPG16: Archaeological Investigations in England 1990-1999*. Bournemouth: Bournemouth University School of Conservation Sciences and English Heritage.

Davies, J. 2010. The Currency of the Past – the Economics of Heritage Tourism, *Conservation Bulletin* 64: 12–14.

Davis, M. E. 2005. *How Students Understand the Past: From Theory to Practice*. Walnut Creek, CA: Altamira.

de Boer, T. 2004. *Shovel Bums: Comix of Archaeological Field Life*. Walnut Creek, CA: Altamira.

Delafons, J. 1997. *Politics and Preservation: Policy History of the Built Heritage, 1882–1996*. London: Spon.

Denhez, M. 2010. *Unearthing the Law: Archaeological Legislation on Lands in Canada*. Montreal: SynParSys Consulting Inc., on behalf of the Archaeological Services Branch of the Parks Canada Agency, http://www.pc.gc.ca/eng/docs/r/pfa-fap/~/media/docs/r/pfa-fap/ pfa%20fap2001_e.ashx.

Doeser, J. 2010. *Diversifying Participation in the Historic Environment Workforce*, http://www .ucl.ac.uk/caa/Projects/Projects/index.htm.

Dromgoole, S. (ed.). 1999. *Legal Protection of the Underwater Cultural Heritage. National and International Perspectives*. New York: Kluwer Law.

Everill, P. 2009. *The Invisible Diggers: A Study of British Commercial Archaeology*. Oxford: Oxbow.

Fagan, G. G. 2006. *Archaeological Fantasies: How Pseudoarchaeology Misrepresents the Past and Misleads the Public*. London: Routledge.

Flannery, K. V. 1982. The Golden Marshalltown: A Parable for the Archeology of the 1980s, *American Anthropologist* (New Series) 84(2): 265–78.

Fritz, J. M. and Plog, F. T. 1970. The Nature of Archaeological Explanation, *American Antiquity* 35(4): 405–12.

Funari, P. P. A. and de Carvalho, A. V. 2009. The Uses of Archaeology. A Plea for Diversity, *Archaeological Dialogues* 16(2): 179–81.

Garrow, B. A., Garrow, P. H., and Thomas, P. A. 1994. Women in Contract Archaeology, in Claassen, C. (ed.). *Women in Archaeology*. Philadelphia: University of Pennsylvania Press, 182–201.

Greenfield, J. 2003. *The Return of Cultural Treasures*. Cambridge: Cambridge University Press.

Guinness, A. 2009. A Mesolithic Site at North Park Farm Quarry Bletchingley, http:// www.surreycc.gov.uk/sccwebsite/sccwspages.nsf/LookupWebPagesByTITLE_RTF/ A±Mesolithic±site±at±North±Park±Farm±Quarry±Bletchingley?opendocument.

References

Henson, D. 2004a. The Educational Framework in the United Kingdom, in Henson, D., Stone, P., and Corbishley, M. (eds.). *Education and the Historic Environment*. London: Taylor and Francis, 13–21.

Henson, D. 2004b. Archaeology in Schools, in Henson, D., Stone, P., and Corbishley, M. (eds.). *Education and the Historic Environment*. London: Taylor and Francis, 23–32.

Henson, D., Stone, P., and Corbishley, M. (eds.). 2004. *Education and the Historic Environment*. London: Routledge.

Heritage Alliance. 2010. *Submission on DCMS Structural Reform Plan*, 20th July 2010, http://www.heritagelink.org.uk/wp/wp-content/uploads/2010/07/THA-sbm-on-SRP-v5.doc.

Heritage Lottery Fund. 2010. *Investing in Success: Heritage and the UK Tourism Economy*. London: HLF.

Hinton, P. and Jennings, D. 2007. Quality Management of Archaeology in Great Britain: Present Practice and Future Challenges, in Willems, W. and Van den Dries, M. (eds.). *Quality Management in Archaeology*. Oxford: Oxbow, 100–12.

Holtorf, C. 2005. *From Stonehenge to Las Vegas: Archaeology as Popular Culture*. Walnut Creek, CA: Altamira.

Holtorf, C. 2007a. *Archaeology Is a Brand! The Meaning of Archaeology in Contemporary Popular Culture*. Oxford: Archaeopress.

Holtorf, C. 2007b. An Archaeological Fashion Show: How Archaeologists Dress and How They Are Portrayed in the Media, in Clack, T. and Brittain, M. (eds.). *Archaeology and the Media*. Walnut Creek, CA: Left Coast Press, 69–88.

Hudson, K. 1981. *A Social History of Archaeology: the British Experience*. London: Macmillan.

Hunter, J. and Ralston, I. (eds.). 2006. *Archaeological Resource Management in the UK: An Introduction*. Stroud, UK: Sutton.

ICOMOS (International Council on Manuments and Sites). 1964. *International Charter for the Conservation and Restoration of Monuments and Sites*, http://www.international.icomos.org/charters/venice_e.htm.

Institute for Archaeologists. 2009. *Code of Conduct*, http://www.archaeologists.net/modules/icontent/index.php?page=15.

Jackson, V. and Sinclair, A. 2010. *Archaeology Graduates of the Millennium: A Survey of the Career Histories of Graduates*. Liverpool: Subject Centre for History, Classics and Archaeology, http://www.heacademy.ac.uk/assets/hca/documents/archaeology/Archaeology_Graduates_of_the_Millennium.pdf.

Johnson, M. 2009. *Archaeological Theory: An Introduction*. Oxford: Wiley-Blackwell.

Jones, B. 1984. *Past Imperfect: the Story of Rescue Archaeology*. London: Heinemann.

King, T. 2002. *Thinking About Cultural Resource Management: Essays from the Edge*. Walnut Creek, CA: Left Coast Press.

King, T. 2004. *Cultural Resource Laws and Practice*. Walnut Creek, CA: Left Coast Press.

King, T. 2005. *Doing Archaeology: A Cultural Resource Management Perspective*. Walnut Creek, CA: Left Coast Press.

King, T. 2009. *Our Unprotected Heritage: Whitewashing the Destruction of Our Cultural and Natural Environment*. Walnut Creek, CA: Left Coast Press.

Kohl, P. L. and Fawcett, C. (eds.). 1995. *Nationalism, Politics and the Practice of Archaeology*. Cambridge: Cambridge University Press.

Lenegan, C. 2005. *Resourcing an Innovative Industry: Minerals Week 2005 Address on "the Minerals Sector and Indigenous Relations."* http://www.atns.net.au/papers/Lenegan.pdf.

Lennon, J. et al. 2001. *Natural and Cultural Heritage Theme Report: Australia State of the Environment Report 2001*, http://www.environment.gov.au/soe/2001/publications/theme-reports/heritage/pubs/heritage.pdf.

Lovata, T. 2007. *Inauthentic Archaeologies: Public Uses and Abuses of the Past*. Walnut Creek, CA: Left Coast Press.

McDermott, C. and La Piscopia, P. 2008. *Discovering the Archaeologists of Europe: Ireland*. Institute of Archaeologists of Ireland, http://www.discovering-archaeologists.eu/national_reports/DISCO_national_Ireland_Final_Web.pdf.

McGhee, R. 2008. Aboriginalism and the Problems of Indigenous Archaeology, *American Antiquity* 73(4): 579–97.

McGill, G. 1995. *Building on the Past: Guide to the Archaeology and Development Process*. London: Taylor and Francis.

McGrail, S. 2001. *Boats of the World*. Oxford: Oxford University Press.

Membury, S. 2002. The Celluloid Archaeologist – an X-Rated Exposé, in Russell, M. (ed.). *Digging Holes in Popular Culture: Archaeology and Science Fiction*. Oxford: Oxbow, 8–18.

Moshenska, G. 2009. Second World War Archaeology in Schools: A Backdoor to the History Curriculum?, *Papers from the Institute of Archaeology* 19: 55–66.

Muckelroy, K. 1978. *Maritime Archaeology*. Cambridge: Cambridge University Press.

Nelson, M. C., Nelson, S. M., and Wylie, A. (eds.). 1994. *Equity Issues for Women in Archaeology*, Washington, DC: Archaeological Papers of the American Anthropological Association No. 5.

Neumann, T. W. and Sanford, R. M. 2001. *Practicing Archaeology: A Training Manual for Cultural Resources Archaeology*. Walnut Creek, CA: Altamira.

Nicholas, G. 2008. Native Peoples and Archaeology (Indigenous Archaeology), in Pearsall, D. (ed.). *The Encyclopedia of Archaeology*. Oxford: Elsevier, 1660–69.

Nicholas, G. 2010. *Being and Becoming Indigenous Archaeologists*. Walnut Creek, CA: Left Coast Press.

Patterson, T. C. 1994. *Toward a Social History of Archaeology in the United States*. New York: Harcourt Brace.

Philips, J. E. (ed.). 2005. *Writing African History*. Rochester, NY: University of Rochester Press.

Philips, T., Gilchrist, R., Hewitt, I., Le Scouiller, S., Booy, D., and Cook, G. 2007. *Inclusive, Accessible, Archaeology: Good Practice and Guidelines for Including Disabled Students and Self Evaluation in Archaeological Fieldwork Training*. London: Higher Education Academy Subject Centre for History, Classics and Archaeology.

Poirier, D. A. and Feder, K. L. (eds.). 2001. *Dangerous Places: Heath, Safety and Archaeology*. Westport, CT: Bergin and Garvey.

Praetzellis, A. 2000. *Death by Theory: A Tale of Mystery and Archaeological Theory*. Walnut Creek, CA: Altamira.

Praetzellis, A. 2003. *Dug to Death: A Tale of Archaeological Method and Mayhem*. Walnut Creek, CA: Altamira.

Quality Assurance Agency for Higher Education (QAA). 2007. *Archaeology Benchmark Report*, http://www.qaa.ac.uk/academicinfrastructure/benchmark/statements/Archaeology.pdf.

Rahtz, P. 1974. *Rescue Archaeology*. Harmondsworth, UK: Penguin.

Ramos, M. and Duganne, D. 2000. *Exploring Public Perceptions and Attitudes About Archaeology*. New York: Society for American Archaeology, http://www.saa.org/Portals/0/SAA/pubedu/nrptdraft4.pdf.

References

Register of Professional Archaeologists. 2009. *Code of Conduct*, http://www.rpanet.org/displaycommon.cfm?an=1&subarticlenbr=3.

Robinson, W. 1998. *First Aid for Underwater Finds*. London: Archetype.

Rothfield, L. 2009. *The Rape of Mesopotamia: Behind the Looting of the Iraq Museum*. Chicago: University of Chicago Press.

Russell, M. (ed.). 2002a. *Digging Holes in Popular Culture: Archaeology and Science Fiction*. Oxford: Oxbow.

Russell, M. 2002b. "No More Heroes Any More": the Dangerous World of the Pop Culture Archaeologist, in Russell, M. (ed.). *Digging Holes in Popular Culture: Archaeology and Science Fiction*. Oxford: Oxbow, 38–54.

Sabloff, J. A. 2008. *Archaeology Matters: Action Archaeology in the Modern World*. Walnut Creek, CA: Left Coast Press.

Schlanger, N. and Aitchison, K. (eds.). 2010. *Archaeology and the Global Economic Crisis: Multiple Impacts, Possible Solutions*. Tervuren, Belgium: Culture Lab Editions, http://ace-archaeology.eu/fichiers/25Archaeology-and-the-crisis.pdf.

Schlatter, N. E. 2008. *Museum Careers: A Practical Guide for Students and Novices*. Walnut Creek, CA: Left Coast Press.

Shennan, S. J. 2002. *Genes, Memes and Human History: Darwinian Archaeology and Cultural Evolution*. London: Thames and Hudson.

Shovelbums. 2009. homepage, http://www.shovelbums.org/.

Smith, C. and Burke, H. 2007. *Digging It Up Down Under: A Practical Guide to Doing Archaeology in Australia*. New York: Springer.

Smith, C. and Jackson, G. 2006. Decolonizing Indigenous Archaeology: Developments from Down Under, *American Indian Quarterly* 30(3&4): 311–49.

Smith, C. and Wobst, H. M. (eds.). 2005. *Indigenous Archaeologies: Decolonizing Theory and Practice*. London: Routledge.

Smith, L. 2001. *Archaeological Theory and the Politics of Cultural Heritage*. London: Routledge.

Smith, L. 2006. *Uses of Heritage*. London: Routledge.

Smith, L. and du Cros, H. 1991. *Equality and Gender in Australian Archaeology*, http://www.anthrosource.net.

Society for American Archaeology. 2009. *Principles of Archaeological Ethics*, http://www.saa.org/AbouttheSociety/PrinciplesofArchaeologicalEthics/tabid/203/Default.aspx.

Society for Historical Archaeology. 2009. *Ethical Principles*, http://www.sha.org/about/ethics.cfm.

Talalay, L. 2004. The Past as Commodity: Archaeological Images in Modern Advertising, *Public Archaeology* 3: 205–16.

TORC (Training Online Resource Centre for Archaeology). 2010. *National Occupational Standards for Archaeology*, http://www.torc.org.uk/nos/nosmap.asp.

Trümpler, C. (ed.). 2001. *Agatha Christie and Archaeology*. London: British Museum.

Two Bears, D. R. 2006. Navajo Archaeologist Is Not an Oxymoron: A Tribal Archaeologist's Experience, *American Indian Quarterly* 30(3–4): 381–87.

Ucko, P., Ling, Q., and Hubert, J. (eds.). 2007. *From Concepts of the Past to Practical Strategies: the Teaching of Archaeological Field Techniques*. London: Saffron.

Ulm, S., Nichols, S., and Dalley, C. 2005. Mapping the Shape of Contemporary Australian Archaeology: Implications for Archaeological Teaching and Learning, *Australian Archaeology* 61: 11–23.

UNESCO. 1970. *Convention on the Means of Prohibiting and Preventing the Illicit Import, Export and Transfer of Cultural Property*, http://portal.unesco.org/en/ev.php-URL_ID=13039&URL_DO=DO_TOPIC&URL_SECTION=201.html.

UNESCO. 1972. *Convention Concerning the Protection of the World Cultural and Natural Heritage*, http://whc.unesco.org/en/conventiontext.

UNESCO. 1999. *Convention for the Protection of Cultural Property in the Event of Armed Conflict*, http://portal.unesco.org/culture/en/ev.php-URL_ID=35261&URL_DO=DO_TOPIC&URL_SECTION=201.html.

UNESCO. 2001. *Convention on the Protection of the Underwater Cultural Heritage*, http://portal.unesco.org/en/ev.php-URL_ID=13520&URL_DO=DO_TOPIC&URL_SECTION=201.html.

UNESCO. 2003. *Convention for the Safeguarding of the Intangible Cultural Heritage*, http://portal.unesco.org/en/ev.php-URL_ID=17716&URL_DO=DO_TOPIC&URL_SECTION=201.html.

UN Department of Economic and Social Affairs Population Division. 2009. *Population Newsletter* 87 (June 2009), http://www.un.org/esa/population/publications/popnews/Newsltr_87.pdf.

Universities and Colleges Admissions Service. 2010a. *Skills Profile for Archaeology*, http://www.ucas.ac.uk/seps/profiles/archaeology.

Universities and Colleges Admissions Service. 2010b. *Archaeology Employability Skills*, http://www.ucas.ac.uk/seps/profiles/abilities/Archaeology1.

UN Economic Commission for Europe. 1998. *Convention on Access to Information, Public Participation in Decision-making and Access to Justice in Environmental Matters*, http://www.unece.org/env/pp/documents/cep43e.pdf.

Vitelli, K. D. and Colwell-Chanthaphonh, C. (eds.). 2006. *Archaeological Ethics*. Walnut Creek, CA: Altamira.

Walz, J. R. 2009. Archaeologies of Disenchantment, in Schmidt, P. R. (ed.). *Postcolonial Archaeologies in Africa*. Santa Fe, NM: School for Advanced Research Press.

Watkins, J. 2000. *Indigenous Archaeology: American Indian Values and Scientific Practice*. Walnut Creek, CA: Altamira.

Watkins, J. 2002. Marginal Native, Marginal Archaeologist: Ethnic Disparity in American Archaeology, *SAA Archaeological Record* 2(4): 36–37.

Watkins, J. 2005. Artefacts, Archaeologists, and American Indians, *Public Archaeology* 4 (2&3): 187–92.

Wheeler, R. E. M. 1954 *Archaeology from the Earth*. Harmondsworth: Penguin.

Whittlesey, S. M. 1994. Academic Alternatives: Gender and CRM in Arizona, in Claassen, C. (ed.). *Women in Archaeology*. Philadelphia: University of Pennsylvania Press, 202–09.

Wright, R. P. 2002. Gender Equity, Sexual Harassment and Professional Ethics, *SAA Archaeological Record* 2(4): 18–19.

Zarmati, L. 1995. Popular Archaeology and the Archaeologist as Hero, in Balme, J. and Beck, W. (eds.). *Gendered Archaeology: The Second Australian Women in Archaeology Conference*. Canberra: ANH Publications. 43–47.

Zeder, M. A. 1997, 1998, 2000. *The American Archaeologist: A Profile*. Walnut Creek, CA: Altamira.

Zorpidu, S. 2004. The Public Image of the Female Archaeologist: The Case of Lara Croft, in Bolin, H. (ed.). *The Interplay of Past and Present*. Huddinge, Sweden: Södertörns Högskola, 101–07.

Index

Index

Index

WITHDRAWAL